7. 18

Despite the exuberance of his verbosity, Browning was at least as reticent as most other great Victorian writers. Barbara Melchiori has never been so interested in the " philosophical " content of Browning's poetry as in the complex imaginative processes by means of which he created it.   In these fascinating studies of several of his poems (including " The Bishop Orders his Tomb," " Andrea del Sarto," " Childe Roland," " Caliban upon Setebos," and *Fifine at the Fair*), she throws much fresh light on his use of sources;   and, by adopting an unrepentantly Freudian approach, she also reveals the hidden wealth of meaning contained in certain themes and images which pervade the whole of his work.

Barbara Melchiori was born in Hull; she is married to Giorgio Melchiori, Professor of English in the University of Rome, and has a son and a daughter.   Since 1957, she has been a lecturer in English, first in Rome, and then in Turin.   She has published many critical essays on Hawthorne, Henry James, Poe, Shakespeare and Browning, but this is her first book.

BIOGRAPHY AND CRITICISM

General Editors
A. NORMAN JEFFARES
R. L. C. LORIMER

10

BROWNING'S POETRY OF RETICENCE

BARBARA MELCHIORI

BROWNING'S POETRY OF RETICENCE

OLIVER & BOYD

EDINBURGH

LONDON

1968

OLIVER AND BOYD LTD

TWEEDDALE COURT
EDINBURGH I

39A WELBECK STREET
LONDON WI

FIRST PUBLISHED 1968

SBN 05 001634 2

PRINTED IN GREAT BRITAIN
BY T. AND A. CONSTABLE LTD
EDINBURGH
SCOTLAND

For Giorgio

Foreword

IN thanking those who have helped me with this book, my gratitude goes first to Professor Norman Jeffares who convinced me that I could write a book on Browning and who helped me by constant encouragement and advice, by the loan of books and by publishing two of my Browning essays in *A Review of English Literature*.

My warm thanks are also due to Mr and Mrs Colin Franklin, and to Dr Adda Corti, for the summer loan of their Hampstead homes which made the London libraries available to me over a number of vacations and research an unhurried pleasure.

Some of the chapters and appendices in the present book have been published separately in a modified form as essays, and I wish to thank the editors of the following periodicals for their permission to republish these: *English Miscellany, A Review of English Literature, Essays in Criticism, Victorian Poetry*.

Counsel and help has come from too many quarters to mention, but I cannot leave unacknowledged the assistance I have had from Professor Vittorio Gabrieli, extending far beyond the covers of this book, and from Professor Clarence Tracy. My debt to Browning scholars and critics has been acknowledged, as far as possible, in the text and notes.

I wish to thank Mr R. L. C. Lorimer for his careful and patient editing and for frequent advice which has made it possible for me to avoid and eliminate a number of inaccuracies and inconsistencies. My husband, who has opinions of his own upon Browning, has helped me by reading and questioning mine, so that I owe to him many revisions and excisions.

B. M.

Rome
May 1967

Contents

I

Browning's Poetry—Good and Bad

Must I lay bare
My heart, hideous and beating, or tear up
My vitals for your gaze, ere you will deem
Enough made known?[1]

WITH these words of Paracelsus Browning outlined, at
the beginning of his poetic career, a problem that
remained central for him throughout his life: the
problem of artistic reticence. Some of the tension which lends
strength to his work arises from the conflict between his wish to
guard jealously his own thoughts and feelings, and the pressing
necessity he was under to reveal them. His first step towards a
solution of this problem was to write very little indeed in his
own person, the wide variety of characters he employed serving,
he trusted, to screen their author. One thing, however, these
characters have in common: they are all taken from out-of-the-
way or little-known sources. This was of the greatest advantage
to Browning. In each of them he sensed some initial sympathy,
some *rapport* with himself, and he was free to develop and play
upon this analogy without being contradicted by the facts. He
was free, in so far as he wished, to invent his characters or
modify them at will. This contradicts the generally accepted
idea of his careful documentation, of his patient following of,
and frequently accurate translation from, his source books.
After following him step by step through a few of the more
important of these sources, through Gerard de Lairesse,[2]

[1] *Paracelsus*, III, 731-34. All quotations of Browning's poetry are taken from
the centenary edition of his *Works*, ed. F. G. Kenyon, 10 vols., London 1912.
[2] Gerard de Lairesse, *The Art of Painting in All its Branches*, tr. J. F. Fritsch,
1778. Originally published under the title *Het Groot Schilderboek*, Amsterdam 1707.

Philippe de Comines,[3] Vasari[4] and Baldinucci,[5] Bartoli,[6] Dante,[7] and the Bible, and above all after checking his use of that major source the "Old Yellow Book",[8] I have come to the conclusion that his quite genuine documentation and accuracy are a cover behind which he could give free rein to his own conception of historical characters. He is describing, in "Sludge", what was substantially his own method, from the starting-point of a sudden intuition or flash of sympathy to the fiction that ensued:

> How did you contrive to grasp
> The thread which led you through this labyrinth?
> How build such solid fabric out of air?
> How on so slight foundation found this tale,
> Biography, narrative?[9]

Nevertheless, the historical framework round the characters he builds up was undoubtedly of immense artistic value. Besides lending verisimilitude to his characters and to their actions, it gave his poems structure and form. In much of his best work the parts are tightly knit, controlled, and related within this given structure. When he broke free there was always the danger that he would be carried away by mere verbalising. His facility in writing was of the greatest danger to him. *Sordello* is the typical example of how not to write a poem, yet *Sordello* is very much better than the later *Inn Album* and than much of *Red Cotton Night-Cap Country*, in that it contains many passages of rich poetry, passages of lyrical beauty and of subtle insight.

This insight into the moving forces behind his characters' words and actions was Browning's great gift. In his early poems he had already theorised about these intimations of psychoanalysis. In his later poetry he was to apply this knowledge. Browning was full of his discovery in *Paracelsus*:

---

[3] Philippe de Comines, *Mémoires*, Paris 1524-8.

[4] Giorgio Vasari, *Le Vite dei più Eccellenti Pittori, Scultori e Architetti*, Florence 1550, 1568.

[5] Filippo Baldinucci, *Notizie de' Professori del Disegno*, Florence 1767-74.

[6] Daniello Bartoli, *Dei Simboli Trasportati al Morale*, Rome 1677.

[7] Dante Alighieri, *Divina Commedia*.

[8] *The Old Yellow Book*, ed. Charles W. Hodell, Washington 1908.

[9] "Mr Sludge, 'The Medium' ", 1456-60.

> Truth is within ourselves; it takes no rise
> From outward things, whate'er you may believe.
> ... and to KNOW
> Rather consists in opening out a way
> Whence the imprisoned splendour may escape,
> Than in effecting entry for a light
> Supposed to be without.[10]

The search for truth is compared, in a later metaphor in the same poem, to a diver plunging for a pearl. With the cry "Festus, I plunge!" Browning sets out on his exploration of the depths of a man's mind. The dramatic monologue, a form which had never been used so effectively before,[11] became his vehicle. The mind into which he plunged was perforce his own, but he succeeded in stringing the pearls with which he rose on to some very different threads.

This gift had fullest play in his major work, *The Ring and the Book*. Here the structure is taken from the "Old Yellow Book", where among the documents pertaining to an Italian trial he found recorded the different versions of an old crime; and it gave him exactly the formula he needed for an investigation into the plurality of truth. His realisation of the possibilities of the Old Yellow Book is recorded in one of the most beautiful passages of descriptive lyrical poetry he ever wrote. After the well-known ring image of the artist-craftsman at work moulding "the lingot truth", Browning tells us how he laid aside the Yellow Book and, his day's work done, stepped out onto the balcony of his house in Florence overlooking the church of San Felice. He had been poring all day long over the story of the ancient murder, disentangling the tissue of lies from which the history of a trial is woven. Now,

> truth thus grasped and gained,—
> The book was shut and done with and laid by. . . . [12]

The sketch that Browning here gives of his room holds, in its atmosphere of calm, a contained emotion. For once Browning

---

[10] *Paracelsus*, I. 726-7, 733-7.

[11] For a thorough study of Browning's use of the monologue, see Robert Langbaum, *The Poetry of Experience* . . ., London 1957.

[12] *The Ring and the Book*, I. 471-2.

is holding open for inspection a moment in his own life—he is
willing to share this rare mood of artistic triumph, of achievement. With the discovery of the Old Yellow Book the material
for artistic success lay to his hand. There had been a shock of
recognition. In his first published poem, *Pauline*, Browning
had given expression to his restlessness as an artist in the following words:

> I cannot chain my soul: it will not rest
> In its clay prison, this most narrow sphere:
> It has strange impulse, tendency, desire,
> Which nowise I account for nor explain,
> But cannot stifle, being bound to trust
> All feelings equally, to hear all sides:
> How can my life indulge them?[13]

The Old Yellow Book brought him the material he needed, gave
him exactly this opportunity "to trust all feelings equally, to
hear all sides"; and with the realisation of this came such peace
and satisfaction that for once he dropped his guard and spoke
openly of his own feelings.[14] Browning laid aside the book, he
tells us:

> On the cream-coloured massive agate, broad
> 'Neath the twin cherubs in the tarnished frame
> O' the mirror, tall thence to the ceiling-top.
> And from the reading, and that slab I leant
> My elbow on, the while I read and read,
> I turned, to free myself and find the world,
> And stepped out on the narrow terrace, built
> Over the street and opposite the church,
> And paced its lozenge-brickwork sprinkled cool;
> Because Felice-church-side stretched, a-glow
> Through each square window fringed for festival,
> Whence came the clear voice of the cloistered ones
> Chanting a chant made for midsummer nights—
> I know not what particular praise of God,
> It always came and went with June.[15]

---

[13] *Pauline*, 593-9.
[14] "By the Fireside", another personal poem, although intended for publication, was addressed to Elizabeth Barrett Browning, so that a more intimate tone
was natural.
[15] *The Ring and the Book*, I. 473-87.

We learn much about Browning from these lines. First, there is his love of Italy, suggested by the sensuous pleasure in the heat, in the marble, in the church. The mention of June, of midsummer nights, of the church-side aglow and of the custom of sprinkling water on the terrace evoke warmth and pleasure. The church differs from a Protestant church; and, while we feel that Browning does not take its festal draperies or ritual singing very seriously as worship, he is the freer to indulge his senses.

Secondly, he gives us only two details of his room. The tall, decorated mirror and the marble slab re-emphasise how Italian the scene is: but they tell us more. Marble Browning always loved and used lavishly for decoration throughout his poetry, yet its two main characteristics offer a striking contrast: for although it is beautiful and precious, it is also very hard and cold. That Browning should have read the Old Yellow Book leaning his elbow on a marble slab fronting a mirror is highly significant. It recalls the many self-portraits in which artists sketch themselves at work seen from behind and at the same time facing us from the canvas, from the picture within the picture. That, I believe, is exactly what Browning was doing throughout his work.

There is one more significant detail. Browning sketches the moment when he has finished work, when

> I turned, to free myself and find the world.

He is ready to descend from his ivory tower, only he does not get very far. What he does, in fact, is to step on to a terrace where he is *over* a street, *opposite* a church; and that is as close as he gets to the world he set out to find. Sensitive to the problem of the isolation of the artist, Browning was taking the first step along the road which was to lead a century later to alienation; and his sense of separation is echoed in the sound of the song of the "cloistered ones", their very segregation part of the essence of the beauty of their song.

Browning, in these lines, was describing what he saw around him, but it is his selection of the significant, the symbolic, details which makes this passage into great poetry. No nineteenth-century room would contain only a book, a marble slab (whether table or mantel-shelf),[16] and a mirror, no Italian street would be empty of life on a summer evening, the sounds among which Browning picked out the chanting of the nuns must have been myriad. Being a great poet, Browning has made the scene his own and caught it in a magic web of words, so simple as to seem no art at all.

Yet few great artists have been more censured for bad workmanship than Browning, and I think it will be useful to analyse some of the reasons for this criticism. Browning was a great experimenter, and while sometimes he succeeded outright, as in "Love in a Life", a complex rhythmical and metrical experiment which caught a dream concept in a delicate lyrical form,[17] many of his experiments were less fortunate. In *Pippa Passes* he put a fine theory of the freedom of the artist into the mouth of Jules:

> One may do whate'er one likes
> In Art: the only thing is, to make sure
> That one does like it—which takes pains to know.[18]

Reading some of his work we are forced back on the conclusion that either he was very easily satisfied, or that he frequently did not take the necessary pains.

He may fairly, I believe, be accused of using inadmissible rhymes, clogged consonants, and forced grammar, and of indulging a tendency to be facetious which grates on the sensitive ear. Worse still, he has offended many by his

---

[16] It is not clear from the poem whether the marble slab was a table-top or the mantelshelf, or whether Browning read sitting or standing. In *Robert Browning, A Portrait*, London 1952, p. 141, Betty Miller notes that Browning and his wife paid "five pounds for an elaborate gilt-framed mirror to hang over the fireplace". This may have been another mirror, the one shown in Mignaty's painting of the drawing-room in the Casa Guidi, which has certainly a heavily decorated gilt frame, but which does not reach anywhere near the "ceiling top" like the one in the poem.

[17] An earlier form of the same dream is to be found in a letter to Elizabeth dated "Monday morning" and postmarked 19 Jan. 1846: "I fancy myself meeting you on 'the stairs'—stairs and passages generally, and galleries (ah, thou indeed!) all, with their picturesque *accidents*, of landing-places, and spiral heights and depths, and sudden turns and visions of half open doors into what Quarles calls 'mollitious chambers'—and above all, *landing-places*—they are my heart's delight—I would come upon you unaware in a landing-place in my next dream!" *The Letters of Robert Browning and Elizabeth Barrett Barrett*, London, 1899.

[18] *Pippa Passes*, II. 308-10.

grotesque realism, and has distressed many more by his prolixity merging into obscurity.

The most obvious of these faults is his use of inadmissible
rhymes. Browning seemed to have very little ear for rhymes
and at the same time an extraordinary facility and inventiveness. Had he been content with the more laboured and
hackneyed rhymes, his inventiveness in other ways would have
kept his poetry alive, but he loved finding rhymes for difficult
words even when it meant misplacing the stress, as in "'mistress"
rhyming with "this 'tress". He clearly expected his readers to
share the delight he felt himself when he rhymed the un-
rhymable: "cock-crow" and "rock-row", "fabric" and "dab
brick" in "A Grammarian's Funeral" are typical examples.
We learn from a letter how Elizabeth, reading over the draft
of "The Flight of the Duchess", drew his attention to the
weaker rhymes. It is interesting to note that, although in both
cases he modified the lines, he retained the offending rhymes.
She attempted to guide him gently away from such combina-
tions as "What meant a hat if it had no rims on" with the
comment:

> Do you like "*what meant*"? I do not quite—and the connection
> is broken. . . . And then "the rims"—a hat has only one rim
> ever—except for the rhyme with crimson.

She also offers a shrewd guess over

> Finding the calendar bid him be hearty,
> Did resolve on a hunting party—

"Does not that first line seem as if it were meditating a rhyme
for the second?"[19]   This deafness to jarring rhymes is
relatively unimportant in poems such as "The Glove" or
"Youth and Art" (rhyming "fortunes" with "long tunes and
short tunes") poems which are intrinsically weak, but it is
startling to find juxtaposed in the same poem, "A Likeness",
lines like

---

[19] See Edward Snyder and Frederic Palmer, Jr., "New Light on the
Brownings", in *The Quarterly Review*, 269 (July 1937), pp. 48-63, which quotes
from an unpublished letter from Elizabeth to Robert, written in July 1845.

B

> That hair's not so bad, where the gloss is,
> But they've made the girl's nose a proboscis:
> Jane Lamb, that we danced with at Vichy!
> What, is not she Jane? Then, who is she?

and the sudden flight of poetry which followed:

> A face to lose youth for, to occupy age
> With the dream of, meet death with,—why, I'll not
>   engage
> But that, half in a rapture and half in a rage,
> I should toss him the thing's self. . . .[20]

Browning had a reason for writing the doggerel lines of the first quotation. He was trying to catch the tone of conversation. The natural effect is, however, wholly destroyed by the insistence on rhyme, with two weak rhymes in succession, and both imperfect, for he cannot resist the temptation to mock the convention of rhyme. The same kind of doggerel mars "Old Pictures in Florence", which Browning presumably meant to be taken seriously. One wishes that he had taken the pains to be sure he really liked stanza xxxi. We must set against this poems such as "The Pied Piper of Hamelin", where his facility as a rhymer came to his aid, and the poem is justly popular; or "My Last Duchess", where the rhymes are present but scarcely heard, absorbed in the tone of the spoken word as in more modern poetry. Much of his best poetry is, however, in blank verse.

A weakness which does even more damage to his poetry than faulty rhymes is that Browning frequently clogs his lines with consonants. These often choke his blank verse, which was particularly vulnerable because it could be written faster than rhymed lines, so that he had less time to control and smooth his work to fluency. In *Aristophanes' Apology* Browning had written of

Vowel-buds thorned about with consonants,[21]

---

[20] "A Likeness", 29-32, 63-66.
[21] *Aristophanes' Apology*, 640.

which suggests that he himself felt consonants to be something of a menace. At times he uses consonant coagulations[22] to obtain a particular effect. The line in "Rabbi Ben Ezra":

> Irks care the crop-full bird? Frets doubt the maw-
> crammed beast?[23]

with its harsh sounds and inverted construction is a deliberate attempt to give the impression of something choked with food. But if we examine this line phonetically—

> Irks care the crop-full bird? Frets doubt the maw-
> crammed beast?

we realise that we have in conjunction, with no intervening vowel-sounds, seven unpronounceable consonant sequences, any one of which would normally be avoided in verse, interspersed with other double, though pronounceable consonants. Was all this necessary? A similar case of deliberately choked consonants is to be found in *Red Cotton Night-Cap Country*:

> That the Pope's self sent two great real gold crowns
> As thick with jewelry as thick could stick,
> His present to the Virgin and her Babe. . . .[24]

This, too, is an exaggeration of his choking formula; it was Browning, this time, who was unable to swallow the Pope's gift, which he considered a serious mis-spending of money that might have gone to feed the poor.

One development which may perhaps have weakened the shock of some of Browning's juxtapositions of rhymes and consonants is that poetry is not so often read aloud as it was in his time; and even more trying to most modern readers is his frequent use of forced grammatical constructions. These can be found even in his best poems and while at times they are the result of the complexity of his thought-patterns, at times they are clearly the outcome of carelessness or downright laziness, as in *Sordello*:

---

[22] J. Hillis Miller, *Of the Disappearance of God*, Cambridge, Mass. 1963, pp. 87-8, writes of Browning, "His words come in bursts of half-coagulated syntax".
[23] "Rabbi Ben Ezra", 24.
[24] *Red Cotton Night-Cap Country*, 1. 460-2.

> his charge, the crazy town,
> Just managed to be hindered crashing down. . . .[25]

Or, in *Red Cotton Night-Cap Country*:

> I never saw what I could less describe.
> The eyes, for instance, unforgettable
> Which ought to be, are out of mind as sight.[26]

Here Browning has just told us that he was having difficulty in describing Madame Miranda, and there is a reason for the grammatical complexity of the sentence: but surely he has no right to pass his problem on to the reader in this way and leave him with it. "Op art" may have accustomed us today to having a do-it-yourself kit thrust into our hands, but it is an attitude on the part of the artist that many are still inclined to resent. Forced grammar and over-complex syntax are to be found even in Browning's good poems. In "The Englishman in Italy", for example, there is a passage which has to be read several times before the reader realises that the mother was eating quails and not spiders for supper:

> Time for rain! for your long hot dry Autumn
>   Had net-worked with brown
> The white skin of each grape on the bunches,
>   Marked like a quail's crown,
> Those creatures you make such account of,
>   Whose heads,—speckled white
> Over brown like a great spider's back,
>   As I told you last night,—
> Your mother bites off for her supper.[27]

Often the bad rhymes or bad grammar accompany deliberate facetiousness on Browning's part. At times this is tolerable, or even successful, and can be appreciated as an ornament in the same way that we appreciate Elizabethan puns. It is worth remembering that Browning was sensitive to metaphysical poetry at a time when it was little appreciated. In Browning's age the metaphysical poets were best known for their harshness, the general Victorian opinion following Ben

[25] *Sordello*, IV. 405-6.
[26] *Red Cotton Night-Cap Country*, I. 847-9.
[27] "The Englishman in Italy", 13-21.

Jonson, that Donne, for not keeping of accent, deserved hanging. Browning was aware of the strength behind the metaphysical poets, but probably identified this strength in part with the harshness accompanying it. He counted, too, on the shock-effect of harsh writing, and on the sense of immediacy it gave:

> word made leap
> Out word, rhyme—rhyme; the lay could barely keep
> Pace with the action visibly rushing past. . . .[28]

On other occasions, even assuming that it is desirable to do so, Browning fails to bring off the intended effect. One example of a passage where his comic verse is completely successful, avoiding the pitfall of facetiousness, is the description of the Duchess Dowager in "The Flight of the Duchess", a passage rivalling and perhaps owing something to Congreve's prose description of Lady Wishfort:

> I could favour you with sundry touches
> Of the paint-smutches with which the Duchess
> Heightened the mellowness of her cheek's yellowness
> (To get on faster) until at last her
> Cheek grew to be one master-plaster
> Of mucus and fucus from mere use of ceruse:
> In short, she grew from scalp to udder
> Just the object to make you shudder.[29]

This is a *bravura* passage in the comic vein, which Browning perhaps never equalled elsewhere. Too often he degenerated into facetiousness, and it is noticeable that this frequently happens in passages describing either eating or learning. In the well-known "Grammarian's Funeral", for example, the funeral is enlivened with a number of un-funny jokes on problems of Greek grammar. "Fust and his Friends" is full of jokes on learning and printing, some better, some worse. "The barrel of blasphemy broached once, who bungs?" is a fair example of the general level, the kind of music-hall humour that was very

[28] *Sordello*, II. 85-7.
[29] "The Flight of the Duchess", 825-32. Browning was certainly familiar with Congreve, as shown by a letter written to Elizabeth, postmarked 13 Apr. 1846, which mentions "the excitement of suspense, and alternating hope and fear, all ending in the marriage day, after the fashion of a Congreve comedy".

popular in the second half of the nineteenth century, and the over-obvious alliteration that was to be used for the same effect by Edith Sitwell in many of her *Façade* poems.   In the "Prologue" to *Ferishtah's Fancies* the facetious effect is achieved by the forced juxtaposition of cooking and poetry.   Long similes from cooking and eating were common in Browning's work.   Dominus Hyacinthus' book in *The Ring and the Book* comes to mind at once in this connexion.   In the "Prologue" to *Ferishtah's Fancies* the whole tone, from the first "Pray, reader", is unacceptable:

> Pray, Reader, have you eaten ortolans
>   Ever in Italy?
> Recall how cooks there cook them: for my plan's
>   To—Lyre with Spit ally.
>
> They pluck the birds,—some dozen luscious lumps,
>   Or more or fewer,—
> Then roast them, heads by heads and rumps by rumps,
>   Stuck on a skewer.[30]

The moral of this complicated simile lies in the lines:

> So with your meal, my poem: masticate
>   Sense, sight and song there![31]

and we feel that all this heavy jocularity has served to lead us nowhere.

The satire of learning is most acceptable, perhaps, in the eighth book of *The Ring and the Book*, where it is in keeping with the character and learning of the lawyer, Dominus Hyacinthus, who is there portrayed.   In his edition (1929) Birrell significantly comments:

> This book is so full of Latin, and the humour of it turns so much upon Latin phrases, as hardly to repay the trouble of reading to any one not acquainted with that language.[32]

One expects a lawyer, especially an Italian lawyer of the seventeenth century, to make free with Latin, a language which lends a certain dignity to even his weaker witticisms, and

---

[30] *Ferishtah's Fancies*, "Prologue", 1-8.
[31] *Op. cit.*, 29-30.
[32] *The Poetical Works of Robert Browning*, 2 vols., new edn., London 1929, II. 173.

which gives the book an attractive air of verisimilitude. Elsewhere Browning's constant satire on learning and pedantry is more surprising. Considering the wide range of his own reading and love of out-of-the-way knowledge it is difficult to grasp why he should have felt so strongly on the subject. Perhaps the fact that he had voluntarily withdrawn from London University after only a few months, to the great displeasure of his father, accounts for the violence of his exclamation in "Sibrandus Schafnaburgensis": "Plague take all your pedants, say I !", and for the satisfaction with which he regards the ruined book:

> Here you have it, dry in the sun,
>   With all the binding all of a blister,
> And great blue spots where the ink has run,
>   And reddish streaks that wink and glister
> O'er the page so beautifully yellow:
>   Oh, well have the droppings played their tricks !
> Did he guess how toadstools grow, this fellow?
> Here's one stuck in his chapter six.[33]

Browning's satire of learning is not always so effective, and scattered throughout his work there are to be found an infinite number of awkward and joyless lines, like those in "Christmas Eve":

> Girding her loins up to perturb
> Our theory of the Middle Verb;
> Or Turk-like brandishing a scimitar
> O'er anapaests in comic-trimeter;
> Or curing the halt and maimed "Iketides",
> While we lounged on at our indebted ease. . . .[34]

This facetiousness which characterises the most boring passages in Browning's poetry contrasts with the grotesque element in his work. His use of the grotesque is to be found in, and lies behind, some of his best poetry. It is the achievement of the synthesis which, when it fails, leaves us with the facetious. At its best it has the quality of Bosch, and is to be found in poems which are deservedly popular, such as " 'Childe Roland to the Dark Tower Came' " or "The Bishop Orders his Tomb at St

[33] "Sibrandus Schafnaburgensis", 89-96.   [34] "Christmas Eve", 1100-6.

Praxed's Church". The triumph of the grotesque is in Guido's second book in *The Ring and the Book*, an extraordinarily subtle analysis of the states of mind of a condemned murderer. On reading it in its context I find that I can accept even the following metaphor for the Pope's refusal to intercede on behalf of the condemned man, in which the Pope is described as vomiting on Guido, who is sitting outside his door:

> but no!
> He sighs, shakes head, refuses to shut hand,
> Motions away the gift they bid him grasp,
> And of the coyness comes—that off I run
> And down I go, he best knows whither! mind,
> He knows, who sets me rolling all the same!
> Disinterested Vicar of our Lord, . . .
>
> He's sick of his life's supper,—swallowed lies:
> So, hobbling bedward, needs must ease his maw
> Just where I sit o' the door-sill.[35]

There is a psychological realism in the disgust evoked here. It is Guido's own disgust and sickness at the unpleasantness of death which is reflected in the whole of the rich imagery throughout this book. The same sort of psychological realism justifies Guido's *lapsus*:

> a master-stroke of argument
> Will cut the spinal cord . . . ugh, ugh! . . . I mean,
> Paralyse Molinism for evermore![36]

Read out of context, this slip could be condemned as facetious. In fact it is tragic, for with it comes the realisation that the condemned man is utterly unable to keep his thoughts from running on his imminent beheading. The dialectic and digressions are on the surface; beneath them the main theme draws on to its foregone conclusion.[37] One more example of this grotesque realism (and there are more in this second book of Guido than anywhere else in Browning) is the curious erotic fantasy into which Guido escapes, as death approaches:

---

[35] *The Ring and the Book*, XI. 73-9, 84-6. [36] *Op. cit.*, XI. 641-3.
[37] Written long before Freud, in *The Psychopathology of Everyday Life*, had drawn attention to the import of this kind of verbal slip, it is a striking example of Browning's intuition.

> O thou Lucrezia, is it long to wait
> Yonder where all the gloom is in a glow
> With thy suspected presence?—virgin yet,
> Virtuous again, in face of what's to teach—
> Sin unimagined, unimaginable,—
> I come to claim my bride,—thy Borgia's self
> Not half the burning bridegroom I shall be!
> Cardinal, take away your crucifix![38]

If we think of the circumstances in which these words were spoken, that they were addressed to a cardinal and an abbot, and that Guido is trying to persuade them to return to the Pope and beg for a reprieve, then the voicing of this fantasy is indeed grotesque. On another level, that of an inner realism, the idea that Guido, half-mad with fear as a violent and inevitable death rapidly approaches, the tortures that he has undergone at the hands of the law a mere foretaste of the torments of Hell which he sees as awaiting him, should take refuge in a dream-plunge into the arms of a supremely beautiful and wicked woman, who holds out the promise of "sins unimagined, unimaginable", is not only credible, but thoroughly convincing. It was the same idea that Browning was to use again in *Fifine at the Fair*[39] and "Numpholeptos", that physical love could ward off, if not death itself, at least the thought of death.

Browning had his own theory for the use of the grotesque. In *Aristophanes' Apology* he explains the theory that underlies this method. The poet, he claims, must not be

> Encircled with poetic atmosphere,
> As lark emballed by its own crystal song, . . .
> No, this were unreality! the real
> He wants, not falsehood. . . .[40]

This reality, this truth, he finds lies rather in ugliness than beauty:

> Strength and utility charm more than grace,
> And what's most ugly proves most beautiful.[41]

---

[38] *The Ring and the Book*, XI. 2214-21.
[39] See below, Ch. VIII, p. 175.
[40] *Aristophanes' Apology*, 2163-7.
[41] *Op. cit.*, 2171-2.

That Browning was not speaking here in his own person does not belie the relevance of this statement to his own art. This was only one side of the question. As always, Browning was ready to argue for both sides, but he did not limit himself to expressing this theory, which was only to become generally accepted in the twentieth century:[42] he put it into practice in much of his verse. In "Bishop Blougram's Apology" Browning was trying to write like Donne, to take the everyday example of a pinch of snuff as a parallel for the great metaphysical questions of doubt and faith. The use of this simile is justified by the setting, an after-dinner talk over the claret in the Bishop's study. Yet, perhaps because the analogy behind the simile is too slight, or because the worldly, society tone of the Bishop does not stretch far enough to cover this kind of humour, Browning does not wholly satisfy us that "faith means perpetual unbelief":

> here's my box—
> I need the excitation of a pinch
> Threatening the torpor of the inside-nose
> Nigh on the imminent sneeze that never comes.
> "Leave it in peace" advise the simple folk:
> Make it aware of peace by itching-fits,
> Say I—let doubt occasion still more faith![43]

These lines are, I feel, a fair example of the risks Browning was running in his use of grotesque realism. They mark, too, a basic difference between Browning and the metaphysical poets. Whereas the metaphysicals were often Baroque, Browning's crowded pages tend to be Biedermeier. We are misled by the historical context of his plots into connecting him with an Italian background, ranging from the Renaissance to the Risorgimento, but he remains fundamentally Victorian in taste and at times even in the lack of it. Like the metaphysicals, he drew his materials from a vast variety of sources, but the resulting whole is rather the harmonious and overcrowded medley of a Victorian drawing-room than the symmetry of a

[42] See W. Kayser, *The Grotesque in Art and Literature*, Bloomington 1963, for a revaluation of the grotesque as a perfectly legitimate category of artistic expression.

[43] "Bishop Blougram's Apology", 669-75.

Baroque structure. This is another way of saying that much of his poetry, with the exception of the best of his dramatic monologues, lacks unity, it is crowded with non-essentials. Take away, for example, from *The Ring and the Book* any of his extended similes, and the structure is no more disturbed than by the removal of a china dog from a littered chimney-piece.[44] Yet it is dangerous to remove many of even the uglier ornaments as irrelevant—their effect is cumulative and in his better work they add up to a whole.

Nevertheless the major weakness of Browning as a poet lay in his prolixity, in a gift of verbalising *ad infinitum* which led, inevitably, to obscurity. It is impossible to give detailed examples of this because the better the example, the more space it would occupy. It was a fault that never left him, from the early *Sordello* to the later *Red Cotton Night-Cap Country*. The extraordinary simile at the end of this latter poem is perhaps worthy of particular attention. Clara is likened to a caterpillar:

> Her quality was, caterpillar-like,
> To all-unerringly select a leaf. . . .[45]

This simile continues for twenty-three lines. After a digression of thirty-nine lines, Browning takes it up again:

> What
> She did believe in, I as little doubt,
> Was—Clara's self's own birthright to sustain
> Existence, grow from grub to butterfly,
> Upon unlimited Miranda-leaf. . . .[46]

This is continued for eighteen lines, then dropped again for one hundred and seven lines, after which it is continued for a further eleven lines. Altogether the caterpillar weaves its way in and out of one hundred and ninety-seven lines. The image of the grub and butterfly which Browning had used so effectively in the prologue to *Fifine* grows like Amedée till Browning most unwillingly lets it drop with the words:

---

[44] See Leonard Burrows, *Browning, An Introductory Essay*, Perth (Australia) 1952, p. 70, which compares Browning's collection of obscure fact to Balzac's collection of *bric-à-brac*.

[45] *Red Cotton Night-Cap Country*, 4037-8.   [46] *Op. cit.*, 4097-101.

> And could she (the grub) still continue spinning,—sure,
> Cradle would soon crave shroud for substitute. . . .[47]

Prolixity is to be found particularly in discursive or dialectic poems. We learn to beware of such words as "Put case that . . .". They are used well in "Caliban upon Setebos", but in "Two Camels", for instance, they plunge us into the useless sort of argument of which Browning was so fond:

> Why, the physician called to help the sick,
> Cries "Let me, first of all, discard my health!"[48]

In *Sordello* Browning, writing of the troubadour, had acknowledged the need of control and brevity:

> He left imagining, to try the stuff
> That held the imaged thing, and, let it writhe
> Never so fiercely, scarce allowed a tithe
> To reach the light—his Language.[49]

To reduce his work to a tithe would have been severe self-censorship, but Browning's strong instinct of conservation prevented him from weeding out anything at all. In 1855 he attempted to revise the poem but found the effort of "filing" instead of "hammering" infinitely irksome, and soon relinquished the project.[50]

Another interesting example of prolixity can be seen in the not unattractive lines in *The Two Poets of Croisic*:

> Our log is old ship-timber, broken bulk.
> There's sea-brine spirits up the brimstone flame,
>   That crimson-curly spiral proves the hulk
> Was saturate with—ask the chloride's name
>   From somebody who knows! I shall not sulk
> If yonder greenish tonguelet licked from brass
>   Its life, I thought was fed on copperas.[51]

I have quoted these lines because they contrast so well with the concise utterance of T. S. Eliot, who in *The Waste Land* concentrates the same idea into only two lines:

---

[47] *Op. cit.*, 4226-7.   [48] "Two Camels", 82-3.   [49] *Sordello*, II. 570-3.
[50] See Betty Miller, *Robert Browning*, p. 141.
[51] *The Two Poets of Croisic*, 34-40.

Huge sea-wood fed with copper
Burned green and orange, framed by the coloured
   stone. . . .

Nor has Browning finished with the sea-wood fire here. He
worries the burning log on and off through the next five
stanzas. I do not wish to suggest that the quality of poetry can
be judged merely by conciseness, but Browning's most definitely
suffered from the lack of it. An attempt to tighten things up
would undoubtedly have eliminated the shockingly weak line:
"From somebody who knows! I shall not sulk." Mere
padding, all of it, and we note again the responsibility of the
rhyme, not forced this time, but only too glib.

It is terribly destructive, and at the same time too easy, to
pick out the faults of an artist: so much harder to show where
his greatness lies. We can at least notice how he turned these
faults to good account. While there is no credit balance to
offset bad grammar or facetiousness, I have already noted that
ostentatious rhymes could be most effective in comic poetry, and
clogged consonants or obtrusive alliteration could be deliberately used to achieve specific technical results.

Much more important are Browning's positive use of
grotesque realism and prolixity. With the former he created
a new style in art, his own style, the style that was to influence
so many of the poets who came after him. He opened the door
which let the false teeth and the soda-water into *The Waste
Land* : [52]   they follow close upon the Bishop's pinch of snuff.

His prolixity opened another kind of door, that of his own
mind, that of the subconscious. In *Sordello*, using the significant
word "escapes", he had written:

        while from true works (to wit
Sordello's dream-performances that will
Never be more than dreamed) escapes there still
Some proof, the singer's proper life was 'neath
The life his song exhibits, . . .[53]

This calls for no examples here, for each one of the following
chapters illustrates the truth of this in Browning's poetry.

[52] An exhibit in the Amsterdam Stedelijk Museum, constructed entirely of
false teeth, is a recent example of how easy it is, missing the grotesque, to fall into
the facetious.   [53] *Sordello*, III. 622-6.

II

Where the Bishop Ordered his Tomb

"THE Bishop Orders his Tomb at Saint Praxed's Church",
first published in *Hood's Magazine* for March 1845
under the title "The Tomb at Saint Praxed's" has, in
the words of DeVane[1], "generally been regarded as the product
of Browning's second Italian tour, taken between August and
December 1844". It is believed that he then visited the
church of Santa Prassede in Rome "and saw the tomb of
Cardinal Cetive there; and it was probably then that the idea
of the bishop ordering his tomb occurred to him". Rome,
however, is full of churches, and these churches are full of
tombs, so that it is possible for even a resident sightseer such
as Browning to confuse his details. I believe that the only
thing which Browning really carried away with him from the
church of Santa Prassede was its name, and something of the
tranquil atmosphere:

> Saint Praxed's ever was the church for peace.[2]

Certainly no tomb there resembles the one Browning's Bishop
orders, either as to position or structure. Furthermore the
Bishop tells us that his niche is so situated that thence one sees

> up into the aery dome where live
> The angels, and a sunbeam's sure to lurk . . .[3]

but Santa Prassede is one of the few Roman churches without a
sunny or even a sunless dome. In spite of his knowledge of
Italian, Browning must have had an English guide-book in his
hands, for the feminine Santa Prassede, named after the virgin
daughter of Pudens, is anglicised as Saint Praxed, a name which
Browning took to be masculine:

[1] W. Clyde DeVane, *A Browning Handbook*, 2nd edn, New York 1955, pp. 166-8.
[2] "The Bishop Orders his Tomb at St Praxed's Church, Rome, 15—", 14.
[3] *Op. cit.*, 23-4.

Saint Praxed at his sermon on the mount.[4]

It is true that the Bishop's mind is shown as wandering here: earlier in the poem he had referred to

> The Saviour at his sermon on the mount,
> Saint Praxed in a glory,[5]

but there is little doubt that this glory, too, surrounded a masculine Saint Praxed, for while Browning might be guilty of mistakes of fact which were wholly irrelevant to the poem, yet he would never have allowed his dying Bishop to change the sex of the patron saint of his church.

If the Bishop and his tomb are not to be found in the Roman church of Santa Prassede, a search has already been made for them elsewhere, and most notably by John D. Rea, Louis S. Friedland, and Lionel Stevenson.

Rea[6] finds the source in the *Vita di Vespasiano Gonzaga* by Ireneo Affò, which was published in Parma in 1780. To summarise his evidence, I hope more fairly, even if more briefly, than Mr Friedland does, he finds in the *Vita* a churchman named Gandolfo, the word "elucescebat", the Duke dictating his will as he lies dying in his state-chamber "Jacens in lecto in quodam camera superiore palatii praefati", and the command to his daughter concerning the erection of his tomb:

> First let my daughter be bound and obligated to erect in that church a tomb of marble, in which my body will be placed, on the construction and adornment of which she will be bound and obligated to spend fifteen hundred scudi, besides the stones necessary to adorn the aforesaid tomb, which I have had brought from Rome.

On the tomb is to be placed, the will goes on, a statue of the Duke.

Friedland[7] challenges only the two weaker arguments put

---

[4] W. Clyde DeVane, *A Browning Handbook*, p. 116; "The Bishop Orders his Tomb", 95.

[5] "The Bishop Orders his Tomb", 59-60.

[6] J. D. Rea, " 'My Last Duchess' ", in *Studies in Philology*, XXIX (1932), pp. 120-2. The English translation of Affò is the one used in Rea's article.

[7] L. S. Friedland, "Ferrara and 'My Last Duchess' ", in *Studies in Philology*, XXXIII (1936), pp. 656-84.

forward by Rea, drawing attention to the common occurrence of the name Gandolfo and the fact that the desire for sumptuous tombs was so general in Renaissance Italy that no particular importance can attach to this one. He carries DeVane along with him, so that the *Handbook* reports Rea's theory as "discredited".

The name Gandolfo as introduced in the *Vita* certainly has no real connexion with anything: "Tali altercazioni spiacevano a tutti i buoni, e specialmente al Papa, siccome abbiamo da una lettera di Gandolfo Porrino a Giulia".[8] There is, however, a further, rather Empsonian argument in favour of Rea's case, which he failed himself to point out. In his article he mentions only Gandolfo, but the name in Affò's *Vita* is Gandolfo Porrino. Had Browning's poem been written twenty-four years later, at the time of *The Ring and the Book*, when his knowledge of Italian enabled him to ring the changes so brilliantly on the name of Hyacinthus-Giacinto, I should have had no hesitation in suggesting that Gandolfo's "paltry onion-stone" came from the Italian surname, for *porrino* is a diminutive of *porro*, meaning "leek". While it is true that a foreigner is often much more conscious of the meaning and origin of names than a native of any language, I cannot tell whether Browning, at this stage, having spent a total of only six months in Italy, and still confused about the sex of Santa Prassede, could have seen the connexion.

To return to Rea's case. The late Latin form *elucescebat* was in use from the fourth century A.D., and Browning may easily have met it in other contexts. Still, the presence of all these elements *together* in a book which may also have served Browning as a source for "My Last Duchess"[9] cannot be too lightly swept aside.

A further theory which still maintains the historical source-link between "The Bishop" and "My Last Duchess" is put forward by Lionel Stevenson,[10] who identifies the Duke of "My

---

[8] P. Ireneo Affò, *Vita di Vespasiano Gonzaga*, Parma 1780, p. 4.

[9] Here again I find Friedland's arguments against Rea specious, although he makes a stronger case for Alfonso II of Ferrara than Rea had made for Vespasiano Gonzaga.

[10] L. Stevenson, "The Pertinacious Victorian Poets", in *The University of Toronto Quarterly*, xxi (1952), pp. 232ff.

Last Duchess" with Ercole II, Duke of Ferrara from 1534 to 1559, and the Bishop of Saint Praxed's with his brother, Cardinal Ippolito d'Este the Younger; but all the support that he offers for the latter is contained in the following passage:

> the Cardinal was notorious for his stinginess (he gave Ariosto no reward in return for his dedication of *Orlando Furioso*); he was defeated as a candidate for the Papacy because of his scandalously worldly conduct; and he is best remembered for the building of the gorgeous Villa d'Este at Tivoli.[11]

If Mr Stevenson fails to explain further to us why he sees the Cardinal as Browning's Bishop, it is because he is too busy explaining why he sees Hermione in *The Winter's Tale* as Browning's Last Duchess—an argument into which there is no need to follow him.

If the question of the origin of Browning's Bishop remains open, whether he was really one man or the sum of a number of Renaissance figures, we can at least determine where he ordered his tomb. Not, as might have been expected, in one of the many Roman churches Browning visited and confused together, and from which he drew much of the atmosphere of his poem, including the richness of coloured marbles and the aery dome, which are not to be found in Santa Prassede. He certainly saw these in "the Jesu Church so gay" mentioned in l. 49 of the same poem, which is the Chiesa del Gesù in Rome, but this is only one of many such ornate churches. Browning did not find the Bishop's tomb ready constructed: he ordered it, and from a man who had taught him a great deal about architecture in general and tomb-making in particular: Gerard de Lairesse.

The name is already familiar to Browning scholars through the article where DeVane first drew attention, in 1925, to *The Art of Painting in All its Branches*[12] as a basic source of the landscape of "Childe Roland".[13] Although much further study has been made of this, the most written-about of Browning's poems, and additional sources have been convincingly

[11] L. Stevenson, *op. cit.*, p. 241.

[12] Gerard de Lairesse, *The Art of Painting in All its Branches*. All my page-refs. are to the 1778 edition, which was the one Browning used.

[13] DeVane, "The Landscape of Browning's 'Childe Roland' ", *PMLA*, XL (1925), pp. 426-32.

C

traced,[14] yet DeVane's examination of parallel passages
between Lairesse's treatise and "Childe Roland" has shown
how thoroughly Browning had imbibed Lairesse.[15] We have,
of course, his declaration, which he wrote in his own copy of
the work:

> I read this book more often and with greater delight, when I
> was a child, than any other; and still remember the main of it
> most gratefully for the good I seem to have got from the prints
> and wonderful text. Robert Browning, Feb. 13, '74.[16]

This treatise on the art of painting takes in the whole range
of the visual arts, including architecture and statuary. DeVane
was chiefly concerned here with the chapters devoted to
landscape, and more especially to "Things deformed and
Broken, falsly called *Painter-like*", which furnished many of the
components of the horrible landscape of "Childe Roland".
But there are other chapters, with such titles as "Of Archi-
tecture in General", "Of immoveable Ornaments; as Tombs,
Houses, etc."; "Of the Matching of the various coloured
Marbles; as well without as within a Building; with the
Management of Tombs, Vasa, and Bacchanalian Terms";
"Of bass-reliefs".

It was from this book, long before his first visit to Rome, that
Browning first learnt of the art of tomb-building. The Bishop
is presented as having long thought on this question, and his
first instructions are very precise. The tomb is to be a basalt
(dark grey) stone, and is to be surrounded by red marble
columns:

> And I shall fill my slab of basalt there,
> And 'neath my tabernacle take my rest,
> With those nine columns round me, two and two,
> The odd one at my feet where Anselm stands:

---

[14] See especially D. V. Erdman, "Browning's Industrial Nightmare", in
Philological Quarterly, xxxvi (1957), pp. 417-35.

[15] The use made of Lairesse in "Childe Roland" shows how completely *The Art
of Painting* had become a part of Browning's mental make-up, even more than the
use he made later of the same text in the *Parleyings with Certain People*, as DeVane
has shown in *Browning's Parleyings: The Autobiography of a Mind*, New Haven (Yale)
1927, for in the latter case Browning was consciously and deliberately writing about
Lairesse.

[16] Cp. DeVane, *A Browning Handbook*, p. 230.

Peach-blossom marble all, the rare, the ripe
As fresh-poured red wine of a mighty pulse.[17]

On this slab is to rest his statue and on the knees of the statue a
lump of lapis lazuli. The forethought which has gone into this
tomb is betrayed by his confession of having previously stolen
and hidden the precious lump:

> Draw close: that conflagration of my church
> —What then? So much was saved if aught were missed!
> My sons, ye would not be my death? Go dig
> The white-grape vineyard where the oil-press stood,
> Drop water gently till the surface sink,
> And if ye find. . . . Ah God, I know not, I ! . . .
>
> Bedded in store of rotten fig-leaves soft,
> And corded up in a tight olive-frail,
> Some lump, ah God, of *lapis lazuli*. . . .[18]

Frank J. Chiarenza[19] convincingly argues that the Bishop's
forethought extends also to the commissioning of the paltry
onion-stone tomb of his predecessor whom he was determined
to outshine, and interprets the line "Tully, my masters?
Ulpian serves his need"[20] as a direction to the craftsmen,
deliberately imposing a low Latin epitaph.

The Bishop, then, had thought long about his tomb, and so,
too, had Browning, for its basic elements are to be found in the
most imaginative part of Lairesse's work, the imaginary walk
the blind painter takes to discover and point out the "Painter-
like Beauty in the open Air" and which Browning refers to in
his *Parleyings* as he describes the boyish ardour of the young
Browning:

> The while that memorable "Walk" he trudged
> In your companionship,[21]

---

[17] "The Bishop Orders his Tomb", 25-30.

[18] *Op. cit.*, 34-42.

[19] F. J. Chiarenza, "Browning's 'Bishop Orders his Tomb at Saint Praxed's
Church' ", in *The Explicator*, XIX (1961), item 22.

[20] "The Bishop Orders his Tomb", 79.

[21] *Parleyings*, "With Gerard de Lairesse", 46-47.

a walk which

> No measurer of steps on this our globe
> Shall ever match for marvels.[22]

In the course of this walk, Lairesse tells us:

> Stepping a little further, I saw another sight as fine as the
> former; I say, fine with respect to art. It was an ancient tomb
> or sepulcher of light red marble, intermixed with dark grey,
> and white eyes and veins, with a lid or cover of lapis lazuli.[23]

So far we have only the basic elements of the tomb, the dark
grey and red marbles and the lapis lazuli. But the Bishop goes
on to specify more precisely what he wishes:

> Did I say basalt for my slab, sons? Black—
> 'T was ever antique-black I meant! How else
> Shall ye contrast my frieze to come beneath?
> The bas-relief in bronze ye promised me.[24]

In the chapter concerning "the Management of Tombs, Vasa,
and Bacchanalian Terms" Lairesse gives more detailed
instructions for tomb-building:

> On brackets of copper or brass, the tomb may be of black
> marble. . . . Note here, that the black must always be under-
> most, especially when divers sorts of colours are placed on one
> another, as we have shewed in the Orders.
> Great vases and urns are always of the same stone as their
> bases, as well in niches as on pedestals.[25]

And earlier in the same chapter: "Between two black marbles
suit best jasper, copper or brass".[26] The brass and copper fuse
together into the Bishop's bronze, and the jasper leaps out
startlingly when the Bishop's mind begins to wander:

> Nay, boys, ye love me—all of jasper, then!
> 'T is jasper ye stand pledged to, lest I grieve.[27]

The jasper has probably come in from the Lairesse context, but
Browning is quick to justify it psychologically for the Bishop—

---

[22] *Op. cit.*, 49-50.   [23] G. de Lairesse, *The Art of Painting*, p. 255.
[24] "The Bishop Orders his Tomb", 53-6.
[25] G. de Lairesse, *The Art of Painting*, p. 297.
[26] *Op. cit.*, p. 295.   [27] "The Bishop Orders his Tomb", 68-9.

he has been reminded of it by his bath, one of the things that
he is so regretfully leaving behind him.[28] As he feels his hold
on life slipping, he appeals to his "nephew" as "child of my
bowels, Anselm", and allows

> strange thoughts . . .
> About the life before I lived this life[29]

to creep into his mind, mixing Saint Praxed with the Saviour,
remembering his mistress and "New-found agate urns as fresh
as day", which may also have come out of the above passage in
Lairesse.

DeVane, in his book on Browning's *Parleyings*,[30] hints at a
further Italian literary source in Daniello Bartoli's *Dei Simboli
trasportati al Morale*: "One of the chapters named above, Il
Teatro di Pompeo . . ., may have supplied Browning with
detail for his poem 'The Bishop Orders his Tomb', which was
written in 1844, when Bartoli was much in Browning's mind.
The rich materials of which the theatre was built are all to be
found in Browning's poem."

DeVane goes no further into the question but the clue is
worth following up, and brings to light an interesting chain.
The rich materials mentioned in the chapter of Bartoli are not
actually those of the theatre itself, the details of which, with the
exception of a description of the huge statue of Sejanus, are left
vague. The marbles are those of a moral reflection by Seneca
which is incorporated in the same chapter:

> Ancor'a'malvagi splendidamente addobbati si fa di berretta e
> s'inchina: ma l'inchino si termina a quella scorza che ne
> apparisce di fuori; ond'è il far con essi quel che Seneca disse
> avvenire a chi vede un muro incrostato di sottilissime falde, e
> quasi foglie di diaspro, di porfido, di nero e giallo antico, di

---

[28] Probably this idea of the Bishop's jasper bath came from the great green
jasper bath of the Emperor Constantine, which stands in the Baptistery of the
Church of San Giovanni in Laterano, Rome.

[29] "The Bishop Orders his Tomb", 91, 93. I do not believe that these lines
mean simply "before I entered the Church", as has been suggested. Why should
such thoughts be "strange"? It seems more probable that he was touching on
metempsychosis, as dying, Browning makes him wonder, if for a moment only,
about the survival of the soul, and this in the midst of struggling for the Renaissance
perpetuity in marble that he desired.

[30] DeVane, *Browning's Parleyings*, p. 57.

lapislazzuli, o d'altra pietra di prezzo; *Miramur parietes tenui marmore inductos, cum sciamus quale sit quod absconditur. Oculis nostris imponimus.*[31]

We find here in common with Browning's poem only jasper, black marble, lapis lazuli, and "other precious stones" (the porphyry is already irrelevant as there is none in the Bishop's tomb), which in itself is a connexion of the slightest. But, on the following page is a much more important passage, again of moral reflexion and not description, which must have led DeVane to think immediately of Browning's Bishop and which explains the link he made in the above note:

> E attoniti parimenti e mutoli rende la compassione i buoni conoscitori e stimatori del merito de' virtuosi, il vederli andarsi tuttodì avvolgendo in cerca di qualche nicchia dove poter, non collocare un pezzo di marmo, ma riparar sè stessi: e i miseri per quantunque cercarne mai non la truovano: perochè ad escluderli da tutte, tutte le nicchie son piene: ma piene, oh quante! di statue d'uomini: d'uomini, oh quanto pochi! Statue poi, voglia il cielo, che son le più d'esse, tiratevi con le machine di Sejano, non portatevi su le proprie spalle, sentendo il peso delle fatiche lungamente sofferte nel rendersi degno e acquistarsi il merito di quell'onore.
>
> Son piene tutte le nicchie, e non riman luogo vuoto per te: cercane altrove, e riparati dove puoi.[32]

Browning's Bishop, who "fought with tooth and nail to save my niche" and who was "cozened" out of it by Gandolfo, surely

---

[31] Daniello Bartoli, della Compagnia di Gesù, *Dei Simboli trasportati al Morale*, III. iv ("Il Teatro de Pompeo dedicato a Sejano"), p. 81. "And to evil men who are splendidly adorned men raise their hats and bow low: but the homage is restricted to the outward surface; so our approach to them is the same as Seneca recorded of a man who sees a wall encrusted with extremely thin slabs, almost leaves, of jasper, porphyry, ancient black and yellow marble, lapislazuli or other precious stones: . . ."

[32] *Op. cit.*, p. 82: "Men who recognise and admire the worth of the virtuous are struck dumb with compassion when they see it employed in searching all day for some niche not to erect there a piece of marble, but to shelter themselves: and however hard the poor wretches try they fail: there is no room for them because all the niches are full; how many of them, full of the statues of men: how few of men! Statues, heaven knows, for the most part raised up by Sejanus' pulleys, not carried there on their own shoulders, feeling the weight of the long-sustained effort rendering them worthy of such honour. All the niches are full, and there is no room left for you: look elsewhere, and take refuge where you may."

owes something to Bartoli here. The niche was no light question for the Bishop: it is a sore point that will rankle for all his temporal "eternity". Something of the pity which Browning betrays for the Bishop condemned to his "not-so-cramped" niche is due to the *cri du cœur* echoing in his ears from Bartoli: "All the niches are full, and there is no room left for you: look elsewhere, and take refuge where you may." The moral of Bartoli too ties up perfectly with that enunciated in the first line of Browning's poem: "Vanity saith the preacher, vanity".

But to return to the earlier instructions for his tomb: we learn that this was not the first time the Bishop had told his sons of his wishes, for he speaks of

> The bas-relief in bronze *ye promised me*,
> Those Pans and Nymphs *ye wot of*, and perchance
> Some tripod, thyrsus, with a vase or so,
> The Saviour at his sermon on the mount,
> Saint Praxed in a glory, and one Pan
> Ready to twitch the Nymph's last garment off,
> And Moses with the tables. . . .[33]

And later in the poem he adds some further details for the frieze:

> Or ye would heighten my impoverished frieze,
> Piece out its starved design, and fill my vase
> With grapes, and add a vizor and a Term,
> And to the tripod ye would tie a lynx
> That in his struggle throws the thyrsus down,
> To comfort me on my entablature. . . .[34]

In juxtaposition with these two passages from Browning should be placed a chapter from Lairesse's book: "Table or Ordonnance of Erisichton; and the Emblem of a Satyr's Punishment: Both serving for the Embellishment of Land-scapes". Subtitle: "Sweet Repose disturbed by Lewdness. An Emblem."

> Here are seen three young nymphs of *Diana's* train, tired with hunting, reposing in the shade of the trees a little off from the road, and near a foamy water: which some *fauni* and satyrs espying, they were resolved to have some sport with

---

[33] "The Bishop Orders his Tomb", 56-62: my italics.   [34] *Op. cit.*, 106-11.

them. Wherefore, acquainting their associates with the matter, they silently advanced towards the place in a body; bringing with them one of the largest *Priapus* terms they had, together with two panthers a vessel of wine and some grapes. Being arrived, and seeing the nymphs almost naked, and fast asleep, they planted before the place the aforesaid hideous scare-crow; and then softly stole their hunting equipage, as quivers, arrows, bows, etc., and hung them on its genitals, fastening them with the straps, which they buckled. They moreover decked its head with one of the nymph's veils, sticking their *thyrses* in the ground round about it, and adorning them with vizors. Not stopping here, they seized as many of the virgins' garments as they could, and tossed them upon the high limbs of an adjoining tree; and to prevent the nymphs climbing up in order to regain, they tied the two panthers under the tree; and after having set down the wine and grapes, pleased with the project, they covertly retired to a peeping place to wait the issue on the nymphs awaking.[35]

Another nymph appears, and shoots one of the panthers:

The satyrs seeing this, came out of their lurking-hole, and pursued her, but she escaped by flight. They then concluded, they had waited long enough; and observing that it grew late . . . they in a full body of satyrs, *fauni*, bacchanals, even all the tribe of *Bacchus*, set up with their instruments so loud a noise, that the nymphs started up on a sudden; and, full of fright, looked for their cloaths; but being now thoroughly awaked, the *term* presented before them, with their hunting equipage hanging about it. . . . Not one durst approach the block in order to take her weapons . . . they above an hundred times invoked the aid of *Diana*; yet in vain. The eldest, named *Cleobis*, at last took courage, and went up to the *term*, with intention to get the veil from it to cover *Carile*, who was naked; saying,—Ah! Why are we such fools as to be thus scared, and only by a wooden black [*sic*] Why are we ashamed? . . . I am resolved to throw it down. Come, sisters, and boldly give an helping hand.—But she had no sooner uttered these words, but all the gang appeared, mocking, scoffing and hooting: any one may determine who was on that overture, most dashed and concerned. A little satyr shot at the *term*, and took the quivers from it, showing the nymphs the unseemly member, with an hearty laughter. This (but especially when other scoffers

---

[35] G. de Lairesse, *The Art of Painting*, pp. 249ff.

shewed them the cloaths on the tree) highly provoked them. To take to flight was not adviseable; one pushed them this way, another that way. During this game a noise of cornets was heard, which suddenly put an end to the laughter; each made off, leaving all things as they stood. The *term* of *Priapus* fell to the ground, and the panther at the tree endeavoured to get loose. Now, *Diana* appears, attended by her train of nymphs, who shot their arrows at the lewd crew. ... The fearful nymphs appeared much ashamed, and prostrated themselves at the feet of the goddess; to whom they related their misfortunes, and the affront put upon them by the gang of satyrs: shewing her at the same time, the *term*, the vizors, their cloaths on the tree, and what else was done in despite to them.[36]

Here we have, in the first place, many of the *words* which went into the ornamenting of the Bishop's frieze: "nymph", "term", "grapes", "thyrses", and "vizors", with the substitutions of satyrs for Pans, and a panther struggling loose as a term is overthrown, in the place of a lynx throwing down a thyrsus. But Browning took more from this passage than mere verbal recollection, more even than the visual picture that he was so obviously conjuring up. The extremely obvious Freudian symbolism of the tale must have made an impression on him as he was reading this as a boy: the guilt not only of the satyrs but the nymphs, who have to prostrate themselves at the feet of their goddess, the chaste Diana, for forgiveness; and the punishment of lewdness following immediately on the heels of the crime: for three of the satyrs, Lairesse tells us, were whipped by the three affronted nymphs "so severely, as almost to kill them", while three others had their tails cut off with a hunting knife, in unquestionable castration symbolism. Had Browning read the text as it was edited thirty-nine years later by Craig in 1817 much of the sexual impact of the story would have been lost, for Craig makes the satyrs hang the quivers of the nymphs "around the waist" of the Priapus term and not *on its genitals* as Fritsch had translated in the 1778 edition in Browning's possession, and the later edition drops completely the details of the satyrs' punishments and the quiver of the nymph used as covering for the term's "unseemly member".

[36] *Ibid.*

Fortunately Browning had the full text in his hands, and must have read this passage many times, for it was a synthesis of many of the elements in the book: like the "Walk" which caught Browning's attention and which he used as the basis for one of his *Parleyings*, it was one of the more imaginative passages. Lairesse's imagination seems, indeed, judging by the amount of Freudian symbolism which has found its way into the tale, altogether to have run away with him. It is a piece of pure creative writing embodied in the treatise on the slender pretext of being "though a feigned story, matter sufficient to furnish many landscapes".[37]

And the tale had a moral:

> You see here the alluring pleasure of committing a crime, and the bashfulness and distress of those who suffer the evil; but at the same time, the grievous consequences, and punishment attending wickedness and insolence. In fine, the sweets and punishment of evil, and the reward and unexpected relief of virtue.[38]

And the moral was appropriate to Browning's Bishop, for his sin lay in the begetting of those "nephews" who stand round his bed, and it is they who are to be the means of depriving him of the only kind of future existence that he believes in or desires: the monument of his rich marble tomb. That such an Edgar-Gloucester relationship is not far-fetched in connection with the Bishop, is suggested by Lairesse's subtitle "Sweet Repose disturbed by Lewdness. An Emblem".

The purpose of a frieze, Lairesse teaches us elsewhere, is

> to set off a figure with emblems, whether on a pedestal, or in a niche, in bass or whole relief, in order to blazon the qualities and virtues of the person it represents.[39]

This, too, Browning has learnt from Lairesse, and what seems at first a *witty* juxtaposition of classical and Christian elements in the Bishop's frieze conveys an overtone of "grievous consequences, and punishment attending wickedness and insolence".[40] How Lairesse helped Browning to make the punish-

---

[37] *Op. cit.*, p. 251.   [38] *Ibid.*
[39] *Op. cit.*, p. 56.   [40] *Op. cit.*, p. 251.

ment fit the crime, and get at his Bishop through his very pride in marble must be considered later; there is more to discuss about the frieze.

In the frieze on the Bishop's tomb Browning's lynx takes the place of Lairesse's two panthers. Elsewhere, in connexion with the ornament of the temple of Bacchus, Lairesse introduces "Two tygers, a thyrsis twined with vine leaves, and bunches of grapes".[41] Why then, among the larger cats, should Browning light on the lynx, an animal Lairesse never mentions, to take the place of these tigers and panthers? It is highly probable that this is simply a verbal compound of lioness and sphinx, two animals which are frequently mentioned by Lairesse in connexion with tombs. A sphinx is coupled with a lioness in the following passages:

> On white sphinxes, lionesses, etc. suits well a tomb of serpentine or porphyry.[42]
> Also termes, niches with figures, ballustrades adorned with lions and lionesses; sphinxes and other ornaments.[43]

In the chapter "Of Painter-like Beauty in the open Air", the chapter to which Browning referred directly in his *Parleyings* with reference to the discovery of Phaeton's tomb, there is a round temple, its steps "adorned with two sphinxes", while "On each side of the before-mentioned steps was a fountain or square bason, adorned with two pretty large lionesses, couching, on pedestals".[44] The description of this temple contains all the following words in common with Browning's poem: entablature, bass-relief, columns, "Pilasters of the Corinthian order, *two and two* together", frieze, dome and sun, so that the lynx can credibly be held to combine the sphinxes and lionesses of the same picture.

All the elements of Browning's frieze recur over and over again interwoven with each other in Lairesse, so that it would be strange if the poet who had "read this book more often and with greater delight, when I was a child, than any other" should not call them to mind when dealing with such a subject. Indeed, the details from Lairesse come tumbling over each other into the

[41] *Op. cit.*, p. 418.   [42] *Op. cit.*, p. 296.
[43] *Op. cit.*, p. 65.   [44] *Op. cit.*, p. 257.

poem and are allowed to do so as being consistent with the dying Bishop's state of mental confusion; for Browning in his better poems, of which this is undeniably one, was capable of the necessary restraint, checking his too fluent rush of recollections, keeping them within the limits of psychological probability.

To return to Lairesse: a lion and a tiger are introduced with a broken thyrsus and grapes in a passage reminiscent of the tiger ornament on the temple of Bacchus:

> Here lie broken thyrses, potsherds, bruised grapes and vine-branches scattered round the body in great disorder: The long-lived stag makes to cover; the dreadful lion and spotted tyger grimly pass each other.[45]

Stone lions and lionesses are to be found in a scene with *vases*, "fragments of *columns*", "pieces of *frizes* and bass-*reliefs*",[46] a scene in which they are followed by mention of "sphinxes", "tombs", and "terms", while another tomb "supported by four white marble sphinxes without wings, resting on a large black marble plinth", stands in front of a pedestal on which had been set "an *urn*, now flung down".[47]   Again later we find "a white marble basis, with a *broken term*, and its trunk lying near it",[48] and a *thyrsus* with *Bacchus* and *grapes*.[49]   The word "entablature" is used in connexion with "frieze",[50] and "term" with "tomb"[51] while "vizards" are to be found in yet another frieze, with playing children and running animals.[52]

The fact that ll. 106-108 of Browning's poem—

> Or ye would heighten my impoverished frieze,
> Piece out its starved design, and fill my vase
> With grapes, and add a vizor and a Term,

—were only added to the poem four years later, for the collected edition of 1849, suggests that Browning had been fully aware of what he was doing when he ordered the Bishop's tomb in the first place.   These lines, added in revision and not in the heat of poetic inspiration, show that he knew at least where to turn

[45] *Op. cit.*, p. 48.   [46] *Op. cit.*, p. 211.   [47] *Op. cit.*, p. 255.
[48] *Op. cit.*, p. 233.   [49] *Op. cit.*, p. 42.   [50] *Op. cit.*, p. 288.
[51] *Op. cit.*, pp. 211-2.   [52] *Op. cit.*, p. 289.

when making a modification to his poem, so that there would
be no change disconnecting the addition from the basic structure. Whatever the reason for the added lines, I am inclined
to think that they, like most of the rest of the poem, came, or
were fetched, from Lairesse.

The elements are jumbled together: the lynx throwing
down the thyrsus in Browning's poem may well be the sphinx-
with-the-urn-flung-down confused with the broken-thyrsus-
grapes-and-lion, and the panther-and-term-thrown-down of
Lairesse's emblematic tale.

Grapes are everywhere, and this brings us to another point
—Browning's obvious interweaving of the persons of Pan and
Bacchus, both of whom are at times equated with the satyrs, and
linked with the term, or God Terminus. In "The Bishop
Orders his Tomb" we find in the bas-relief of the frieze

> Those Pans and Nymphs ye wot of . . .
> . . . and one Pan
> Ready to twitch the Nymph's last garment off.[53]

This is no casual ornament, but an integral feature of the tomb
as planned by the Bishop, a feature he had already discussed
previously with his sons. It conveys, and is intended to convey,
a deeper understanding and revelation of the Bishop's character,
something over and above the surface joke contrasting the
naughtiness of the Pan with the solemnity of Moses, his hands
full of the *Thou Shalt Nots*. It draws attention to the Bishop's
essentially pagan nature. The mixture of classical and
Christian elements is in no way surprising on a Rennaissance
tomb, but the introduction of Pan, the pagan and Arcadian
earth-god, is interesting.

The Pan of the Bishop's frieze is the Pan of "Pan and Luna"
which Browning wrote much later, in 1880, basing it on Virgil's
third Georgic. This Pan, as Luna is wrapped in wraiths of
cloud, holds "a treacherous hand wide ope to grasp her":

> So lay this Maid-Moon clasped around and caught
> By rough red Pan, the god of all that tract.[54]

---

[53] "The Bishop Orders his Tomb", 56, 60-1.
[54] "Pan and Luna", 65-6.

The Pan of "Pan and Luna" is at the same time the satyr of Browning's *Parleyings*, "With Gerard de Lairesse" who spies on Lyda, one of the "train of forest-thridding nymphs", as she lies asleep:

> Thy greedy hands disclose the cradling lair,
> Thy hot eyes reach and revel on the maid![55]

and Pan's love for Echo is evoked as an analogy in the same passage.[56]

But the satyr of Browning's *Parleyings* is also the troop of satyrs in Lairesse's "feigned story of a satyr's punishment: Sweet Repose disturbed by Lewdness. An Emblem". Here the satyrs spied on the sleeping nymphs of Diana's train, and "seized as many of the nymphs' garments as they could".[57] They also decked the head of the Priapus term with one of the nymphs' veils, sticking their thyrses in the ground round about it, and adorning them with vizors.

While the satyr of Browning's *Parleyings* is connected with the satyrs of Lairesse, so the nymph Lyda of "With Gerard de Lairesse", x, who is linked with the Diana of "With Gerard de Lairesse", ix,

> Moon-maid in heaven above and, here below,
> Earth's huntress queen[58]

is at the same time connected with the nymphs of Diana's train in Lairesse.

The Art of Painting in All its Branches makes no mention of Pan, but Lairesse's Bacchus "is adorned with *vine-sprigs*, crowned with *grapes*, and armed with a *Thyrsis*",[59] connecting

---

[55] *Parleyings*, "With Gerard de Lairesse", 306-7.

[56] In *Browning's Parleyings*, pp. 247-8, DeVane points out that this is the story told by Moschus and translated by Shelley. DeVane sees this as a picture "that Lairesse might have envied", but fails to link it up with Lairesse's own picture in his emblematic tale. His conclusion, however, that Lairesse could never, like Browning, have thrown himself into the feelings of the satyr, is unquestionably true, for Browning could always look at a moral question through the eyes of a sinner, even although he allows moral condemnation and retribution so inevitably to follow, and this moral having-it-both-ways may in part account for his popularity.

[57] G. de Lairesse, *The Art of Painting*, p. 250.

[58] *Parleyings*, "With Gerard de Lairesse", 230-1.

[59] G. de Lairesse, *The Art of Painting*, p. 42.

him with the satyrs of the emblematic tale, who carried a vessel of wine and some grapes, thyrses and a Priapus term. These terms he tells us,

> anciently used in the *Bacchanalia*, were mostly of wood, not very large, and pointed underneath for conveniency of carriage from place to place, whither the gang of satyrs, fauni and bacchanals, determined to go. . . . These terms were sometimes painted of a brick colour, sometimes also white; about the mouth and breast they were smeared with blue grapes. [60]

Of another term, Lairesse tells us

> This term, was down to the lower belley, like a man, yet very musculous, and the head resembled that of a satyr, and guarded with two large crooked ram's horns. . . . [61]

In "Pan and Luna" the maid-moon is caught by "rough red Pan" (the terms in Lairesse were sometimes painted a brick colour), is raked by his "bristly boar-sward" (the "furry-framed" visage of the *Parleyings*), and a complex analogy of purity and defilement is introduced into the passage from Virgil, figuring a forefather ram. The maid recoils, feeling Pan's horns when he kisses her, reminding us of the term's satyr-like head with its crooked ram's horns. In "Pan and Luna" and in the *Parleyings* Browning develops more fully the scene of nymphs and satyrs he took from Lairesse. In "The Bishop Orders his Tomb" he can only introduce it in an emblematic form, but, like so much that goes into poetry, it carries added weight from its original context, a weight which can be sensed even before its origin is traced.

So Lairesse furnishes not only the marbles which went into the construction of the Bishop's tomb, but almost all the emblems which went into the frieze. And as the Bishop's heart was wholly set on lying "through centuries" in his magnificent tomb, so his growing fear was lest his sons should cheat him and leave him for eternity "Bricked o'er with beggar's mouldy travertine". [62] The conviction that this will ultimately be the case, becoming increasingly intense throughout the poem,

---

[60] *Op. cit.*, p. 297.   [61] *Op. cit.*, p. 254.
[62] "The Bishop Orders his Tomb", 66.

builds up the dramatic tension which is so effective, until the reader, as so often in Browning, is led to suspend all moral judgment in his pity for the predicament of a sinner, presented so vividly from that sinner's own point of view.

Clearly Browning wanted to stress this damnation which was awaiting the Bishop, a damnation in his own terms,

> Gritstone, a-crumble! Clammy squares which sweat
> As if the corpse they keep were oozing through—
> And no more *lapis* to delight the world.[63]

Lairesse, when considering the qualities of various marbles, draws attention to the same type of stone:

> Some stones, being more weak and brittle than others, and corroded by the air, dampness and drought, are broke in pieces by the pressure of those over them, and thus leave gaps and breaks. . . .[64]

The idea of the escaping corpse may have come from another passage in Lairesse, the chapter which DeVane has shown to be such a basic source for "Childe Roland". Here Lairesse writes:

> It was here so lonesome and gastly, that I was seized with a cold sweat; wherefore I mended my pace, in order to get out of it; and, being got to the other side, and ten or twelve paces from it, I found myself again at the lake before-mentioned; near which lay a shattered tomb, with the corpse half tumbled out.[65]

Browning had already used this corpse in *Sordello*: "As shows its corpse the world's end some split tomb" and it is possible that this, too, lay behind the Bishop's revulsion and dread. Like the *danse macabre*, such a scene was one peculiarly likely to impress a child as intensely shocking, a revelation striking out against all sense of decency, and Browning, who was born in 1812, when the swaddling and swathing which was so to characterise the Victorian era was just beginning, was liable to be peculiarly sensitive to such shocks.

The position of these lines, near the close of "The Bishop Orders his Tomb", stresses the basic meaning of the poem: Browning, like Lairesse in his emblematic tale, is dealing with

---

[63] *Op. cit.*, 116-8.   [64] G. de Lairesse, *The Art of Painting*, p. 297.
[65] *Op. cit.*, p. 261.

"the sweets and punishment of evil". For, together with the many verbal echoes he took more or less consciously from his source, there is the borrowing of the basic idea, the punishment of lewdness, which in Christian terms can be expressed as a sin against chastity and damnation, or in Freudian terms as a violation against taboo and retribution.

It has been argued that Browning's popularity with his contemporaries was largely due to a dual morality which condoned the sins of his characters: this can certainly never be argued of the Bishop, and it is doubtful whether it can be convincingly argued of his other personae. For the Bishop meets at Browning's hands with comprehension, pity—and punishment, a punishment more classical than Christian in nature, as the Bishop is more classical than Christian in outlook, or perhaps we can say more neo-classical than either, toning down the tortures of a Tantalus or a Prometheus to an eternity spent oozing through an inferior grave-stone subject to the mockery of his hated rival. Browning might sympathise with his sinners, but he never suggests that the offender can or should be allowed to get away with it. Salvation for Browning could only be in strictly Christian terms, through repentance, and the Bishop shows no signs of repenting. The last line of the poem "As still he envied me, so fair she was!" leaves him where the first line had found him: "Vanity, saith the preacher, vanity!" This text was no casual choice. Scripture for Browning was never mere proverb: he remembers texts in their Biblical contexts. As to the interpretation to be put on Browning's poem: his first words were also his last word, for the quotation is taken from Ecclesiastes:

> Then shall the dust return to the earth as it was: and the spirit shall return unto God who gave it. Vanity of vanities, saith the preacher, all is vanity.[66]

---

[66] Ecclesiastes, xii, 7-8.

III

Bright Gold

A KEY word, I might say the key word, in Browning's poetry is "gold". He uses this word and its compounds approximately 390 times in his poetical works, and is (so far as we can judge from concordances) the only English poet in whose work the word occurs more frequently than it does in the Bible. To see the relevance of this figure we need only note that in the Old and New Testaments together the word occurs approximately 334 times, in the whole of Shakespeare's work 296 times, and in Browning's contemporary Tennyson 302 times.[1] These figures have no scientific value as proportions whatsoever, as the works in question are of varying lengths (though all long), but they serve to make my main point incontestably clear: that Browning's interest in and concern with gold was inordinate. Gold meant much, so much, to him, that I am proposing in the present study first to find out what, and secondly why.

Gold has had many meanings for man; and it is hardly surprising that Browning, with his constant awareness of ambiguities, should have been attracted by its plurisignificance. For not only does he use it in many different ways in different contexts: often he concentrates a number of meanings into the single reference.

Old and New Testament gold

In this, as in everything, the Bible was one of the deepest influences on Browning's thought. The Old Testament takes

[1] It is interesting to note the use of the word by other major English poets. Spenser comes high in the list, with 279 references, as opposed to Milton's 98. Chaucer strikes a balanced 182, Yeats 153, Wordsworth 136, and Coleridge only 67. Shelley, whose early influence on Browning was great, comes high, with 260; and Keats, considering his relatively small output, was likewise much travelled in the realms of gold, with 148 references. These figures are based on concordances, and have only, I must repeat, a curiosity-value.

the primitive view of gold—something of unquestionable value, the attribute of kings and the adornment of temples. This is the basic meaning of the word, its oldest meaning: the most precious metal known to man. In Old Testament times it is either a material good, or a symbol of something positive. Abraham, we are told, was rich "in silver and in gold",[2] and it is felt to be good and right that he should be so. Gold was the Jews' most valued possession (they made their idols of it); the Queen of Sheba brought it as a gift to Solomon just as, at the changing of the epochs, the least wise, surely, of the three wise men brought it to the infant Christ. For with Christianity a change came over the nature of gold. While the Hebrew sense of gold as a priceless possession continued, by which it represented purity as opposed to baser metals, the new Christian concept of gold as something evil entered. Preachers began to ask such questions as "Whether is greater, the gold, or the temple?"[3] A division had come about between what was divine and what was material. These were the distinctions which fascinated Browning. He may even have had the above question in mind when he quotes from Lamentations[4] both in *Fifine at the Fair*—

Where the fine gold grew dim i' the temple . . .[5]

and in *The Ring and the Book*—

"How is the fine gold of the Temple dim!"[6]

—the first time in connexion with the ruin and change wrought in a city by time, and the second as an ironical reference by the lawyer to the besmirching of Pompilia's good name.

But gold was to be still further purified in the New Testament. In Revelation, where it is used to describe the vision of Heaven, the heavy metal of which Solomon had built his temple is felt to be too earthly a substance, and we have the further refinement, "And the city was pure gold, like unto clear glass, . . . and the street of the city was pure gold, as it were transparent glass",[7] in a poetical attempt to transcend the grosser material quality of the gold. Gold had lost all reality

---

[2] Genesis XIII. 2.   [3] Matthew XXIII. 17.

[4] Lamentations IV. 1.   [5] *Fifine at the Fair*, 2000.

[6] *The Ring and the Book*, XII. 735.   [7] Revelation XXI. 18, 21.

here, gold as transparent as glass is inconceivable as matter: we are dealing with pure symbol. The grossness of the metal has been transmuted, it has become a wholly unreal and ætherial substance. Henry James was trying to create just this material for his golden bowl, but he had to be content with the approximation of crystal covered with gold.

Browning had this transparent gold in mind already in an early poem in a passage clearly deriving from Revelation, where he describes heaven as

> ... a place in the other world ...
> All glass and gold, with God for its sun. ....[8]

But the glass and gold are still separate here, as in James. In "Abt Vogler" instead, where the gold is a symbol of music, itself the most disembodied form of artistic creation, Browning achieves the transmutation and writes of

> Raising my rampired walls of gold as transparent as
> glass. ...[9]

Like all artists, Browning was deeply interested in his art; and much of his writing, despite the dramatic disguise it often took, is more or less openly concerned with aesthetics and technique. It is significant that in order to find an expression for the *achievement* of artistic creation (the *process* is magnificently described by another golden symbol in *The Ring and the Book*, and the *materials* by that elemental gold I shall consider further in the next chapter) he has recourse to the purest symbol he knows, something beyond the material wonders of the earthly paradise, beyond the Tree of Life itself or another tree whose fruit never lost its attraction for him, the Tree of the Knowledge of Good and Evil: the substance of the Heavenly Paradise, over and beyond this earth. For Browning, the solid, comfortable, respectable Victorian writer, who wrote so much of the time about earthly gold, and whose interests may have seemed almost wholly bound up in this, conceived art as belonging to another sphere. He did not leave gold wholly behind him, but found, as so often, in the Bible the symbol he wanted, transcending the baser metal.

[8] "The Worst of It", 95-6.   [9] "Abt Vogler", st. iii.

Elsewhere, however, the metal itself, pure and unmixed with dross, is used as a symbol for art or poetry, as in

> With poetry, the gold, and wit, the gem . . .[10]

or again in *The Two Poets of Croisic*,[11] where the gold in the crock to be found where the rainbow ends is poetry—the crock holding, like the artist's cup, the purest distillation of the actual.[12] This surely provides us with a definition of what Browning was trying to do throughout his work: when he failed, as so often he did, it is because he fed in so much of "the actual" that the distilling process broke down under the strain and too many of the impurities are left.

Alchemical and Refined Gold

Most frequently Browning expressed the work of the artist through two metaphors, seeing him first as the magician and secondly as the craftsman. As a magician he was an alchemist, transmuting baser materials, either clay or brass, into gold. And gold in these contexts represents, to a greater or lesser extent, both art and truth, art for Browning being equated with truth, the artist's sole aim. This transmutation is described at some length in "Mr Sludge, 'The Medium' ":

> "He dug up clay, and out of clay made gold"— . . .

> How many of your rare philosophers,
> In plaguy books I've had to dip into,
> Believed gold could be made thus, saw it made
> And made it?[13]

Browning believes in the possibility of this transformation on a symbolic level, but it puzzles him, for it is a magical process, the operation of which cannot be clearly understood. Therefore he reasons it out, placing the arguments, with his usual perversity, into the mouths of such untrustworthy characters as Mr Sludge or Dominus Hyacinthus de Archangelis, the lawyer in *The Ring and the Book*, as though to see how, in these

[10] *Aristophanes' Apology*, 2412.   [11] 839.
[12] Cp. Henry James, "The Author of 'Beltraffio' ", in *The Complete Tales*, ed. Edel, Vol. V, London 1963, pp. 332.
[13] "Mr Sludge, 'The Medium' ", 114, 121-4.

adverse circumstances, it will stand up. The lawyer, preparing a defence for the four rustics concerned with Guido in the murder of Pompilia and her parents, is meditating on how the confessions of his clients under torture can waste all the artistry with which he has built up his speech:

> So, doubtless, had I needed argue here
> But for the full confession round and sound!
> Thus might you wrong some kingly alchemist,—
> Whose concern should not be with showing brass
> Transmuted into gold, but triumphing,
> Rather, about his gold changed out of brass,
> Not vulgarly to the mere sight and touch,
> But in the idea, the spiritual display,
> The apparition buoyed by winged words
> Hovering above its birth-place in the brain,—
> Thus would you wrong this excellent personage
> Forced, by the gross need, to gird apron round,
> Plant forge, light fire, ply bellows,—in a word,
> Demonstrate: when a faulty pipkin's crack
> May disconcert you his presumptive truth![14]

Browning is troubled by the paradox of the "presumptive truth", by the fact that the work of the artist can apparently be diverted to a wrong end.

But Browning's questioning of "presumptive truth" goes even deeper than this, and again he uses a metaphor from alchemy. Not only is the artistry of man called in question, but even the artistry of God, that Power "who undertook to make and made the world". Where, the Pope asks, is

> the gloriously-decisive change,
> Metamorphosis the immeasurable
> Of human clay to divine gold, we looked
> Should, in some poor sort, justify its price?
> Had an adept of the mere Rosy Cross
> Spent his life to consummate the Great Work,
> Would not we start to see the stuff it touched
> Yield not a grain more than the vulgar got
> By the old smelting-process years ago?[15]

---

[14] *The Ring and the Book*, VIII. 383-97.
[15] *Op. cit.*, x. 1615-23.

If we are surprised by the failure of the Rosicrucians to achieve
the alchemical transformation promised, how much more so
by the apparent failure of God to keep his promise and meta-
morphose man? After tracing this huge question mark, the
Pope hurriedly turns his back on it and disowns it—

> I
>
> Put no such dreadful question to myself, . . .
> No,—I have light nor fear the dark at all[16]

—in a gesture typical enough of Browning himself when, as so
often happened, his reasoning seemed to have turned against the
fundamentals of his faith.

The difficulties, even the despair of the artist, are likewise
set out by Browning in another metaphor from the refining of
gold. Even the "perfect man, as we account perfection"
working with the

> most pure
> O' the special gold, whate'er the form it take,
> Head-work or heart-work, fined and thrice-refined
> I' the crucible of life, whereto the powers
> Of the refiner, one and all, are flung
> To feed the flame, . . .[17]

holds out triumphant a block which

> breaks,
> Into some poisonous ore, gold's opposite. . . .[18]

The alchemical process fascinated Browning, as it was later to
fascinate Yeats, suggesting the supernatural element in artistic
inspiration and creation, and he returns to the crucible image
in "Jochanan Hakkadosh", and again in "A Pillar at Sebzevar",
where he gives the metaphor a personal twist, adapting it to his
favourite theory that it is not the result which counts, but the
effort:

> cast in fining-pot,
> We learn,—when what seemed ore assayed proves dross,—

---

[16] *Op. cit.*, x. 1630-1, 1660.
[17] *Prince Hohenstiel-Schwangau, Saviour of Society*, 1319-24.
[18] *Op. cit.*, 1325-6.

> Surelier true gold's worth, guess how purity
> I' the lode were precious could one light on ore
> Clarified up to test of crucible.
> The prize is in the process: knowledge means
> Ever-renewed assurance by defeat
> That victory is somehow still to reach. . . .[19]

"The prize is in the process"—here, an old man, Browning is still preaching the theory of art which was also his theory of life, the theory which underlies so many of his poems in *Men and Women* such as "Andrea del Sarto" and "A Grammarian's Funeral", that it is not the result but the effort that counts.

The Goldsmith or Craftsman

Alchemy then, though a fascinating process, is more or less unsatisfactory, and Browning is happier with his second metaphor for the artist: the goldsmith or craftsman. The legend of an actual goldsmith was the subject he took for his long poem *Red Cotton Night-Cap Country*, the goldsmith with a Paris shop on the Place Vendôme and a country residence at the Clairvaux Priory:

> A jeweller—no unsuggestive craft!
> Trade that admits of much romance, indeed.
> For, whom but goldsmiths used old monarchs pledge
> Regalia to, or seek a ransom from,
> Or pray to furnish dowry, at a pinch,
> According to authentic story-books?[20]

Though the trade may "admit of much romance" there is little in the tale, yet Browning was clearly drawn to Monsieur Léonce Miranda, its masochistic hero. Even the description of the park at Clairvaux betrays how intimately the fact that Miranda was a goldsmith was bound up with Browning's whole conception of the man, for I suspect that underlying the description of the park landscape, we have the goldsmith's shop window in Paris, where the jewels are displayed on a velvet background, viewed perhaps through the trellis of a safety-grate:

[19] "A Pillar at Sebzevar", 17-24.
[20] *Red Cotton Night-Cap Country*, 588-93.

> Look through the railwork of the gate: a park
> —Yes, but *à l'Anglaise*, as they compliment!
> Grass like green velvet, gravel-walks like gold,
> Bosses of shrubs, embosomings of flowers. . . .[21]

The bushes remind him of those large circular Victorian brooches, and the flower-beds of parures. But Miranda is no craftsman: indeed, burning off his hands at the wrists[22] in a fit of madness, and finally committing suicide, he is the very negation of one, so that the tale is concerned with the negative values of gold, and the greed it inspires. Before considering how deeply the evil in gold interested Browning, I wish, however, to complete this survey of its "good" meanings.

The finest use Browning makes of gold is perhaps as a symbol of art and artistry in *The Ring and the Book*. Here he studies the craftsmanship by which gold can be made malleable, and finds a symbol (he calls it just that) for the part played by the artist in transforming the raw material into a work of art. First he tells us of the find on a Florentine stall of the Old Yellow Book from which he drew his plot

> thus far take the truth,
> The untempered gold, the fact untampered with,
> The mere ring-metal ere the ring be made![23]

and of how he recognised its value

> From the book, yes; thence bit by bit I dug
> The lingot truth, that memorable day,
> Assayed and knew my piecemeal gain was gold. . . .[24]

This connoisseurship, this selection and recognition of his material, he acknowledges to be part of the work of the artist. It is perhaps regrettable that, like many other connoisseurs, he let himself be drawn away too often by the merely curious at the

[21] *Op. cit.*, 656-59.
[22] Read in conjunction with some extraordinary mutilation images in Browning's early letters to Elizabeth Barrett, 26 May and 25 Sep. 1845, this gesture of Miranda's may well be seen as castration symbolism.
[23] *The Ring and the Book*, I. 364-6.
[24] *Op. cit.*, I. 458-60.

expense of what he himself had the instinct and experience to recognise as good. This time there is no mistaking:

> Now, as the ingot, ere the ring was forged,
> Lay gold, (beseech you, hold that figure fast!)
> So, in this book lay absolutely truth,
> Fanciless fact.[25]

It is with this precious material that the artist works—and Browning succeeds in adapting his "gold" metaphor to allow for his own contribution. He cannot accept that the artist merely beats out the raw material of the gold, and hammers it into shape, which is the usual poetic metaphor. The artist, he feels, adds something of himself to the material at his disposal, and his reading furnishes him with the technical process which serves as metaphor:

> There's one trick,
> (Craftsmen instruct me) one approved device
> And but one, fits such slivers of pure gold
> As this was,—such mere oozings from the mine,
> Virgin as oval tawny pendent tear
> At beehive-edge when ripened combs o'erflow,—
> To bear the file's tooth and the hammer's tap:
> Since hammer needs must widen out the round,
> And file emboss it fine with lily flowers,
> Ere the stuff grow a ring-thing right to wear.[26]

The artist, that is to say, is more than a craftsman, it is his own substance which interfuses the gold. This concept is more usually expressed in terms of giving birth to the work of art, but Browning has sought for and found a symbol which is more suited to his own method of composition. It is the recognition of the essential rightness of this whole concept which has made the introductory lines to *The Ring and the Book* one of the best-loved passages in Browning. Gestation may fitly serve to express much poetic creation (one thinks at once of a Blake, a Coleridge or a Shelley—of Browning's own "Childe Roland" or his *Fifine*), but *The Ring and the Book* was forged along the lines Browning so clearly explains to us, as

[25] *Op. cit.*, I. 141-4.   [26] *Op. cit.*, I. 8-17.

That trick is, the artificer melts up wax
With honey, so to speak; he mingles gold
With gold's alloy, and, duly tempering both,
Effects a manageable mass, then works:
But his work ended, once the thing a ring,
Oh, there's repristination! Just a spirt
O' the proper fiery acid o'er its face,
And forth the alloy unfastened flies in fume;
While, self-sufficient now, the shape remains,
The rondure brave, the lilied loveliness,
Gold as it was, is, shall be evermore:
Prime nature with an added artistry—
No carat lost, and you have gained a ring.
What of it? 'Tis a figure, a symbol, say. . . .[27]

Gold here is used by Browning in its highest sense as "absolutely truth". To refine it still further was to reach the "gold transparent as glass" which, as we have seen, was not of this world.

Sexual Gold: The Bee-Honey-Lily Image Cluster

The opening lines of *The Ring and the Book* are intensified, too, by the introduction of a key image-cluster, the bee-honey-lily flowers. All these are, in different contexts, separately linked with gold, through their yellow colour. In "Aeschylus' Soliloquy" he writes of "golden bees",[28] while in *Sordello* June lilies are "soiled by their own loose gold-meal",[29] and in the *Parleyings*

Only to ope a lily, though for sake
Of setting free its scent, disturbs the rough
Loose gold about its anther.[30]

and in *Sordello* again we have the arum lily

The gold-rough pointel, silver-blazing disk
O' the lily![31]

---

[27] See Paul A. Cundiff, "The Clarity of Browning's Ring Metaphor", in *PMLA*, LXIII (1948), pp. 1276-82; *The Ring and the Book*, I. 18-31.

[28] "Aeschylus' Soliloquy", *New Poems*, ed. Kenyon. London 1914. p. 65.

[29] *Sordello*. III, 687.

[30] "With Francis Furini", 30-2.

[31] *Sordello*, V. 130-1.

Although the lily is a traditional symbol of chastity, in Browning's work it has other associations. Browning uses the bee-honey-pollen cluster, again and again, with sexual connotations; and there is no doubt that gold for him was mingled with these symbols and its value enhanced by them. This was, perhaps, one more reason why Browning used the word "gold" so freely in his poetry: it brought with it pleasurable though often unidentified associations which only became conscious, or partially so, in some of his flower imagery. The use of the words "womb", "ardours", and "groom", for example, in "Popularity" is unequivocal:

> Most like the centre-spike of gold
> Which burns deep in the blue-bell's womb,
> What time, with ardours manifold,
> The bee goes singing to her groom,
> Drunken and overbold.[32]

Here the golden pistil-spike of the blue-bell is equated with the gold-rough pointel of the lily, a link being provided perhaps by "Saul",[33] where the lilies are blue, suggesting that Browning thought of the blue-bell and the lily in the same way.[34] The lily itself becomes a symbol of exotic temptation in *Fifine*, where the heart of the flower is twice referred to as a "golden gloom" and we are told that

> About each pistil spice is packed,
> Deliriously-drugged scent.[35]

Though gold was pollen for Browning, it was even more inextricably bound up with honey, and the parallel is drawn again in *Aristophanes' Apology*,[36] and in *The Ring and the Book*,[37] while the bee as a sexual symbol is most fully developed in "Women and Roses":

[32] "Popularity", x.

[33] "Saul", 12.

[34] "Saul", 6. In a letter to Elizabeth postmarked 16 Mar. 1846, in answer to her repeated query about "blue lilies", Browning furnished the following explanation: "Lilies are of all colours in Palestine—one sort is particularised as *white* with a dark spot and streak—the water lily, lotos, which I think I meant, is *blue* altogether".

[35] *Fifine at the Fair*, 178.

[36] *Aristophanes' Apology*, 2722.   [37] *The Ring and the Book*, III. 905-3.

Deep, as drops from a statue's plinth
The bee sucked in by the hyacinth,
So will I bury me while burning,
Quench like him at a plunge my yearning,
Eyes in your eyes, lips on your lips!
Fold me fast where the cincture slips,
Prison all my soul in eternities of pleasure. . . .[38]

Other elements form part of this image-cluster,[39] which re-appears over and over again (although in more fragmentary forms) throughout Browning's work, but what interests us here is the bee-honey-gold association. Although this cluster was probably the most potent in influencing him, as it represented the pleasure of the sexual act itself, yet it by no means exhausts the sexual connotations of gold for Browning.

Male Gold: Danae's Golden Shower

Gold and silver coins have also, on occasion, a sexual signifi-cance in his work, where they are the equivalent of the golden shower Jove rained on Danae. This sexual symbolism is to be found in *Fifine at the Fair*,[40] and can also be seen as underlying Pompilia's definition of her marriage as "the coin, a dirty piece",[41] and it may even be an under-reading of the famous lines in "The Statue and the Bust":

The counter our lovers staked was lost
As surely as if it were lawful coin. . . .[42]

The equation is drawn up clearly in the line "Whose last faint sands of life, the frittered gold",[43] where the sand is running out of the hour-glass, but the "frittered gold" is also at the same time humanity itself,[44] the seed of Adam mentioned in the lines immediately preceding:

[38] "Women and Roses", vi.
[39] The Shakespearian fly as a symbol of lust becomes in Browning that strange hybrid, the "gadbee", cp. "Artemis Prologizes", 21-2: "A noisome lust that, as the gadbee stings, /Possessed his stepdame Phaidra for himself".
[40] *Fifine at the Fair*, 109.   [41] *The Ring and the Book*, vii. 407.
[42] "The Statue and the Bust", 244-5.
[43] *The Ring and the Book*, viii. 1445.
[44] Guido is seen as part of this humanity, and therefore as redeemable, and at the same time the sands running out of the hourglass are the numbered days of his life before his execution.

> . . . world like ours
> Where Adam's sin made peccable his seed![45]

recalling God's promise to Abraham: "I will multiply thy
seed as the stars of the heaven, and as the sand which is upon
the sea shore";[46] so that Browning is presenting us with the
equation sand = seed = gold. A gold coin carries sexual
implications in *Fifine*, where Don Juan slips a double *louis d'or*
between two silver coins into the tambourine of the gypsy girl,
describing this action as the laying of an egg in "the nest, her
tambourine":

> Between two silver whites a yellow double yolk![47]

Further evidence that gold was bound up with sex in
Browning's mind can be found in a passage on banking in *The
Inn Album* where he uses the same imagery in reverse, speaking
of the banking process through metaphors drawn from breeding,
generation, and, again, eggs:

> I know, my banker makes the money breed
> Money; I eat and sleep, he simply takes
> The dividends and cuts the coupons off. . . .
>
> But you, spontaneous generator, hatch
> A wind-egg; cluck, and forth struts Capital
> As Interest to me from egg of gold.[48]

While in "Sludge" we have mention of "cackling o'er a golden
egg".[49] It is natural that Browning should make use of the
common expression "lust" in connexion with gold, as in
"Cenciaja",

> Blinded by so exorbitant a lust
> Of gold . . .[50]

or in *The Ring and the Book*, where it is put into the mouth of the
Pope:

> but all to instigate,
> Is what sinks man past level of the brute
> Whose appetite if brutish is a truth.

---

[45] *The Ring and the Book*, VIII. 1442-3.   [46] Genesis XXII. 17.
[47] *Fifine at the Fair*, 2350.   [48] *The Inn Album*, 437-9, 442-4.
[49] "Mr Sludge, 'The Medium' ", 643.   [50] "Cenciaja", 54.

> All is the lust for money: to get gold,—
> Why, lie, rob, if it must be, murder! Make
> Body and soul wring gold out, lured within
> The clutch of hate by love, the trap's pretence![51]

Lust, the strongest term available to the Pope, is used here to condemn the love of gold (it is significant that the Bible condemns the *love* of money, the term "lust" here is Browning's own). But the use of sexual terminology to describe money is sufficiently usual to be uninteresting if it were not for the reverse image of money terminology applied to sex, as we have seen earlier, which would suggest that there is nothing casual about the interchange, but that the two were closely fused in Browning's mind.

In "Gold Hair" the sexual suggestion behind gold coins, to which references are frequent in Browning, is fully exploited. The "stainless", "inviolate" girl is buried, and many years later a hoard of gold, all in double *louis d'or*, is found hidden in the wealth of her gold hair. The lines

> Gold! She hoarded and hugged it first,
> Longed for it, lean'd o'er it, loved it—alas—[52]

show a remarkably modern sensitivity to the psychological implications of such avarice, an instinct which was to find its fullest artistic expression only many years later through the cinema in Eric von Stroheim's classic *Greed* (based on Norris's novel *McTeague*), where the obsessed woman takes the piles of coins into her bed.

This sexual suggestion is hinted at again in other poems. The cloak of the mysterious gypsy woman in "The Flight of the Duchess", who represents the sexual awakening of the heroine, is bordered with gold coins, which seem to have a meaning over and above that of mere barbaric ornament,

> For where its tatters hung loose like sedges,
> Gold coins were glittering on the edges,
> Like the band-roll strung with tomans
> Which proves the veil a Persian woman's. . . .[53]

---

[51] *The Ring and the Book*, x. 540-6.
[52] "Gold Hair: A Legend of Pornic", 107-8.
[53] "The Flight of the Duchess", 478-81.

The analogy which suggests itself to the author's mind is that
of the veiled Persian woman, indicating the cloistered state in
which the Duchess is kept, and from which, by following the
gypsy, she is to escape.　It is interesting that this passage occurs
in a sequence where the gypsy is undergoing a dream change:

> For first, she had shot up a full head in stature, . . .
> And the ignoble mien was wholly altered,
> And the face looked quite of another nature,[54]

and I am inclined to think that, as the dream technique is
extended to her garments—

> And the change reached too, whatever the change meant,
> Her shaggy wolf-skin cloak's arrangement[55]

—the interpretation of the passage should be in the same key.[56]

Royal Gold

Naturally the more usual associations played their part as well:
gold represented wealth, power, and magnificence, for
Browning as for all men.　The glance of a god or a king is
described as a "gold gaze", and the link with the ray of sunshine occurs in a passage in *Balaustion's Adventure:*

> Apollon stood a pitying moment-space:
> I caught one last gold gaze upon the night . . .[57]

and again in "Rudel to the Lady of Tripoli":

> Oh, Angel of the East, one, one gold look. . . .[58]

In "Andrea del Sarto", which, like *The Ring and the Book*, is one
of Browning's golden poems, the painter describes working
under the eye of King Francis himself:

> In that humane great monarch's golden look,—[59]

implying both the King's magnificence (the golden symbol of
his authority is directly referred to as "the jingle of his gold

---

[54] *Op. cit.*, 471, 474-5.　　　　　　　　　[55] *Op. cit.*, 476-7.
[56] See Appendix E, pp. 216-19.　　　　　[57] *Balaustion's Adventure*, 495-6.
[58] "Rudel to the Lady of Tripoli", 19.　　[59] "Andrea del Sarto", 153.

chain in my ear"), and his munificence, around which the
story of Andrea's life turns, while the "gold look" recalls the
"gold gaze" of the sun, implying warmth and benevolence. All
this Andrea has thrown away to build a house for Lucrezia,
building it, as it seems to his tormented mind, out of the very
substance of the stolen gold itself:

> oft at nights
> When I look up from painting, eyes tired out,
> The walls become illumined, brick from brick
> Distinct, instead of mortar, fierce bright gold,
> That gold of his I did cement them with![60]

He has sacrificed the patronage and friendship of the king who
used to watch him paint at Fontainebleau "one arm about my
shoulder, round my neck". Gold here, the gold of the French
court, is presented by Browning as something good—it creates
the atmosphere in which Andrea can paint, it is untarnished
even by his theft, but it remains "fierce bright gold", accusing
him not only of the theft of the gold itself, but also of the
greater crime of betraying his art, of leaving the place and the
conditions where he could produce great work, to please the
wife he knows to be unworthy. I wish to return later, in
another context, to this tragedy of Andrea, but at present must
follow up Browning's use of gold as a symbol of authority,
power, and magnificence: gold as it was understood in the Old
Testament of the Bible, as it was used in the courts of kings.
Throughout his work, from the early poems through to the late
ones, we have a wealth of gold crowns, gold chains, gold collars,
and gold rings, gold gates, gold steps, cloth of gold. The legend
of the Golden Fleece is referred to in both *The Ring and the Book*
and *Fifine*, while the golden apples of the Hesperides are
recalled even more frequently than Danae's golden shower.
Even St George, a figure of whom Browning was particularly
fond,[61] makes his first anonymous appearance in *Paracelsus*, an
early poem, wearing a scarf "heavy with rivelled gold". All
these things are felt to be good—Browning is not here question-

---

[60] *Op. cit.*, 214-8.

[61] Browning sometimes fuses St George slaying the Dragon with the myth of
Perseus slaying the sea monster, to which he so often refers. See DeVane, "The
Virgin and the Dragon", *Yale Review*, xxxvii (1947), pp. 33-46.

E

ing the value of gold but lavishing it, taking pleasure in it, revelling in it.

Gold of Happiness and Glory

By analogy Browning uses gold to represent all that he values most, hope and happiness, the praise of friends, glory, truth itself. The mood of *Pippa Passes* is set by the morning which

> Boils, pure gold, o'er the cloud-cup's brim . . .
>
> Till the whole sunrise, not to be suppressed,
> Rose, reddened, and its seething breast
> Flickered in bounds, grew gold, then overflowed the
> world.[62]

The same mood is suggested, much more concisely, in *The Ring and the Book*, where "Rome lies gold and glad";[63] and the building of Giotto's campanile for the Florence cathedral is likewise seen as a symbol of hope which will "soar up in gold some fifty braccia":

> Shall I be alive that morning the scaffold
> Is broken away, and the long-pent fire,
> Like the golden hope of the world, unbaffled
> Springs from its sleep, and up goes the spire.[64]

In "Numpholeptos" gold is equated with love:

> . . . heart-pulse ripened to a ruddy glow
> Of gold above my clay—I scarce should know
> From gold's self, thus suffused! For gold means love.[65]

In all these contexts gold is associated with pleasurable emotions, and it is interesting to note that what for Browning was clearly one of the things he valued most highly, the praise of

---

[62] *Pippa Passes*, Intro., 4, 10-12.

[63] *The Ring and the Book*, I, 907; Browning's vision of gold in nature as the colour of happiness is remarkably close to that of Agnes Varda in her film *Le Bonheur*. The dancing yellow sunflowers of the title sequence are in the same key as Browning's: "Fancy the Pampas' sheen!/Miles and miles of gold and green/ Where the sunflowers blow/In a solid glow . . .", from "A Lovers' Quarrel", 36-39. The sense of something threatening in so much beauty, so much happiness, is conveyed visually in the film and verbally by Browning.

[64] "Old Pictures in Florence", 281-4: an idea expressed not dissimilarly in William Golding's novel *The Spire*.

[65] "Numpholeptos", 13-15.

friends or fellow-artists, he equates with gold, too.[66] In "Gold Hair", this praise seems to be the highest good he can name on earth:

> With heaven's gold gates about to ope,
> With friends' praise, gold-like, lingering still. . . .[67]

And in *Luria*:

> You have the fellow-craftsman's sympathy.
> There's none cares, like a fellow of the craft,
> For the all-unestimated sum of pains
> That go to a success the world can see:
> They praise then, but the best they never know
> While you know![68]

Even the envy or hate of the fellow-craftsman cannot lessen, Browning says, the value of his praise:

> that drop's pure gold!
> —For nothing's like it; nothing else records
> Those daily, nightly drippings in the dark
> Of the heart's blood, the world lets drop away
> For ever—so, pure gold that praise must be![69]

The craft of which Luria is speaking is the art of war, but here, as so often, Browning is writing as much about himself as about his character. The passage may even have a biographical value, for he was already in correspondence with Elizabeth Barrett, and one of her attractions for him must have been the warm admiration of his work (as well as criticism) which she poured into her letters to him. To ensure for himself a steady domestic flow of such precious drops may have seemed almost a sufficient reason in itself for marrying his fellow-craftsman.

The Golden Grail

While most of the meanings of gold are present throughout Browning's work, its connexion with the quest theme is only to be found in his early poems. The most open enunciation of

---

[66] In one of his early letters to Elizabeth Barrett (11 Feb. 1845) he writes that a dozen pages of verse "ought to bring me a fair proportion of the Reviewers' gold currency".

[67] "Gold Hair", 121-2. [68] *Luria*, III, 78-83. [69] *Op. cit.*, III. 85-9.

this theme is in *Pauline*, his first published poem, where his early conception of his task as a poet is defined as

> to weave such lays
> As straight encircle men with praise and love.[70]

Significantly enough, praise is the reward he is already looking for:

> So, I should not die utterly,—should bring
> One branch from the gold forest, like the knight
> Of old tales, witnessing I had been there. . . .[71]

This passage was written some sixty years before Frazer turned everybody's attention to the full significance of the Golden Bough. Gold is used again in *Paracelsus* in relation to the Grail, and more subtly hinted at in *Sordello*, but by the time Browning wrote "Childe Roland" it had ceased to be identified with the quest theme (gold being the colour of hope, not despair). In *Sordello*, where the poet is arguing that

> 't were too absurd to slight
> For the hereafter the to-day's delight!

he finds his golden Grail not in

> some rocky fount
> Above i' the clouds

but in this first rivulet, with its

> silver globules and gold-sparkling grail
> At bottom. . . .[72]

The "gold-sparkling grail" here is the gravel bed of the stream, and the unconscious punning with the word aptly substitutes this grail for that, the link being the cup from which he drinks. The Grail here suggests a renunciation of the quest, it is the poet's refusal of further effort as he pleads with Fate to be allowed to wear

> Home-lilies ere strange lotus in my hair![73]

---

[70] *Pauline*, 524-5.
[71] *Op. cit.*, 526-8.
[72] *Sordello*, VI. 378-83.
[73] *Op. cit.*, VI. 386.

He has (he is suggesting in the unconscious pun) found his Grail, and is therefore entitled to take his rest. The noting and recording of this pun shows the kind of psychological subtlety which Browning at times achieved.

Browning has his golden bowls, his ewers, chalices, and communion cups, but he made comparatively little use of them as accepted Christian symbols. The Christian meaning is always there as an overtone whenever the Grail words are used, but Browning's main interest lay in the failure of the quest. The Grail may contain "abominations", as we shall see in the next chapter, or it may be sexual in significance, as in *Fifine* and "The Flight of the Duchess", but the main sense is often of evil or failure.

Gold as Truth

It was the gold itself, the substance of which these bowls were made, that he took as his symbol of truth, and not the artefact. In *The Two Poets of Croisic* he was to state this attitude clearly:

> But truth, truth, that's the gold! and all the good
> I find in fancy is, it serves to set
> Gold's inmost glint free, gold which comes up rude
> And rayless from the mine. . . .[74]

The "fume and fret" of the artist could do nothing to add to this truth:

> All fume and fret
> Of artistry beyond this point pursued
> Brings out another sort of burnish: yet
> Always the ingot has its very own
> Value, a sparkle struck from truth alone. . . .[75]

Truth is at times seen, not as the refined ingot, but as gold in the mine, regarded as the purest gold, in apparent contradiction of the smelting and refining metaphors. So that whereas in "Rabbi Ben Ezra" the gold of truth is refined by life itself—

> Youth ended, I shall try
> My gain or loss thereby;
> Leave the fire ashes, what survives is gold[76]

---

[74] *The Two Poets of Croisic*, 1209-12. [75] *Op. cit.*, 1212-16.
[76] "Rabbi Ben Ezra", 85-87.

—in *Paracelsus* the liquid gold of truth undergoes a natural smelting process in the heat of the earth:

> For some one truth would dimly beacon me . . .
>
>   and tremble
> Into assured light in some branching mine
> Where ripens, swathed in fire, the liquid gold. . . .[77]

In "Saul" Browning develops the same metaphor: once more it is the heat of the earth which, by a great natural struggle, refines the gold:

>   (like the throe
> That, a-work in the rock, helps its labour and lets the
>   gold go). . . .[78]

In all these gold-in-the-mine contexts Browning is emphasising that truth is something natural, a part of nature herself. The stress has shifted from Donne's:

> On a huge hill,
> Cragged, and steep, Truth stands, and hee that will
> Reach her, about must, and about must goe;
> And what the hills suddennes resists, winne so. . . .[79]

Both Donne and Browning were thinking of truth in Christian terms, but Browning shows an awareness of the new climate of nineteenth-century thought, and the changes wrought by such men as Huxley and Darwin. He arrives at the conclusion that gold is to be found in nature, and that art may be wrongly used to hide truth. In "Master Hugues of Saxe-Gotha" the roof of the church in which the organist is playing is described with "its gilt moulding and groining, under these spider webs lying". Art (which in this poem as elsewhere is symbolised by the spider's web) is here found obscuring the gold of truth. The web of music "blots" the gold. The final assertion that

> Truth's golden o'er us although we refuse it—
> Nature, thro' cobwebs we string her . . .[80]

---

[77] *Paracelsus*, II. 161, 163-5.
[78] "Saul", 93-4.
[79] John Donne, "Satyre III".
[80] "Master Hugues of Saxe-Gotha", 134-5.

is of the truth of Christianity (the roof of the church here
representing the sky). The poem is, on one level, an attack on
religious controversy, and the spider's web stands for scriptural
commentary. Yet I believe it contains a reference, at the same
time, to one of Browning's basic personal problems: the
function of the artist.[81] He was already filled with the doubts
he was to voice again much later in *The Two Poets of Croisic*:
doubts as to whether the gold of truth had any need of the
fume and fret of artistry. In *The Two Poets of Croisic*, written
twenty-four years after "Master Hugues of Saxe-Gotha",
when Browning had found time to think out and justify his
position as an artist, he admits that art may add "another sort
of burnish to the gold", but in "Master Hugues" he sees it as
veiling truth or shrouding "Heaven's earnest eye".

For an artist so concerned with truth this problem was
bound to arise, and Browning solves it best, as we have seen, in
the introductory passage to *The Ring and the Book*, where he sees
the artist as infusing something of himself into the gold of his
material to make it malleable and fashion it to form a ring, but
his return to the question later in *The Two Poets of Croisic*
suggests that he never really put it from him as satisfactorily
solved.

Gold for Browning, besides being the truth of God and of
Christianity, represented virtue, knowledge and love.

> . . . a virtue golden through and through. . . .[82]
> Knowledge, the golden. . . .[83]
> . . . some noble love, all gold. . . .[84]

It was the metaphor for all that was highest and most pure.

Graven Gold

First and foremost, however, Browning was an artist, a poet,
and one of his prime concerns was with the problems of his art.

---

[81] In *The Ring and the Book*, he speaks (I. 1179-81) of "the gift of eloquence! /
Language that goes, goes, easy as a glove, /O'er good and evil, smoothens both
to one", and uses (I. 1168-9) an image which has analogies with Hawthorne's
artificial butterfly: "some finished butterfly /Some breathing diamond-flake with
leaf-gold fans".

[82] "The Statue and the Bust", 229.   [83] "A Pillar at Sebzevar", 15.
[84] "In a Balcony", 589.

Although at times, as we have seen, he had his doubts, and art became a web to obscure the gold of truth, yet most often he saw his art in terms of gold. References to gold writing, gold lettering, gold graving, gold books, and even to gold binding, and golden plates of books, abound in his work. A few examples will suffice to show what was a simple, straightforward instinct in a writer. Gold represented for him not only the truth contained in the works, but the intrinsic value of the works themselves. Writing was something to be regarded as precious, no lesser material than gold was seen as fitting for the pages, no meaner colour suited to the bindings. Also there was the idea of the durability of the material, and therefore of the contents, and there was, too, the idea of wealth and riches which the work of art should bring its author, and the glory and fame. When he wrote in *Sordello*

> They laughed as they enrolled
> That name at Milan on the page of gold. . . .[85]

Browning was thinking of a roll of honour. So, whenever the context permits, Browning allows himself the indulgence of speaking of gold writing, graving, or books. The number of such references increased in his later poetry, and was extremely rare in his early, more autobiographical works, although they were all concerned to a large extent with his youthful views on art and his conception of himself as an artist. Perhaps these early poems were too personal; perhaps he did not wish to admit to himself any non-idealistic impulses. But possibly, too, his appetite for material things, his sense of their value, grew with the years, as his sense of the passing of time, and of the importance of durability in a work of art, must inevitably have done. It is not that Browning ever refers directly to his own work in these terms, but it obviously gives him pleasure to contemplate the handing-down of this work to others. In "Saul" we have the praise of David

> whereon they shall spend
> (See, in tablets 't is level before them) their praise, and
> record

---

[85] *Sordello*, I. 249-50.

With the gold of the graver, Saul's story,—the statesman's
  great word
Side by side with the poet's sweet comment. . . .

So the pen gives unborn generations their due and their
  part
In thy being! . . .[86]

The poem of "Cleon" is likewise described as engraved on "a
hundred plates of gold" and Browning tells us something more
in *Balaustion's Adventure*:

> any who could speak
> A chorus to the end, or prologize,
> Roll out a rhesis, wield some golden length
> Stiffened by wisdom out into a line, . . .

> Any such happy man had prompt reward. . . .[87]

Here it is the actor, the mere speaker and vehicle of the poet's
golden words, who receives high honour:

> If he lay bleeding on the battle-field
> They staunched his wounds and gave him drink and
>   food;
> If he were slave i' the house, for reverence
> They rose up, bowed. . . .[88]

In the same poem Browning uses this metaphor to describe the
words of Elizabeth:

> I know the poetess who graved in gold,
> Among her glories that shall never fade,
> This style and title for Euripides,
> *The Human with his droppings of warm tears.*[89]

Whether or not we feel that this definition of Euripides is worth
the metaphorical gold on which it is engraved is irrelevant.
What concerns us is the form of expression used by Browning,
for there can be no doubt as to his own opinion.

In "Bishop Blougram's Apology" it is Shakespeare's books

---

[86] "Saul", 184-7, 189-90.

[87] *Balaustion's Adventure*, 165-8, 171.

[88] *Op. cit.*, 172-5.

[89] *Op. cit.*, 2668-71. Cp. Elizabeth Barrett Browning, "Wine of Cyprus": "Our Euripides, the human /With his droppings of warm tears . . .".

that are "bound in gold". In *Aristophanes' Apology* the "books which bettered Hellas" are "beyond graven gold or gem indenture", and later the poet speaks of "a gold-graved writing".

In "Fust and his Friends" the whole question of printing is raised, for Browning had chosen as subject a German printer whom he held to be the inventor of movable types. Browning acknowledges the value of printing, the importance of spreading "truth broadcast o'er Europe". But there is a wry humour in his presentation of the first reception of Fust's new process of black and white printing by his friends:

> FUST. Word for word, I produce you the whole, plain enrolled,
>   Black letters, white paper—no scribe's red and gold!
> OMNES. Aroint thee!
> FUST. I go and return.[90]

The rational Browning must accept and praise the invention, yet his first irrational reaction was surely that of OMNES, and his employment of "Aroint thee!" with its slightly comical overtones is, I believe, in rather rueful self-reproach. For he has caught himself regretting the passing of the age of illuminated manuscripts, and may have suspected the reason. He would—as what writer would not—have wished to see his own works presented in all the splendour that gold could provide, with gold binding, gold lettering, or better still, graven on plates of gold, and to be paid, too, in gold. As he considers the history of printing this poet's fantasy comes to the surface, and is recognised for what it is worth.

Nor does this exhaust all the positive connotations of gold in Browning's work—there are such wonderful expressions as "girl-gold-beetling-beauty" from *Aristophanes' Apology* that I have not even touched on, but which would imply a detailed examination of Browning's hidden sexual imagery, leading too far from my main subject. There are, to catch up some loose threads, the golden strings of a harp in *Fifine*—

> the harp, whose every golden fret
> Still smoulders with the flame, was late at fingers' end—[91]

---

[90] "Fust and his Friends", 204-7.
[91] *Fifine at the Fair*, 1305-6.

which seem to me to link up with the golden plates of the graver, suggesting the transmutation wrought by art. Also in *Fifine* we find some "snakes of gold", which clearly belong to Cleopatra and are the beams of the sun which the magic of her "Asian mirror" has transformed to adorn her. For this is one of the virtues of gold, whether as a symbol or a metaphor: the vast range of transformations to which it is quite naturally subject. As colour it can enter into the nature of other materials. As a substance it can assume an endless variety of forms.

The Ambiguity of Gold

This ambiguity of gold is stressed in *Aristophanes' Apology* where the variety of forms that can be assumed by the same substance, and the uses to which it can be put, are pointed out by means of a very deliberate pun:

> Gold, leaf or lump—gold, anyhow the mass
> Takes manufacture and proves Pallas' casque
> Or, at your choice, simply a cask to keep
> Corruption from decay.[92]

The helmet enclosing the wisdom of the Goddess is at the same time the casket of the coffin. Twice before, in "Waring" and "Gold Hair" the pall over the coffin had been gold, and I think the link here is made not only through the open pun of casque/cask but through an unvoiced Pallas/pall association. This double pun shows how closely the two concepts of gold are interwoven, as the words themselves interweave. The following lines—

> Your rivals' hoard
> May ooze forth, lacking such preservative[93]

—transfer the gold from the containing cask or coffin to the contents, which become hoarded gold. To interpret these lines in full, they should be read in connexion with "Gold Hair", where the coffin was found to be heaped with hoarded gold coins hidden in the hair of the dead girl, and "The Bishop

[92] *Aristophanes' Apology*, 3360-3.
[93] *Op. cit.*, 3363-4.

Orders his Tomb",[94] where the dread of "oozing through" seems to be connected with an abnormal longing for privacy and sense of shame, explainable in physiological terms by early associations of the poet, related to the gold = dung equation I make at the end of the following chapter. For there I propose to examine the dark gold, the gold of money and evil, which played no less a part in Browning's works than did the bright gold, the gold of sunshine and splendour, the gold of pleasure and truth.

[94] See Ch. II, above, p. 38.

IV

Dark Gold

"THE love of money is the root of all evil". This text, the truth of which they never questioned, was a source of great distress to the Victorians. Their consciences were far from clear. To say that the Victorian age was an age of hypocrisy is begging the question: the need for hypocrisy arises when there is something to hide. It was an age, rather, of deep moral self-searching; men looked into their actions and found much of which they were ashamed, much that they sought to disguise. Many characters in the fiction of the time were obsessed with money, characters against whom both authors and readers could release their accumulated moral condemnation, censuring what they felt to be wrong in society, and in their own lives. The "good" characters either gave money away or sacrificed it to marry for love (whereupon it was frequently returned to them). But money, whether greedily grasped or nobly refused, was of paramount interest in Victorian fiction. Bulwer Lytton's play, "Money" had a record run for the period, being given at the Haymarket for eighty consecutive nights. For money was pouring into the country, the great banks were building their palatial establishments—the banks which Butler in his satire of the era was to substitute for the churches as the centres of national worship. Wealth was in the air, it was visible in the building going on in London, in the increase of trade. As its importance grew, the fear of losing it became greater, and, at the same time, a feeling of guilt over its unequal distribution began to creep in. The more wealth was revered, the more poverty was feared and hated. The sense of guilt which came with the possession of money was offset by the sentimental idealisation of the labourer in literature as "poor but honest". This was a common feature in novels at the time, although Trollope, at least, had the sense to

poverty could have not only a narrowing but also a
—ng influence, as in the parish of Hogglestock. Browning
—ed to the traditional view, not only in *Pippa Passes*, but
also in the gate-keeper who refuses Guido's bribe in *The Ring
and the Book*:

> Whose palm was horn through handling horses' hoofs
> And could not close upon my proffered gold![1]

Browning, whose subject-matter was so often drawn from
the past and from other countries, might well have been
expected to free himself more easily than the rest of his contemporaries from this preoccupation with money. But in fact
he was obsessed by it beyond all measure. We have only to
take two of his best-known poems and compare them with
their Italian sources to see how the emphasis has shifted:
"Andrea del Sarto" and *The Ring and the Book*.

Money in "Andrea del Sarto"

"Andrea del Sarto" was based on Vasari's *Le Vite de' Pittori* and
Baldinucci's *Notizie de' Professori del Disegno*.[2] In the Italian
histories Andrea's wife, Lucrezia, is accused not of greed but
of bullying. Vasari, who was a pupil of Andrea's, and had
lived in his house as an apprentice, writes with feeling on this
point. The misappropriation of the loan from the French King
is recorded in the source-books, but not emphasised. Browning
has developed the money question far beyond its original
significance. The reason is probably not purely sociological.
The money which passes from the husband's hand to the lover
through the wife may be partly sexual in interpretation, for
Browning was a fine instinctive psychologist. But what
interests us here is that out of hints in the Italian art-historians
and De Musset,[3] Browning has made so much of the question of
money, which is seen in Victorian terms. The "cousin", for
whose whistle the wife is so restlessly waiting, has "gaming
debts to pay". Anyone familiar with eighteenth-century and

---

[1] *The Ring and the Book*, XI. 1672-3.
[2] See W. Clyde DeVane, *Handbook*, pp. 244-8.
[3] See Appendix A, below, pp. 199-204.

Victorian fiction will realise how much worse these seemed, how much more vicious, than other debts—for gaming was the squandering of money. It is true that in another detail Browning has one of his characteristic flashes of intolerance, and breaks away from accepted Victorian money-making morality. Meditating on the fact that he has allowed his parents to die of want, a detail suggested by Vasari—"And he made provision for her father and sisters; but not for his own parents, whom he never wished to see; so that in a short time they died in poverty"—Andrea tries first to put forward an unconvincing plea in self-excuse:

> They were born poor, lived poor, and poor they died:
> And I have laboured somewhat in my time
> And not been paid profusely.[4]

Then he pushes aside this hypocrisy, to exclaim

> Some good son
> Paint my two hundred pictures—let him try! . . .[5]

arguing that his dedication to his art was of more value than filial virtue, and that art has nothing to do with moral conduct. Despite this, his sense of wrong-doing remains, and the thought that Lucrezia's infidelity is a punishment to him for having neglected his parents follows immediately:

> No doubt, there's something strikes a balance. Yes,
> You loved me quite enough, it seems to-night.[6]

It is the same idea of punishment conceived as payment that we find later in Browning's poem on the drowned men lying in the Paris Morgue.

This one short monologue, "Andrea del Sarto", which deals with subjects of such interest as the relations between a husband and an unfaithful wife, and investigates the whole question of the assessment of an artist's achievement, contains the following words connected with money, showing how the theme ran in an undercurrent through the whole poem: "price, money, count, saves, dear, grasp, gain, profitless, given,

---

[4] "Andrea del Sarto", 253-5.
[5] *Op. cit.*, 255-6.
[6] *Op. cit.*, 257-8.

give, gain, compensates, award, golden, gold-chain, crown, reward, golden, gold, fortune, earn, give, gold,[2] loans, debts, pay, buy, spend, worth, pay, worth, pay, thirteen scudi, coin, want, poverty, riches, rich, poor,[3] paid".

Money in "The Ring and the Book"

This basic theme is to be found over and over again in Browning's poetry. The well-known lyric "The Lost Leader" is completely in this key. But it is in *The Ring and the Book* that we notice how far this emphasis is exaggerated and abnormal. This long poem is a detailed examination and presentation of the truth as it emerges from a long law-suit, or rather a series of law-suits. And the facts of the case are taken, with great accuracy of detail, from its famous source, the Old Yellow Book, the volume which Browning picked up on a stall in Florence. But what has never been sufficiently noted by the commentators, is that the whole emphasis in Browning's version has been changed. In the source the crime is conceived in Italian terms—the motive is Honour. Or it might be more correct to state that the defence, including Guido himself, stakes everything upon this plea —the one most likely then, as now, to be regarded at least in the light of an extenuating circumstance by Italian justice.

Some mention of money is made in the Old Yellow Book, for the facts of the case are those elaborated by Browning. There is the question of the Comparinis' need of a legal heir, there is the wrangle over Pompilia's dowry, and her alleged theft from her husband, and there is Pietro's will. But sums of money are mentioned on relatively few occasions—only the inventory of stolen goods (all of which are valued in *scudi*) makes anything like a show. *Scudi* are the only currency mentioned, with the exception of the *gratie* paid for a lamb to show the parsimonious house-keeping at Arezzo, of which Pietro and Violante complain so bitterly:

> For the food of all this tableful, the Franceschini bought on Saturday a sucking lamb, on which they spent, at most, twelve or fourteen gratie. Then Signora Beatrice cooked it and divided it out for the entire week. And the head of the lamb she

divided up for a relish three times, and for the relish at other times she served separately the lights and intestines.[7]

A sum of three hundred *scudi* is mentioned as the security or bail, under guarantee of which Pompilia is released to give birth to her child in the home of her foster-parents, where the murder takes place, and the sum bequeathed in Pietro's will is recorded. This, as far as the source-book is concerned, is the extent of the interest in money.

Not so in Browning. Even a casual reading of *The Ring and the Book* is enough to show how differently he viewed the question. To start with, we are told of his purchase of the Old Yellow Book itself:

> I found this book,
> Gave a *lira* for it, eightpence English just. . . .[8]

It is most significant that he not only should mention the Italian sum (a very small one), but should trouble to give the English translation, showing, not only his extreme accuracy over money matters, but also his pride in the trivial bargain he has achieved, which he does not intend his readers (unfamiliar perhaps with contemporary conversion tables) to miss. It lay he tells us, among

> A pile of brown-etched prints, two *crazie* each,[9]

a detail which seems insignificant enough, but to which he returns over three hundred lines later

> The etcher of those prints, two *crazie* each, . . .[10]

It is, however, extremely significant for a fuller understanding of Browning and of his poem. For gold, money, coins, pour out of it on every page. Only Pompilia herself uses these words less often than the other characters, thereby suggesting her purity—for money throughout *The Ring and the Book* suggests soiling. Pompilia mentions money only to disown it:

> I no more own a coin than have an hour
> Free of observance.[11]

---

[7] *The Old Yellow Book*, ed. Charles W. Hodell, p. 40.
[8] *The Ring and the Book*, I. 38-9.
[9] *Op. cit.*, I. 66.   [10] *Op. cit.*, I. 370.   [11] *Op. cit.*, IV. 815-6.

F

whereby the imagery seconds the argument for her chastity in that coins, for Browning, are the golden shower of Danae. That "coin" can have this meaning for Pompilia as well as for Fifine is shown later in her confession:

> Here, marriage was the coin, a dirty piece[12]

—while the idea of the sullying of chastity by gold goes back in Browning as early as *Sordello*: "Shook off, as might a lily its gold soil" and "soiled by its own loose gold-meal".[13]

Pompilia's confession apart, the rest of *The Ring and the Book* is impregnated with gold. The Pope is in no way spared. He may be economical, as indeed he is, for we are told, quite gratuitously, at the beginning of the poem, of Pope Innocent, that

> His own meal costs but five carlines a day,[14]

but he is involved to this small extent in the general corruption.

For money, and gold in so far as gold is used as money, is regarded by Browning as fundamentally evil. The sociological reasons I have already glanced at—a growing feeling that its unequal distribution was wrong, the frame of mind which was preparing the way for the economic doctrines of socialism and communism. And Browning, who was married to Elizabeth Barrett[15] must have felt increasingly guilty on this count—indeed Erdman[16] in an exciting study of "Childe Roland" suggests that that poem contains suppressed guilt feelings over the working conditions and economic hardships of the life of industrial workers, linking it up with Elizabeth Barrett Browning's campaign against child labour.

---

[12] *Op. cit.*, VII. 407.

[13] Much the same words were used in 1831 by W. S. Landor in his "Fæsulan Idyl": "... the ever-sacred cup/Of the pure lily hath between my hands /Felt safe, unsoil'd, nor lost one grain of gold". Landor does not, however, make the same point as Browning, that it is the gold itself which may soil the lily.

[14] *The Ring and the Book*, I. 324.

[15] The best example of her attitude is to be found in her poems "The Cry of the Children" and "The Cry of the Human", which contain lines such as "The plague of gold strikes far and near", and "The curse of gold upon the land /The lack of bread enforces."

[16] See David W. Erdman, "Browning's Industrial Nightmare", in *Philological Quarterly*, XXXVI (1957), pp. 417-35.

Gold and the Roman Catholic Church

These doubts were strengthened by the Christian condemnation of money and gold. In the New Testament it is referred to as "filthy lucre", and the young Browning must often have heard sermons wherein the money-changers were cast out of the Temple. Moreover the Scarlet Woman of Revelation, who by Protestant interpretation represents the Church of Rome, must have left an indelible impression on the mind of the child:

> I will show unto thee the judgement of the great whore that sitteth upon many waters. . . . And the woman was arrayed in purple and scarlet colour, and decked with gold and precious stones and pearls, having a golden cup in her hand full of abominations and filthiness of her fornication.[17]

The gold cup in her hand is the communion cup or Grail; and for the abominations in it we need only recall

> Had a spider found out the communion-cup, . . .[18]

The particular form taken by the "abomination" as a spider (a creature of which Browning was fond) is probably from *The Winter's Tale* "I have drunk and seen the spider". In "A Forgiveness", instead, a barber's basin (which in medieval times may well have contained abominations) is changed into God's sacramental cup. It is difficult today to grasp the strength of the religious intolerance underlying this concept— to realise how much Protestants *hated* the Church of Rome. The evil seemed so insidious, the filth was to be found in the Communion cup itself.

This ambiguity in the Bible, whereby gold represented not only good, as we have seen in the preceding chapter, but also the worst form of evil, may have encouraged Browning's own highly ambiguous use of the symbol.

Evil in Gold

In the introduction to *The Ring and the Book* Browning had used gold as a symbol for his art itself. Yet elsewhere he often uses it in its darker meanings. Gold, in the sense of money, was

---

[17] Revelation XVII. 1, 4. [18] "Gold Hair", 104.

often for him a bribe or the reward of crime. Already in
Sordello the Kaiser's gold is seen as an evil, and we have a
situation foreshadowing "The Bishop Orders his Tomb" with
the children waiting greedily for their father's death (the
situation Trollope touches upon with such subtle comprehension in *Barchester Towers*). In *Sordello* the father, like the
dying Bishop of St Praxed's, is afraid of his children:

> I am sick too, old,
> Half-crazed I think; what good's the Kaiser's gold
> To such an one? God help me! for I catch
> My children's greedy sparkling eyes at watch. . . .[19]

In *King Victor and King Charles* the gold is extorted, while in
"The Laboratory" it is both the "gold oozings" of the poison
and the gold to be "gorged" in reward. In "Instans
Tyrannus" gold is used for temptation, while in "The Italian
in England" it is offered for betrayal:

> the State
> Will give you gold—oh, gold so much!—
> If you betray me to their clutch.[20]

In "Andrea del Sarto", as we have seen, the gold is stolen, while
in "Gold Hair" it is hoarded. This last poem alone would raise
suspicions as to the normality of its writer's interest in gold.
The morbid elements of this legend of Pornic are, to say the
least, curious: there seems to have been something about this
particular corner of France which set all Browning's neuroses
on edge, some atmosphere to which he was peculiarly sensitive,
for it is the setting of his much later poem *Fifine*.[21] In "A
Death in the Desert" the value of gold to man is contrasted
with that of fire, and a parallel drawn with the value of Christ:

> will he give up fire
> For gold or purple once he knows its worth?
> Could he give Christ up were His worth as plain? . . .[22]

---

[19] *Sordello*, II. 873-6.
[20] "The Italian in England", 66-8.
[21] See Browning's letter to Elizabeth postmarked 5 Jan. 1846.
[22] "A Death in the Desert", 292-4.

in what may be an allusion to his betrayal by Judas—to which Browning makes frequent references throughout his work, as the greatest evil wrought by money.

Gold is offered as a bribe by Guido in *The Ring and the Book*, Hervé Riel accuses the men of St Malo of being "bought by English gold", and in "Doctor—" a monarch tries to buy off death itself by bribing the Doctor:

> Be saved I will!
> Why else am I earth's foremost potentate?
> Add me to these and take as fee your fill
> Of gold—that point admits of no debate
> Between us: save me, as you can and must,—
> Gold, till your gown's pouch cracks beneath the weight!
> This touched the Doctor.[23]

In this late poem, written when Browning was almost seventy, there is probably some personal consideration as he weighs the ultimate uselessness of gold, even while humorously noticing the doctor's greed. The greed inspired by gold is also the subject of "Cenciaja" where "blinded by so exorbitant a lust of gold" a youth sets out to kill the Marchesina Costanza, his widowed mother.[24] Gold inspires greed not only in this juvenile delinquent but also in the Roman Catholic Church, which Browning is ever-ready to censure. The "golden grist" of Monsieur Léonce Miranda's charity in *Red Cotton Night-Cap Country* pours steadily

> From mill to mouth of sack—held wide and close
> By Father of the Mission, Parish-priest,
> And Mother of the Convent, Nun I know,
>   . . . in these same two years, expenditure

---

[23] "Doctor—", 160-6. Here "these" are "half my subjects rescued by your skill". The source of this poem is probably to be found in the account of Louis XI's fear of death and attempt to bribe the doctors, given in the *Mémoires* of Philippe de Comines: "son medicin, maistre Jacques, en qui il avoit toute esperance, et à qui chascun moys donnoit dix mil escus, esperant qu'il luy alongeast la vie, . . ."

[24] A subsidiary source for this matricide may be found in Vidocq's museum "of knives and nails and hooks that have helped great murderers to their purposes". Browning describes his visit there in a letter to Elizabeth dated 1 July 1845. He tells us "thus one little sort of dessert knife *did* only take *one* life. . . . 'But then' says Vidocq, 'it was the man's own mother's life, with fifty-two blows, and all for' (I think) 'fifteen francs she had got' ".

> At quiet Clairvaux rose to the amount
> Of Forty Thousand English Pounds. . . .[25]

The capital letters are Browning's own, clearly impressed by
the enormity of the sum which seemed to him exorbitant and
sadly misspent, in that a "trifle" went

> to supply the Virgin's crown
> With that stupendous jewel from New-York.[26]

This theme of the ill-gotten wealth of the Catholic Church had
always been popular with Protestants: it is perhaps best
expressed in Hawthorne's *Marble Faun*, where the fascination
and repulsion exerted by the combined sense of beauty and evil
are very close to Browning's own.   Henry James's *Roderick
Hudson* catches something of the same atmosphere, but the
sense of sin is best typified in the figure taken from Revelation:
the whore of Babylon—a fitting symbol, not for the Church
herself, but for the uneasy attraction she exerted over these
Protestant writers.   The Pope himself is allowed by Browning
in *The Ring and the Book* to have doubts as to the utility of so
much wealth, and to wonder, though only to wonder, whether
it has not had a corrupting influence on one of his foremost
prelates.   Faced with the failure of the Archbishop of Arezzo
to help Pompilia when she turned to him for advice in her
distress, the Pope ponders

> Have we misjudged here, over-armed our knight,
> Given gold and silk where plain hard steel serves best,
> Enfeebled whom we sought to fortify,
> Made an archbishop and undone a saint?[27]

The corrupting influence, as the Pope sees it, has been the gold.

"*The Heretic's Tragedy*"

In "The Heretic's Tragedy" the negative aspects of gold, both
religious and sexual, come to a head in a forceful and somewhat
frightening poem in which Browning concentrated all his
major symbols.   The nightmarish quality of the poem springs,

---

[25] *Red Cotton Night-Cap Country*, 3153-8.
[26] *Op. cit.*, 3162-3.
[27] *The Ring and the Book*, x. 1467-70.

I believe, not so much from the horror of the subject (the details of the burning of Jacques du Bourg-Molay at the stake in Paris in 1314), as in a strange distortion in the symbolism— for here many of Browning's habitual symbols are seen, as it were, in reverse.[28]   Instead of the bee of the flowercup image cluster (in which the associations of sex and gold are habitually linked together) we find John (as he calls Jacques):

> a-buzzing there,
> Hornet-prince of the mad wasps' hive,
> And clipt of his wings.[29]

And the honey, another symbol for sex and gold, has been degraded:

> Alack, there be roses and roses, John!
> Some, honied of taste like your leman's tongue. . . .[30]

The rose is the rose of Sharon, taking us back to the Song of Solomon, where the rose and lily are one:

> I am the rose of Sharon, and the lily of the valleys . . .
> And his fruit was sweet to my taste.[31]

So Browning's lily, which in the later poem *Fifine* was to become the symbol of the harlot, has already taken on some of these negative connotations with the association with the "leman's tongue".   The climax comes in stanza ix, where the burning heretic takes the shape of a flower (rose + lily) to become

> . . . a coal-black giant flower of hell!

The "deliriously-drugged scent" of the flower in *Fifine* is here "a gust of sulphur".   This detailed description of the burning man in terms of a flower is peculiarly horrible just because of the contrast it offers with the earlier connotations (already present

---

[28] Browning seems to have arrived at a literary technique comparable with the negative-print sequence which is fairly frequently introduced into modern films. But while the visual inversion is used (when it is used intelligently, as in *Une Femme mariée*) to suggest alienation from the scene portrayed, this inversion of the symbols gives not only a sense of unreality, but of abnormality and horror.

[29] "The Heretic's Tragedy", ii.

[30] *Op. cit.*, viii.

[31] Song of Solomon II. 1-2.

in "Women and Roses", although they find their fullest
expression in the later *Fifine*):

> Lo,—petal on petal, fierce rays unclose;
>   Anther on anther, sharp spikes outstart;
> And with blood for dew, the bosom boils;
>   And a gust of sulphur is all its smell;
> And lo, he is horribly in the toils
>   Of a coal-black giant flower of hell![32]

This reference to Hell, the destination of the heretic, and the
lurid imagery, remind us that Browning as a child, and a
sensitive child, must have heard a number of Hell-fire sermons.
These, however completely discounted later, must have
remained as material for dreams and poetry. The burning off
at the wrists of Miranda's hands in *Red Cotton Night-Cap
Country* is a further example of the use of the same background
material. The crime of the heretic Jacques is twice equated
with the crime of Judas

> Jesus Christ—John had bought and sold,
>   Jesus Christ—John had eaten and drunk;
> To him, the Flesh meant silver and gold.[33]

and

>   the Person, he bought and sold again. . . .[34]

A great many meanings are entangled in the complex imagery
of this poem. The burning flower is Sharon's rose, a figure of
the Church, but it is also the Rosa Mundi named in the motto
to the poem, thereby involving the whole world in the sin of
Judas. The thirty pieces of silver have become, less specifically,
"silver and gold", likewise extending the sin to all humanity.
The Flesh is the body of Christ which to man "meant silver and
gold" and for trafficking with this he is punished by the
burning of Hell. The details of the pyre, with gallows, fork,
and tumbrils, are a foretaste of the punishments of hell,
emblems which are developed much more fully in Guido's
second book in *The Ring and the Book*, where the torments of hell
become dramatically present to the condemned man. At the

---

[32] "The Heretic's Tragedy", ix.   [33] *Op. cit.*, vi.   [34] *Op. cit.*, x.

same time here the burning of the heretic recalls details of the crucifixion, seen, as it were, in a distorting mirror:

> Then up they hoist me John in a chafe,
>   Sling him fast like a hog to scorch,
> Spit in his face, then leap back safe,
>   Sing "Laudes" and bid clap-to the torch.[35]

so that the heretic appears as an inverse personification of Christ.[36]

Interwoven with the theme of the betrayal and crucifixion of Christ, involving the theme of gold, is the theme of sex, and the Puritan idea that this, too, carried with it the tortures and punishments of Hell. The burning man takes on the form of Browning's "sexual" flower emblem. The comment is unmistakable:

> What maketh heaven, That maketh hell.[37]

The fact that the rose is the rose of Sharon, the rose of the Song of Solomon, marks the association with sexual pleasure. But the root of the tree, with its roses, some "honied", some "bitter", grows, significantly, out of devil's dung:

> Their tree struck root in devil's dung.[38]

Browning is not using the term "devil's dung" in the sense of the plant, asafoetida, but as a synonym for manure.[39] At the same time, the word carries the metaphorical meaning of gold and, by analogy, money. The tree striking root there reminds us that "the love of money is the root of all evil",[40] harking

[35] *Op. cit.*, iv.

[36] The same pattern is visible in the description of the execution in *The Ring and the Book*, where, with the peasants hanging on either side, Guido is the inverted Christ figure: "To mount the scaffold steps, Guido was last /Here also, as atrocious-est in crime. /We hardly noticed how the peasants died, /They dangled somehow soon to right and left . . .". *The Ring and the Book*, XII, 167-70.

[37] *Op. cit.*, ix.

[38] *Op. cit.*, viii.

[39] Browning was to use "devil's dung" in the same sense many years later in *Red Cotton Night-Cap Country*, 1508: "the florist bedded thick /His primrose root in ruddle, bullocks' blood /Ochre and devils' dung for aught I know". Here the primrose is Clara de Millefleurs, the "rarity" raised in "social manure", and seen at this stage of the poem as a corrupting influence on the young Miranda.

[40] I Tim. VI. 10.

back to the buying and selling of Christ earlier in the poem.
Freud has drawn attention to this association of gold or money
with dung:

> Wherever archaic modes of thought have predominated or
> persisted in the ancient civilisations, in myths, fairy tales and
> superstitions, in unconscious thinking, in dreams and in
> neuroses—money is brought into the most intimate relationship
> with dirt. We know that the gold which the devil gives his
> paramours turns to excrement after his departure. . . .[41]

The term "devil's dung" seemed to Browning peculiarly
expressive of the evil at the root, an implication of extreme
importance, for over and over again in his work gold has these
overtones. We have already noted how gold pollen *soiled* the
lily, how the pure Pompilia is less tainted by gold than the
other characters of *The Ring and the Book*. Not only does she
refer less to money, she also declares that she possesses none,
implying not only her poverty, but also her purity.

In *Red Cotton Night-Cap Country* there is a long and amusing
simile in which the Priest and Nun, carrying away Monsieur
Léonce Miranda's money, are seen as carting manure. First
they are compared to the Egyptian scarab which rolls dung, and
then Browning presents

> the couple yonder, Father Priest
> And Mother Nun, who came and went and came,
> Beset this Clairvaux, trundled money-muck
> To midden and the main heap oft enough,
> But never bade unshut from sheathe the gauze,
> Nor showed that, who would fly, must let fall filth,
> And warn "Your jewel, brother, is a blotch:
> Sister, your lace trails ordure . . .".[42]

---

[41] Sigmund Freud, *Complete Psychological Works*, London 1949, IX, 175.

[42] *Red Cotton Night-Cap Country*, 4131-8. A complex simile which would bear
full psychoanalytical investigation is to be found in *The Ring and the Book*, VI, 668-82.
Browning returns to it again in VI, 910-1. Here the soul of the liar issues from the
body "By way of the ordure corner". A parallel is drawn with the scorpion
issuing from the Madonna's mouth, and the same scorpion is referred to as a
"blotch", linking it with the dung in the lines from *Red Cotton Night-Cap Country*.
The elements of dung and painting are complicated here by reptile, birth, and
death symbolism in a passage which challenges full interpretation, although the
"argument" is clear enough.

The closeness of the relationship is evident in the above passage of Browning, where the manure actually stands for the money. Sometimes, as in *The Ring and the Book*, the two are merely brought into contact:

> Grime is grace
> To whoso gropes amid the dung for gold. . . .[43]

Or in *Easter Day*:

> The filthy shall be filthy still:
> Miser, there waits the gold for thee![44]

and in *Parleyings* "With Daniello Bartoli":

> Choose muck for gold?[45]

A similar connexion is made again in *The Ring and the Book* in the speech of the Fisc or lawyer for the defence:

> the lady here
> Was bound to proffer nothing short of love
> To the priest whose service was to save her. What?
> Shall she propose him lucre, dust o' the mine,
> Rubbish o' the rock, some diamond, muck-worms prize.[46]

There is a further subtlety in this passage, for the introduction of [filthy] lucre and muck-worms implies, without in any way stating, that the lawyer here is fouling Pompilia's fair name with his worldly argument that she should have committed adultery with the priest out of common gratitude. For while it is interesting to trace why, as a man, Browning was so often led to these images, it is even more so to realise the use that, as an artist, he makes of them. In *The Ring and the Book* Guido twice uses "muck" for "money":

> My dowry was derision, my gain—muck . . .[47]

and again

> No better gift than sordid muck? Yes, Sirs![48]

---

[43] *The Ring and the Book*, IX. 552-3. [44] *Easter Day*, 713-4.
[45] "With Daniello Bartoli", 196. [46] *The Ring and the Book*, IX, 509-13.
[47] *Op. cit.*, XI. 1215. [48] *Op. cit.*, XI. 2182.

where the ambiguity is quite deliberate, for besides implying
the worthlessness of money, there are further implications of the
disgrace of Pompilia's shameful birth:

> The babe had been a find i' the filth-heap, Sir, . . .[49]

And:

> Daughter? Dirt
> O' the kennel! Dowry? Dust o' the street![50]

And the soiling of the family name:

> Another of the name shall keep displayed
> The flag with the ordure on it, brandish still
> The broken sword has served to stir a jakes?[51]

All these connotations underlie the use of "muck" in the first
quotation.   Perhaps Browning has escaped the accusation of
coprophilia, to which lines such as these might well lay him
open, chiefly because he does make poetry out of this, as out of
other unlikely material.   Another reason is the screen provided
by the dramatic monologue.   Were he to write in his own
person, as Swift did, he could hardly have escaped censure, but
the speaker is never Robert Browning, and is at times some
evil-doer such as Guido or Sludge.   But it was Browning who
felt this sense of evil in money, who made this equation with
dung and who transferred it to so many of his characters.   Mr
Sludge simply wallows in money—he refers to dimes, dollars,
and V-notes with every breath.   Fitly enough, it is to him that
another coprophilic passage is attributed:

> And the cash that's God's sole solid in this world!
> Look at him!   Try to be too bold, too gross
> For the master!   Not you!   He's the man for muck;
> Shovel it forth, full-splash, he'll smooth your brown
> Into artistic richness, never fear!
> Find him the crude stuff. . . .[52]

And he continues in the same vein, but with an even more
surprising turn:

---

[49] *Op. cit.*, II. 558.
[50] *Op. cit.*, V. 772-3.
[51] *Op. cit.*, V. 1490-2.
[52] "Mr. Sludge, 'The Medium' ", 753-8.

That man would choose to see the whole world roll
I' the slime o' the slough, so he might touch the tip
Of his brush with what I call the best of browns—
Tint ghost-tales, spirit-stories, past the power
Of the outworn umber and bistre![53]

What is remarkable is that Browning is here sullying the very art of painting for which he had so great a respect. His suggestion that a painter might use "what I call the best of browns"[54] goes beyond the most daring of recent experiments and reaches back, we can only imagine, to some infantile fantasy. The idea is not exhausted here, for Browning touches on it again in *Red Cotton Night-Cap Country* where the full significance of the verb "daub" would probably go unnoticed if not read in conjunction with the Sludge passage above:

And most of all resent that here town-dross
He daubs with money-colour to deceive![55]

Painting, for Browning, often represented art in general, and just as he considers his own problems as a poet in his "painter" poems, so, too, "painting" is a cover for poetry. He seems here to be hinting at a basic question for him, the justification for the use of what Bagehot has defined as the "grotesque" in art.

Throughout his work Browning makes free use of words and compounds relating not only to "dung", but to "muck", "mire", "dirt", "filth", "ordure", and "manure". As we should expect, these words emerge most easily in his longer poems, where he was exerting least control. The shorter and more tightly-knit poems were subject to more conscious censorship. Nor were such terms by any means restricted to his evil characters. For instance, his contemporary Tennyson

---

[53] *Op. cit.*, 768-72.

[54] Browning had already used this image, in a modified form, over ten years earlier, in a letter written to Elizabeth on 7 Jan. 1846, apropos of the colloquial language introduced into a poem by their friend Horne: "The Sailor Language is good in its way; but as wrongly used in Art as real clay and mud would be, if one plastered them in the foreground of a landscape in order to attain to so much truth, at all events—the true thing to endeavour is the making a golden colour which shall do every good in the power of the dirty brown".

[55] *Red Cotton Night-Cap Country*, 947-8.

uses the word "muck" only three times, and then always in dialect poems: but Browning uses it in *Sordello*, "The Heretic's Tragedy", *Easter Day*, "Mr Sludge", *Aristophanes' Apology*, *The Ring and the Book*, *Red Cotton Night-Cap Country*, "Numpholeptos", *Parleyings* ("Bartoli"), "Ned Bratts", and *Strafford*.

In *Paracelsus*, an early poem in which Browning is much concerned with the task of the artist, Paracelsus states:

> Ne'er shall boat of mine
> Adventure forth for gold and apes at once.[56]

He wishes gold here to represent purity, art itself, and deliberately dissociates it from the apes, which represent filth, as is stated in an early play:

> though I warrant there is filth, red baboons.[57]

While for Shakespeare apes were associated with lechery, for Browning they were associated rather with dirt. The association is again a childish one, and it is curious to find Browning retaining it in his adult poetry. In *Colombe's Birthday* there is a styleme echoing the "gold and apes at once" in "gems and mire at once", where "gold" is replaced by "gems", and "apes" by "mire", showing how closely the two were inter-related.

The equation "money = dirt" is, after all, of universal application; and it is only in drawing the analogy so often and so thoroughly that Browning differs from many other writers. The extent of Browning's obsession with money can be substantiated by listing some of the varieties of currency which are mentioned in his poems: "carline, crazie, cross, crown, dime, doit, dollar, drachma, ducat, farthing, florin, franc, half-penny, lira, louis, louis d'or, obol, paul, penny, penny-piece, pound, scudi, soldo, sous, talent, V-note, zechines". Browning's word-hoard was a formidable one, and nothing did he hoard more jealously than these coins—many of which are to be found time and again in his work. A perceptive passage of Edmund Wilson's in a study of Ben Jonson seems relevant in this connexion:

[56] *Paracelsus*, I. 650-1.
[57] *A Soul's Tragedy*, II. 373.

His learning [Jonson's] is a form of hoarding; and allied to it is his habit of collecting words. He liked to get up the special jargons of the various trades and professions and unload them in bulk on the public—sometimes with amusing results, as in the case of the alchemical and astrological patter reeled off by the crooks of *The Alchemist*, and even of the technique of behaviour of the courtiers in *Cynthia's Revels*, but more often, as with the list of cosmetics recommended by Wittipol in *The Devil is an Ass* and, to my taste, with the legal Latin of the divorce scene in *The Silent Woman*, providing some of his most tedious moments. The point is that Ben Jonson depends on the exhibition of stored-away knowledge to compel admiration by itself.[58]

How easily this judgment could be fitted to Browning! In his lists of technical details he outdoes Jonson himself (whether he is retailing varieties of Italian marble or juggling with variants of "Hyacinthus"; and while the theatre must have exercised some form of restraint on Jonson, no actor could have got through, or audience sat through, the legal Latin which Browning poured in a torrent of quibbles and puns into *The Ring and the Book*. And, as we read the frequent food and cooking interpolations with which Dominus Hyacinthus de Archangelis lards the speech he is preparing:

> (May Gigia have remembered, nothing stings
> Fried liver out of its monotony
> Of richness, like a root of fennel, chopped
> Fine with the parsley: parsley-sprigs, I said—
> Was there need I should say "and fennel too"?
> But no, she cannot have been so obtuse!
> To our argument! The fennel will be chopped.)[59]

we are reminded again of Wilson's definition of the "type" to which Jonson belongs:

> They are likely to have a strong interest in food both from the deglutitionary and the excretory points of view; but the getting and laying by of money or of some other kind of possession which may or may not seem valuable to others is likely to

---

[58] Edmund Wilson, *The Triple Thinkers*, Harmondsworth 1962, p. 246.
[59] *The Ring and the Book*, VIII. 543-9.

substitute itself for the infantile preoccupation with the contents of the alimentary tract.[60]

Edmund Wilson goes on to compare this trend in Jonson to James Joyce:

> Joyce, too, hoarded words and learning and attempted to impress his reader by unloading his accumulations; he, too, has his coprophilic side.[61]

Browning's word-hoarding is, I believe, of the same compulsive nature as that of Jonson and Joyce—and we can add another writer to the list in Thomas Carlyle. James Halliday has drawn attention to this in *Mr Carlyle, My Patient*, a book in which he examines Carlyle's neuroses.[62] This book has only a marginal interest for us, in that it is based mainly on biographical and medical details. But Betty Miller, in her study of Browning, shows, I think, considerable penetration in commenting on Browning's friendship for Carlyle. Seeking to explain Browning's admiration for Carlyle, she suggests:

> It was, perhaps, because he saw in Carlyle's attitude the mirror-image of his own that he felt so closely, so peculiarly bound to him.[63]

An attitude that was "the mirror image of his own". Now what Halliday demonstrates for Carlyle, and what Wilson demonstrates for Ben Jonson, is that they fitted exactly into one of the Freudian psychological types, classified as anal-erotics, and of which Freud wrote:

> They are especially orderly, parsimonious and obstinate. . . . It is therefore plausible to suppose that these characteristic traits of orderliness, parsimony and obstinacy which are so often prominent in people who were formerly anal-erotics, are to be regarded as the first and most constant results of the sublimation of anal eroticism.[64]

---

[60] Wilson, *The Triple Thinkers*, p. 246.

[61] *Op. cit.*, p. 259.

[62] James Halliday, *Mr Carlyle, My Patient: A Psychosomatic Biography*, London 1949.

[63] Betty Miller, *Robert Browning*, p. 56.

[64] Freud, *Complete Psychological Works*, ix. 169-71.

There is no need to look far in Browning's biography to find instances of these basic traits in his character. The standard biography by Hall Griffin and Minchin tells us:

> This extreme carefulness became a fixed habit, and pervaded his own expenditure after it had ceased to be necessary. He habitually rode in omnibuses and practised various small economies.[65]

This fits in with what he told us himself of his purchase of the Old Yellow Book for one lira, "eightpence English just". His obstinacy is well attested by his refusal to continue his university studies, and by the well-known story of his marriage. He wrote to Elizabeth on 26 February 1845:

> For when did I once fail to get whatever I had set my heart upon? As I ask myself sometimes, with a strange fear.

His parsimoniousness and orderliness can be seen together in a letter of his wife's which complains of his "morbid" horror of owing five shillings five days:

> I laugh insolently sometimes at Robert and his accounts, and his way of calculating for the days and weeks. . . . And *if* you were to see his little book, with our whole income accounted for to the uttermost farthing, week by week, and an overplus (yes, an overplus!) provided for casualties.[66]

In his poetry this horror of debt, moral as well as pecuniary, is shown in the grim comment of "Apparent Failure", where the poet stands in the Doric little Morgue looking through a sheet of glass at the bodies of those suicides who had drowned themselves in the Seine: "One pays one's debt in such a case". Elizabeth herself attributed his fear of debt to early training, in that he was "descended from the blood of all the Puritans, and educated by the strictest of dissenters", but it seems probable that character combined with training and heredity. Fortunately for his art, Browning hoarded, not money, but words. Yet it is scarcely surprising that words conjuring with money

---

[65] W. Hall Griffin and H. C. Minchin, *The Life of Robert Browning*, London 1938, p. 289.
[66] Letter from E. B. Browning to her sister Henrietta, dated Florence, August 2, 1847, and quoted by Betty Miller from the Huxley typescript.

G

should have been among those hoarded most jealously. Where another poet decorates his work with gems (which Browning used but sparingly, though he had a weakness for marbles), Browning adorned his work with ducats, drachmas, and doits. And, everywhere and always, gold.

Conclusions

To break down the conclusions reached, for the sake of clarity, we are back with Browning's constant antithesis of good and evil. Gold is good in the Old Testament sense of what is of value, what is durable, what is pure. It is evil in the New Testament sense of filthy lucre—and was seen also by Browning as a characteristic of the Catholic Church, typified in the whore of Babylon. This Biblical duality (for the New Testament takes over also the *good* sense of gold from the Old) may have influenced Browning's own awareness of its ambiguity. Then gold is good in so far as it can be equated with sexual pleasure (as I have shown in the honey, pollen, egg-yolk, semen imagery), but is bad in so far as sex was regarded as wicked "What maketh heaven, that maketh hell". Finally, it was good in so far as it represented excrement (good, that is, in the unconscious childish memory which comes to the surface with Browning when he treats of it as material for art and connects it with monkeys), but bad, above all, in this sense, too, as the first thing that the child was taught to abhor as filthy and vile, and which became mixed in this sense, too, with sin.

The conscious recognition of these ambiguities helps us, first of all, on the level of interpretation—often no mean task where Browning is concerned—for one passage can be read in the light cast by another. But more than this, it can aid us in the appreciation of the poems by showing not only what they meant but what they implied, and when the apparent meaning and the implication are at odds, then we have Browning at his most stimulating.

Poetry is more, much more, than a musical arrangement of words—it is the use of words in such a way as to evoke a wealth of echoes and associations. If the old definition of "memorable prose" were enlarged to mean, not only prose which can be memorised, but also prose which is full of memories, we begin to approach a definition. By tracing this one theme of gold (and its debased form, money) through Browning's work I have tried to show some of the associations it has had for him, to help us to realise consciously what his readers have already recognised unconsciously: the wide range of reference covered in the single word, and the ambiguities it holds.

V

Browning and the Bible:
an Examination of "Holy-Cross Day"

"Holy-cross day", which was first published in *Men and Women*, is not one of Browning's great poems; it lacks the perfection of "Andrea del Sarto" or "The Bishop Orders his Tomb". It is, rather, an experimental poem: an experiment in irony, an experiment, too, in the use of colloquial language, and an experiment into that investigation of the plurality, or apparent plurality, of truth which was to lead Browning on to *The Ring and the Book*. It is above all an extraordinary texture of ambiguities, which, even when exploited for their value as irony, are fundamentally the expression of an awareness of underlying plurality.

The fact that the poem falls a little apart of its own accord makes it all the easier to take to pieces, and the paradox is that, having once laid it out in pieces, we realise how singularly well it all fits together. The key lies in the prose introduction, which must be read as part of the poem, underlying as it does the philosophical second part as much as the colloquial opening.

The poem consists of the prose introduction, which is the most wholly successful part, and which must have been written after the poem itself; the colloquial first eleven stanzas, describing the Jews being herded into the church to hear a compulsory Christian sermon; and the final nine stanzas, purporting to be taken from Rabbi Ben Ezra's Song of Death. One of the purposes of this study is to question the existence of a Jewish original for this part of the poem. Most commentators seem to take Browning's declaration at its face value, and to assume that he was re-working a Jewish text. I feel considerable doubt as to this supposed source. Rabbi Ben Ezra, or Abraham Ibn Ezra, was an eleventh-century Jewish commentator on the Scriptures, of Spanish birth, some of whose writings are preserved in the Vatican Library. But nobody has actually seen this song, nor can I find any record of Ben Ezra's ever having written it. The internal evidence of Browning's supposed translation, as detailed analysis demonstrates, points strongly against a Jewish original. That Browning was versed in Rabbinical lore and knew and admired Ben Ezra we know from his poem of that title, but even there the philosophy is rather Browning's own. Ben Ezra was for Browning a symbolic figure, such as Michelangelo was for Yeats, but it is of course typical that Browning should have sought as symbol a little-known Jewish commentator on the Scriptures rather than a universally acknowledged genius.

To take these questions in their order, and to begin at Browning's own beginning, his prose introduction ran as follows:

> Now was come about Holy-Cross Day, and now must my lord preach his first sermon to the Jews: as it was of old cared for in the merciful bowels of the Church, that, so to speak, a crumb at least from her conspicuous table here in Rome should be, though but once yearly, cast to the famishing dogs, under-trampled and bespitten-upon beneath the feet of the guests. And a moving sight in truth, this, of so many of the besotted blind restif and ready-to-perish Hebrews! now maternally brought—nay (for He saith, "Compel them to come in") haled, as it were, by the head and hair, and against their obstinate hearts, to partake of the heavenly grace. What awakening, what striving with tears, what working of a yeasty conscience! Nor was my lord wanting to himself on so apt an occasion: witness the abundance of conversions which did incontinently reward him: though not to my lord be altogether the glory.

Arthur Symons (one of Browning's early critics) described this as "a deliciously naïve extract from an imaginary *Diary by the Bishop's Secretary*, 1600".[1] And that is what, on the surface, it is. Packed as tightly as a parish magazine with wholly probable Biblical quotations, it sets the tone for the following poem, with its roughly ironical contrast: "What the Jews really said, on thus being driven to church, was rather to this effect: . . ."

The many Biblical quotations in this introduction seem as

[1] Arthur Symons, *An Introduction to the Study of Browning*, new edn, 1906, p. 117.

obvious as they are "right"—they seem, that is, to be just those which a bishop's secretary might choose. But Browning knew his Bible well, and the irony of these quotations lies in the contexts from which they are uprooted. One and all, these Biblical references are taken from passages (in the New as well as in the Old Testament) which teach the supremacy of the Jewish race, and its final triumph.

How far Browning knew what he was doing it is impossible to judge. He knew his Bible consciously, as his poetry everywhere shows, but he must have known the most symbolic of all books unconsciously, too. The Victorian tradition of Bible-reading chapter by chapter, making the chapter a unit in itself as sufficient unto the day, irrespective of continuity or discontinuity, serves to link together certain episodes, certain verses, even certain words which have otherwise no logical connexion. And the fact that as a child he must have heard so much Bible-reading in this form would allow unconscious associations to take over at the point where conscious ones broke off.

By a close examination of this poem and its introduction, line by line, and even, where necessary, word by word, it is possible to see not only that the poem is rich in quotations and associations, but above all in irony. In his book entitled *Guidance from Robert Browning in Matters of Faith*,[2] John A. Hutton understandably ignored "Holy-Cross Day", even though he was not afraid to confront some of the more complex and baffling of Browning's works, drawing thence, in the words of the *Dunfermline Journal*, "a powerful confirmation of his evangelical faith", and producing a book, this time in the words of the *Aberdeen Journal*, fit "to put into the hands of any youth or maiden who wants to read to good purpose".[3] Such a youth or maiden would have found "Holy-Cross Day", to say the least, disconcerting.

The title "Holy-Cross Day" (on which the Jews were forced to attend an annual Christian sermon in Rome) refers to a festival on 14 September[4] commemorating the dedication, in

---

[2] Edinburgh 1903.
[3] Extracts from reviews quoted in the publisher's advertisements.
[4] See W. Clyde DeVane, *Handbook*, pp. 260-1.

the year 335, of churches built near Jerusalem on the sites of the Crucifixion and the Holy Sepulchre. It was therefore held to be an appropriate date on which to attempt the conversion of the Jews: "Father, forgive them; for they know not what they do". In 1853 and 1854, when the poem was probably written, this sermon had already been abolished,[5] but Browning may have attended one of the other services for the Jews such as are described by his friend G. S. Hillard in *Six Months in Italy*, or at least have read the account and heard talk of the services. Hillard's report runs:

> By a bull of Gregory XIII. in the year 1584, all Jews above the age of twelve years were compelled to listen every week to a sermon from a Christian priest, usually an exposition of some passage from the Old Testament, and especially those relating to the Messiah, from the Christian point of view. This burden is not yet wholly removed from them; and to this day, several times in the course of a year, a Jewish congregation is gathered in the church of S. Angelo in Pescheria, and constrained to listen to a homily from a Dominican friar, to whom, unless his zeal have eaten up his good feelings and his good taste, the ceremony must be as painful as to his hearers.[6]

Another account of these compulsory services for the Jews which Browning may have read was that in Evelyn's *Diary* for 7 January 1645, which gives a description in much the same tone as Browning's own:

> A Sermon was preach'd to the Jewes at Ponte Sisto, who are constrain'd to sit, till the houre is don; but it is with so much malice in their countenances spitting, humming, coughing and motion, that it is almost impossible they should heare a word, nor are there any converted except it be very rarely.

This, whether or not Browning had read of it in Evelyn, is the "situation" on which he bases his poem. In Browning's poem, as in Evelyn's *Diary*, not one word spoken by the Bishop is retailed. The words are all those of the Jews, and the Bishop's point of view is given in the prose introduction, purporting to

---

[5] As Browning tells us in his own note, it was abolished, during the papacy of Gregory XVI, in 1846, shortly before the Brownings came to Italy.

[6] G. S. Hillard, *Six Months in Italy*, New York 1853, II, 51. See W. Clyde DeVane, *Handbook*, p. 260.

be an extract from the diary of the Bishop's secretary. Whether
this idea of the diary was suggested by Evelyn's we cannot say,
but the suggestion is attractive. Whatever its origin, this prose
"extract" is a most remarkable piece of writing, throwing
considerable light on Browning himself, and on the subtleties
of which he was capable.

The first quotation from the Bible "as it was of old cared for
in the merciful bowels of the Church" is the prophecy of
Zacharias concerning the great preacher, John the Baptist: "for
thou shalt go before the face of the Lord to prepare his ways;
to give knowledge of salvation unto his people by the remission
of their sins, through the bowels of the mercy of our God".[7]
The reference is highly appropriate for a Christian bishop
preaching a sermon to the Jews, the "my people" of the text.
But the irony lies hidden in the context, which is the Lord's
promise to Abraham to free the Jews from their enemies

> To perform the mercy promised to our fathers, and to remem-
> ber his holy covenant; the oath which he sware to our father
> Abraham, that he would grant onto us, that we being delivered
> out of the hand of our enemies might serve him without fear, in
> holiness and righteousness before him, all the days of our life.[8]

This promise to Abraham is mentioned openly in the third
section of the poem, the Song of Rabbi Ben Ezra. Here in the
introduction it is merely in the background, hidden behind the
words of the Bishop's secretary. But what I want to stress, both
here and later, is how much the background of context existed
for Browning, and indeed for his contemporary readers.

The same sentence of the introduction contains further
Biblical references: "a crumb at least from her conspicuous
table here in Rome, should be, though but once yearly, cast to
the famishing dogs, undertrampled and bespitten upon ...".
Once more the quotation rings true: these are words the
Bishop's secretary might very well have used in his diary.
Yet once more the context is revealing. The quotation is from
Matthew xv, where the woman of Canaan (a Gentile) appeals
to Jesus for help:

[7] Luke i. 76-8.
[8] Luke i. 72-5.

But he answered and said, I am not sent but unto the lost sheep of the House of Israel. Then came she and worshipped him, saying, Lord, help me. But he answered and said, It is not meet to take the children's bread, and to cast it to dogs. And she said, Truth, Lord: yet the dogs eat of the crumbs which fall from their masters' table.[9]

So while the dogs referred to by the Bishop's secretary are the Jews, once again the context illuminates Browning's irony, for in the Bible it is the Gentile woman who is the dog and the Lord is concerned primarily with the saving of the house of Israel. The words "undertrampled" and "bespitten upon" further the same idea, for trampling is almost exclusively an Old Testament term used in connexion with the vengeance of the Lord on his enemies, *i.e.* the enemies of Israel. The single exception is the New Testament use in the "Cast not thy pearls before swine" context, which we shall come to later. "Bespitten upon" recalls again the spitting of the Gentiles upon the Lord, and is used only in this sense in the New Testament, except in some of the miracles.

The turning of the tables, which is the main point of the poem, is already suggested in this masterpiece of irony, but Browning manages to mark a nice distinction. The Gentiles here are the Roman Catholics rather than the Protestants. For the crumbs of the Church fall "from her conspicuous table here in Rome". In the one adjective he sums up many of the criticisms of the Catholic Church which were formulated by foreign visitors to Rome in the last century: the richness of the church buildings themselves and all the paraphernalia of religion which fill the town and which both shocked and fascinated generations of Protestant tourists. A letter from a friend of the Brownings', W. W. Story, to J. R. Lowell, written from Rome on 18 April 1848 reveals the same attitude:

Holy Week it has been, and all sorts of ceremonies have been going on, most of them senseless and superstitious, with a penny worth of religion to a ton of form.[10]

---

[9] Matthew xv. 24-7.
[10] See Henry James, *William Wetmore Story and his Friends*, Edinburgh 1903, Vol. I, p. 100; reprinted in *Browning to his American Friends*, ed. Gertrude Reese Hudson, London 1965, p. 237.

The secretary continues by describing the moving sight of "so many of the besotted blind restif and ready-to-perish Hebrews!" "Blind" is used in one of the most common scriptural connotations of such as are wilfully and obstinately ignorant in matters which concern salvation, a sense still current in salvationist and gospel preaching. There may perhaps be the further idea of the blind leading the blind[11] which is what the Catholic sermon to the Jews must have seemed to the Protestant Browning. "Restif" seems to recall Evelyn's description of the Ponte Sisto sermon, and is as concentrated in its way as "conspicuous", combining the idea of physical restlessness with mental intolerance and impatience. "Ready-to-perish" is once more from the Bible, where it is first used in Deuteronomy in a chapter dealing with the delivery of the Jews from their slavery in Egypt and their arrival in the pleasant land, speaking of them as God's chosen people:

> A Syrian ready-to-perish was my father, and he went down into Egypt, and sojourned there with a few, and became there a nation, great, mighty and populous: And the Egyptians evil entreated us, and afflicted us, and laid upon us hard bondage: And when we cried unto the Lord God of our fathers, the Lord heard our voice, and looked on our affliction, and our labour, and our oppression: And the Lord brought us forth out of Egypt with a mighty hand, and with an outstretched arm, and with great terribleness, and with signs, and with wonders: And he hath brought us into this place, and hath given us this land, even a land that floweth with milk and honey. . . . And the Lord hath avouched thee this day to be his peculiar people, as he hath promised thee, and that thou shouldest keep all his commandments; And to make thee high above all nations which he hath made, in praise, and in name, and in honour; and that thou mayest be an holy people unto the Lord thy God, as he hath spoken.[12]

Concealed behind the belittling adjective is a reference to the two great hopes of the Jewish people; the promised land, and that they shall be honoured "high above all nations".

Another "ready-to-perish" occurs in Proverbs:

[11] Luke VI. 39.
[12] Deuteronomy XXVI. 5-9, 18-19.

> Give strong drink unto him that is ready to perish, and wine unto those that be of heavy hearts.   Let him drink, and forget his poverty, and remember his misery no more.[13]

This context may explain the adjective "besotted" which otherwise is difficult to account for, in that drunkenness is not generally regarded as characteristic of the Jews, even by their detractors.

The diary of the Bishop's secretary now quotes from the parable of the Great Supper, the principal text on which this idea of the forcible feeding of the sermon down the Jewish throats was based: "Will ye nill ye they are to be made to *partake of the heavenly grace.*"[14]   With these words Browning sends us to I Corinthians, from which come several of the elements fused together in the last lines of the diary:

> If any of them that believe not bid you to a feast. . . .

> For if I by grace be a partaker, why am I evil spoken of for that for which I give thanks?   Whether therefore ye eat, or drink, or whatsoever ye do, do all to the glory of God.   Give none offence, neither to the Jews, nor to the Gentiles, nor to the church of God.[15]

Here we have the feast which is the Feast of the Great Supper of the parable that gave rise to the compulsory sermon, and which is at the same time the Communion.   Browning links it to the parable with the words "to partake of the heavenly grace", in this way recalling the injunction to give none offence, neither to the Jews, nor to the Gentiles, nor to the Church of God, for to Browning, as to Evelyn and Hillard, this *bad business of the sermon* must have seemed an offence against the Church itself.

Nor does this close the irony underlying the secretary's platitudes, for the last words of the Diary, with reference to the abundant conversions are *though not to my Lord be altogether the glory.*   Setting aside the charm of "altogether", richly suggestive of the dependent position of the secretary, this contains a pregnant cross-reference to the preceding chapter in I Corinthians.   In I Corinthians, x, quoted above, we find "do all to the

---

[13] Proverbs xxxi. 6.   [14] "Holy-Cross Day", prose introduction.
[15] I Corinthians x. 27, 30.

glory of God", while on the opposite page there is a passage of St Paul's relating to preaching which points the irony and shows how mistaken Browning believed the compulsory sermon to be:

> For though I preach the gospel, I have nothing to glory of: for necessity is laid upon me; yea, woe is unto me, if I preach not the gospel!... What is my reward then? Verily that, when I preach the Gospel, I may make the gospel of Christ without charge, that I abuse not my power in the gospel. For though I be free from all men, yet have I made myself servant unto all, that I might gain the more. And unto the Jews I became as a Jew, that I might gain the Jews.[16]

The Bishop set about his sermon to the Jews in a very different frame of mind from St Paul, and I believe that it was Browning's intention to emphasise the difference.

After the subtlety of the prose introduction, the poem itself, or rather the first colloquial part of the poem, seems very coarse.[17]   There is indeed a marked contrast between the first part, which is in the roughly humorous "Pied Piper" vein (a tone which is even improbable, for the Jews are made to speak of themselves without true sympathy, but rather from the outside as they must have appeared to sightseers), and the second part where Browning achieves that identification with his subject which characterises his best poetry.   The poem opens with a description of the crowding into the church and the trickery of the arranged "conversions" but in Ben Ezra's "Song of Death" it breaks into a different mood showing sympathy and understanding with the centuries of persecution and spiritual oppression suffered.

The point of view in this first part is strictly Protestant; the

---

[16] I Corinthians ix. 16-20.

[17] Of the many recent books concerned with Browning, one of the very few which take note of "Holy-Cross Day" is J. Hillis Miller, *Of the Disappearance of God*, Cambridge, Mass., 1963.   This book contains a perceptive stylistic analysis of the colloquial opening of the poem.   Miller writes (p. 122): "Sometimes the effect is produced by a cascade of grotesque metaphors.   In Browning's world anything can be a metaphor for anything else, and often he gets an effect of uncouth vitality by piling up a heap of idiosyncratic things, each living violently its imprisoned life;" He quotes the first three lines of "Holy-Cross Day" as direct appeals to the kinesthetic sense and onomatopoeia.

Jews are shown as vulgar and cheating and Catholic obser-
vances and ritual are presented as absurd and ridiculous. It
was only gradually that Browning became involved and
identified himself emotionally with the Jews' predicament.
His first concern was with the comedy of the situation, however
broad.

The poem opens with the exclamation:

> Fee, faw, fum! bubble and squeak!
> Blessedest Thursday's the fat of the week.[18]

The first words are from Edgar's song in *King Lear*, III, iv, 93:
"Fie, foh, fum, I smell the blood of a British man"—obviously
familiar to Browning in that words from the same song had
provided the title of his " 'Childe Roland to the Dark Tower
Came' ". The expression sprang originally from the story of
Jack the Giant Killer, and is probably introduced here because
of another version which reads "Christian man".[19] The speaker
is a Jew, and the surface value is simply to recall an old
rhyme dealing with the traditional hatred of Jews and
Christians for each other. Dare one go further? The rhyme
continues:

> Be he alive or be he dead
> I'll grind his bones to make me bread.

Jew, that is, threatens to eat Christian, which is the reason for
the continued popularity of the rhyme with its traditional figure
of the Bogey Man. But the doctrine of transubstantiation in the
service of the Mass or Holy Communion was based on Christian
eating Jew. That Browning may have had this further sense in
mind is suggested by his following words which are concerned
once again with ritual eating. "Bubble and squeak" recalls a
line from Elizabeth Barrett Browning's *Aurora Leigh*

> Boiling cabbage for the fast-day's soup
> It smelt like blessed entrails . . .

---

[18] "Holy-Cross Day", 1-2.
[19] See *Illustrations of Northern Antiquities from the Earlier Teutonic and Scandinavian
Romances* . . ., Edinburgh 1814. The lines "With *'fi, fi, fo,* and *fum* !' / I smell the
blood of a Christian man !" are taken from the section on popular heroic and
romantic ballads translated from the Northern languages, with notes and illustrations, by R. Jamieson, p. 402.

linking up with the next line, with its reference to Holy Thursday (in Italian *giovedì grasso*): "Blessedest Thursday's the fat of the week" and to l. 54 "To usher in worthily Christian Lent". That is to say that although Browning here is speaking with the voice of a Jew, his words and his criticism of the Catholic customs and ritual are essentially Protestant and Nonconformist, for the Jewish ritual is as elaborate and the fasts as strict as those of the Catholics.

The following words "Rumble and tumble" are those used in stanza vii of "The Pied Piper of Hamelin" to describe the hurrying of the rats into the street and the contrasting adjectives which follow (sleek and rough, etc.) recall the same treatment of the rats. The two scenes of the Jews hurrying to church and the rats crowding after the Pied Piper were clearly linked in Browning's mind, showing a vital lack of sympathy and suggesting again that his only aim at this stage was to write a piece of colourful description. The rats, swine, wasps, frogs, worms, and fleas, all used as figures for overcrowding in stanza iii, are equally unsympathetic. Yet they are an integral part of the poem, the rats harking back to the Pied Piper vocabulary of the first stanza, the swine forward to the "acorned hog" of the Bishop in the fourth. The wasps are a verbal link with the following "buzz for the Bishop" and probably, too, with the "humming" of Evelyn's description of the Jews packed in the church:[20] "Bow, wow, wow—a bone for the dog!" With these words of stanza iv we are back with Old Mother Hubbard in the realm of nursery rhymes, already recalled in "Fee, faw, fum!" and in the lesser known:

> Higgledy-piggledy
> Here we lie,
> Picked and plucked
> And put in a pie.
> My first is snapping, snarling, growling. . . .

---

[20] There is an obscure passage in Isaiah (VII. 18-20), a book with which Browning was very familiar, and to which he refers again and again in his work, which may have provided verbal links for a number of elements in the second and third stanzas of "Holy-Cross Day", and may account for the presence of the "shaving-shears". In the poem this is probably a reference to the shaving of converted Jews (see II, 39-41 for a further development of this theme), but in Isaiah it is the razor of the Lord and the judgment on Judah (of which the enforced sermon may be seen as part).

That Browning should have recalled three nursery rhymes in twenty lines is significant—their crude alliteration and popular *motifs* fitted in well with his colloquial style, while the direct appeal of their associations to the reader added considerable strength to his verse. It may be, too, that they were intermixed in his own mind with the Biblical texts which, in Lowesian terms, hooked them up, and this would only confirm how very early in his training the Bible had been absorbed. The simple rhythms and verse forms of the nursery rhymes, which so deliberately mark the beat of the lines, as in all popular poetry, and their unashamed alliteration going back to the roots of English poetry, have probably done much to fashion the metre and form of "Holy-Cross Day". Miller notes the "syncopated rhythm" of the line

> Boh, here's Barnabus! Job, that's you?
> Up stumps Solomon—bustling too?[21]

Browning is trying, I believe, to do what Stravinsky was aiming at through a similar technique in the ragtime section of his *Histoire du soldat*, likewise deliberately popular in form. Both use and indeed exaggerate pronounced rhythms, but the effect is in neither case that of parody. While deliberately comic, the use is fundamentally serious; it is a straight appeal, an attempt to get under the skin. What is lost in elegance is gained in directness. Browning's metrically primitive "Bow, wow, wow" is at the same time surprisingly modern in its tone of colloquial irreverence, and brings us back to the text referred to in the prose introduction: "Give not that which is holy unto the dogs, neither cast ye your pearls before swine, lest they trample them under their feet, and turn again and rend you".[22]

---

[21] "Holy-Cross Day", 7-8, J. Hillis Miller, *Of the Disappearance of God*, p. 121.

[22] Matthew vII. 6. Although Minnie Gresham Machen's book, *The Bible in Browning*, New York 1903, is much better, being both more informative and more balanced, than most of the more recent books and articles dealing with Browning and the Bible, or Browning and religion, surprisingly she misses the use of this text in "Holy-Cross Day", while pointing out a number of other examples of Browning's use of it. She writes (p. 2): "Another phrase which Browning has assimilated is derived from our Lord's injunction in Matt., vII, 6: 'Give not that which is holy unto the dogs, neither cast ye your pearls before swine.' Whenever his aim is to indicate utter waste of the best things, he reverts to 'pearls before swine'. This figure occurs twice in *The Ring and the Book*, again in 'The Flight of the Duchess' (concluding line), in *The Two Poets of Croisic*, in 'Pacchiarotto'."

The dogs were the "famishing" and "trampled . . . under" Jews before whom the "pearl" of the sermon was to be cast. By one of his masterly twists of ironical compression Browning makes a double point out of this text. First that the sermon itself is unjustified, for as long as the Bishop considers the Jews as dogs he is under the express injunction not to cast that which is holy before them. Secondly, with the following line it is the Bishop who is the hog, an image kept up throughout the stanza with the words "chine", "laps", and "fresh-singed swine".

In the description of the Bishop it is the Browning with the Congregationist upbringing that comes to the fore,[23] finding everything about the Bishop ridiculous simply because it is ornate and ceremonious, and rendering this ridicule in deliberately comic words:

> And the gown with the angel and thingumbob![24]

No Jew with a synagogue background would take exception to such details, nor treat them so lightly or disrespectfully, and it is a failure to realise this that weakens this part of the poem, otherwise so effective in its description, and lively in its visualisation of the scene, with image dovetailing into image to make a vivid whole, so that the Bishop's cheeks with "laps like a fresh-singed swine" contrast with the bearded faces of the Jews, some of whom are to undergo the shaving-shears after their false conversions, the "doomed black dozen", probably twelve because of the twelve disciples, and with "black" suggesting both "dark-bearded" and "sinful", but with perhaps a further sense in which it is found in Jeremiah, Lamentations, and the Minor Prophets, where the Jews' countenance changed and turned black like persons ready to be strangled, being struck with terror at the approach of God's judgments.

Not only the vestments, but also the ritual is ridiculed with "Now you've his curtsey", and the Bishop himself is shown as borrowing money from the Jewish money-lenders:

[23] This aspect of Browning is stressed by James Benziger, *Images of Eternity*, Carbondale 1963, p. 197: "In Browning's case the chief early sympathy had been not with nature but with the Christianity of his youth; the first worship, reinforced by his devotion to his mother, had been directed toward the God of the Chapel."

[24] "Holy-Cross Day", 28.

> I meddle no more with the worst of trades—
> Let somebody else pay his serenades.[25]

Browning, who in "Fra Lippo Lippi" could show so much sympathy with the Friar's amorous escapades (though never with the Church that enjoined celibacy in its priests) is here decidedly hard on the Bishop. Even worse things are glanced at. "What, a boy at his side, with the bloom of a lass"[26] suggests that the Bishop, too, may have had his eccentricities and reminds us of "the bloom and fleeting folly of Don Apple-cheeks", the apotheosis of all such "boys" in *Cardinal Pirelli*; while the lines "which gutted my purse" recall the Bishop who ordered his tomb in St Praxed's and who was also a thief.

The change of mood in the poem hinges round the words "it's awork" in l. 50, which mean literally that the heavenly grace is active and that the Jews are feigning "the working of a yeasty conscience" with their cry of "woe is me". But the *it* of l. 50 is also the *it* of l. 51 referring to the persecution of the Jews, for which the "woe is me" is a lamentation. From this point onward the Jews are no longer seen as dirty, vulgar, and cheating, but as God's chosen race, suffering persecution, but sustained by the promise of a final vindication and triumph:

> It began, when a herd of us, picked and placed,
> Were spurred through the Corso, stripped to the waist . . .[27]

refers to the traditional scene of the *corsa dei Berberi* or race of Barbary horses, spurred but riderless along the main street in Rome. This race took place even in the nineteenth century and Browning either witnessed it himself or heard first-hand reports. He must have been impressed by the report that at Carnival time during the persecutions "Jew brutes" had been substituted for the horses "to usher in worthily Christian Lent", which follows hard upon Carnival. This recollection of the persecution of the Jews is reinforced through the use of animal vocabulary, suggesting that the Jews were treated as beasts: "herd", "spurred", "brutes", "sweat", "hounds", "gutted", "scape-goats", "flock".

[25] *Op. cit.*, 47-8.   [26] *Op. cit.*, 21.

[27] *Op. cit.*, 51-2. The spurs were heavy spiked balls strapped to swing under the horses' bellies to make them run.

H

The bitterness of the persecution of the Jews calls forth all Browning's sympathy[28] and is expressed with fierce irony in the line:

> Men I helped to their sins help me to their God.[29]

Yet it is still Browning the Protestant who is writing, for while the first meaning of help is simply "assist", there is the under-lying sense of "serve at table", bringing us back with a deli-berately ironic effect to the doctrine of transubstantiation and the idea of partaking of the body of Christ in the Mass.

As the "scapegoats" go forward for their feigned conversion the poem passes on to a new mood with Ben Ezra's "Song of Death". From this point on Browning's sympathies are wholly with the Jews and with their aspirations. The song purports to be a translation of the Song of Death of Rabbi Ben Ezra who lived A.D. 1092-1167 and who is remembered today chiefly for his Old Testament commentaries. Some of his poetry also exists, both in the Hebrew text and in Latin and German translation.[30] Yet there is room for considerable doubt as to whether Browning really had access to such a song.

Although it is true that Browning used the most out-of-the-way sources and that both he and his wife could read Hebrew,[31]

---

[28] Browning was to return to the same theme as late as 1876 with the poem "Filippo Baldinucci on the Privilege of Burial (A Reminiscence of 1676 A.D.)". Here again, Browning, in DeVane's words, heightens "the unconscious satire of the speaker" as he recounts an anti-Semitic story narrated by Baldinucci. Browning's whole approach to the subject, a practical joke played on the Jews as told in Baldi-nucci's "Life" of Ludovico Buti, is similar to that in "Holy-Cross Day", written over twenty years earlier, showing that Browning's attitude was an established one.

[29] "Holy-Cross Day", 60.

[30] See *Carmina rhythmica de ludo shah mat* (*De historia shahiludii*) 1689, and the German edition, published thirty years after the poem, of *Reime und Gedichte des Abraham Ibn Ezra*, ed. David Rosin, Breslau 1885-8.

[31] See Judith Berlin-Lieberman, *Robert Browning and Hebraism*, 1934, a study of those of Browning's poems which are based on Rabbinical writings and other sources in Hebrew Literature. Although the book does not deal specifically with "Holy-Cross Day", the comment on Abraham Ben Meir Ibn Ezra is of interest to anyone studying the sources of this poem. Dr Berlin-Lieberman notes (p. 11): "Two works in Hebrew belonged to Robert Browning and Elizabeth Barrett. The Books of the Prophet Isaiah (in Hebrew) and the Biblia Hebraica in four volumes have the inscription 'My wife's book and mine Robert Browning'. The Hebrew Bible and its pages are of extreme interest to us for the many illuminating glimpses they reveal of the author. They abound with Browning's notes on textual matters. And it is important to point out here that the Bamberg edition of the Bible was one of the first to include Ibn Ezra's commentaries."

yet, supposedly written on the night of Ben Ezra's death, this song may well be merely apocryphal.[32] Nor does it contain anything which Browning could not have read for himself in the Bible, and, more strikingly, a number of the texts underlying the argument are taken from the New Testament, which was a source much more likely to be known and used by Browning than by the Rabbi.

But stronger evidence for Browning's *authorship* (for even the New Testament texts could have crept in with a very free *translation*) is the point of view which, under the surface, remains Protestant. A key line is

> In one point only we sinned, at worst[33]

and the whole of stanza xvi. This sin is the failure to accept Christ as the Messiah, but it could hardly be acknowledged by a Jew in these terms. Apparently Furnivall took this point up in correspondence with Browning, although as Furnivall's letter is lost or unpublished we can only reconstruct his argument from Browning's reply. In February 1888 Browning wrote to Furnivall:

> in Holy Cross Day, Ben Ezra is not supposed to acknowledge Christ as the Messiah because he resorts to the obvious argument "even on your own showing, and accepting for the moment the authority of your accepted Lawgiver, you are condemned by His precepts—let alone ours".[34]

I feel very certain that Browning here is defending his own words and not those of the Rabbi, especially as he used the phrase "Ben Ezra *is not supposed* to acknowledge", and that the

---

[32] See M. Friedlaender, *The Commentary of Ibn Ezra on Isaiah*, 1873, Vol. 1 (Isaiah, xxvii). The account of the death of Ibn Ezra given by Friedlander in his biographical sketch is as follows: "Ibn Ezra died seventy-five years old, in Kalahorra, on the frontier of Navarre, as some report, or in Rome according to other authorities. When he felt death was approaching, he applied to himself the words of the Bible 'And Abraham (Ibn Ezra) was seventy-five years old when he departed from Horan', that is from the troubles of this life (Gen., xii, 4)." The relevance of this account to "Holy-Cross Day" is that this authoritative biography of the Rabbi (written more recently than the poem) makes no mention of any report or attribution of a death-bed song.

[33] "Holy-Cross Day", 72.

[34] See DeVane, *A Browning Handbook*, p. 261.

inconsistency that Furnivall seems to have noticed in the poem
is therefore a real one.

The effect of the poem is not seriously marred by this
inconsistency for the majority of readers, probably because their
outlook and upbringing being Christian rather than Jewish,
they stand in the same relation toward the subject as Browning
himself, and fail altogether to perceive the anomaly. And the
Old Testament backing which Browning gives to his poem
shows a thoroughness of reading which is worthy of a Jewish
scriptural commentator of the Middle Ages. Stanzas xiii and
xiv are a close following of Isaiah:

> For the Lord will have mercy on Jacob, and will yet choose
> Israel, and set them in their own land: and the strangers shall
> be joined with them, and they shall cleave to the house of
> Jacob. And the people shall take them, and bring them to their
> place: and the house of Israel shall possess them in the land
> of the Lord for servants and handmaids; and they shall take
> them captives, whose captives they were; and they shall rule
> over their oppressors.[35]

In the poem "border" is substituted for Isaiah's "land",
probably in recollection of a passage in Jeremiah: "And there is
hope in thine end, saith the Lord, that thy children shall come
again to their own border",[36] thereby recalling God's promise
to the Jews in the preceding verses, "and they shall not sorrow
any more at all . . . for I will turn their mourning into joy, and
will comfort them, and make them rejoice from their sorrow".[37]
This kind of enriching of the text by interweaving quotations
could very well have been the work of the learned Rabbi. But
it is interesting to see what actually was the Rabbi's commentary on the verses from Isaiah xiv: "1. When Babylon was
taken, Cyrus allowed the exiled Jews to return home. 2. When
people will see how Cyrus honours Israel, they will like to be
servants of the Israelites." What interests us here is that
Browning was *not* drawing on the Rabbi. The Song which
Browning purports to be translating quotes exactly the same
passage, but the explanation given by Ibn Ezra in his Com-

[35] Isaiah XIV. 1-2.   [36] Jeremiah XXXI. 17.
[37] Jeremiah XXXI. 12-13.

mentary (in Friedlander's translation)[38] is simply historical, and quite unlike the interpretation Browning attributes to him in the Song.

Still more revealing of the subtle way in which Browning manipulated Biblical references in reconstructing the supposed Song is stanza xv. It is still further away from what should have been a Rabbi's argument, in so much as its substance is from the New Testament with only one significant interpolation from the Old:

> God spoke, and gave us the word to keep,
> Bade never fold the hands nor sleep
> 'Mid a faithless world,—at watch and ward,
> Till Christ at the end relieve our guard.
> By His servant Moses the watch was set:
> Though near upon cock-crow, we keep it yet.[39]

This follows the text so closely as to be almost a transcription:

> Heaven and earth shall pass away: but my words shall not pass away.... Take ye heed, watch and pray: for ye know not when the time is.... Watch ye therefore: for ye know not when the master of the house cometh, at even, or at midnight, or at the cockcrowing, or in the morning: Lest coming suddenly he find you sleeping. And what I say unto you I say unto all, Watch.[40]

But l. 89,

> By His servant Moses the watch was set . . .

comes instead from the very last chapter of the Old Testament, from Malachi:

> Remember ye the law of Moses my servant, which I commanded unto him in Horeb for all Israel, with the statutes and judgements. Behold, I will send you Elijah the prophet.[41]

This Elijah who is promised to the Jews was the prophet for whom they were all looking at the time of Christ. The

---

[38] M. Friedlaender, *The Commentary of Ibn Ezra on Isaiah*, i. 69. The text is given in ii. 22-9.

[39] "Holy-Cross Day", 85-90.

[40] Mark xiii. 31-7.

[41] Malachi iv. 4-5.

Christians claimed that he was John the Baptist, the prophet who prepared the way for the coming of Christ, the Messiah: "This is Elias,[42] which was for to come".[43]   But the Jews were unconvinced, and the debate goes on throughout the New Testament: "Art thou Elias, art thou the Prophet?"[44]   This question was a vital one for the Christians, for in order to win over the Jews they had to convince them of the continuity of the tradition.   That it was bitterly debated is shown by the words of the jibe of the Jews to Christ on the Cross, which in Mark are the last words addressed to him:

> And some of them that stood by, when they heard it, said, Behold, he calleth Elias.   And one ran and filled a sponge full of vinegar, and put it on a reed, and gave him to drink, saying, Let alone; let us see whether Elias will come to take him down. And Jesus cried with a loud voice, and gave up the ghost.[45]

Browning was well aware that this debate was crucial, that indeed it was one of the main questions on which it would be necessary to convince the Jews before they could be converted, and such was his knowledge of the Scriptures that he could insert the one line from Malachi into a Gospel context in a way which condenses the whole problem.   This raises the question, as often in Browning, of how he expected his readers to follow him.   It would seem, however, that he never allowed this thought to worry him unduly, and it is also true that for many of his contemporary readers the Bible was by no means a closed book.

Stanza xvi is based once more on a New Testament text, and once again the words of Browning are almost a transcription of the words of the Bible:

> Thou! if thou wast He, who at mid-watch came,
> By the starlight, naming a dubious name!
> And if, too heavy with sleep—too rash
> With fear—O Thou, if that martyr-gash

---

[42] "Elias" comes from the Greek transcription of the Hebrew name "Elijah".
[43] Christ speaking of John the Baptist: Matthew XI. 14.
[44] Addressed to the Apostle John: John I. 21.
[45] Mark XV. 35-7.

Fell on Thee coming to take thine own,
And we gave the Cross, when we owed the Throne. . . .[46]

And he cometh unto the disciples, and findeth them asleep, and saith unto Peter, What, could ye not watch with me one hour? Watch and pray, that ye enter not into temptation: the spirit indeed is willing, but the flesh is weak. . . . And he came and found them asleep again; for their eyes were heavy.[47]

Just before this text are the words "I say unto thee, That this night, before the cock crow, thou shalt deny me thrice".[48] This provides the verbal link of the crowing cock which may easily have brought together the two passages in Browning's mind. The starlight refers to the star of Bethlehem and the birth of Christ, the Jews' unrecognised Messiah. Yet in spite of the "if" this argument, with its implied apology, is hardly credible as coming from a Rabbi, however broadminded. No Rabbi would have expressed himself in these terms, appealing to a risen Christ with the words, "Thou art the judge".

In stanza xviii the Rabbi makes a bargain with Christ (and it must always be remembered that it was unthinkable that a Jew should admit of the Resurrection) by which he asks that the Jews shall be forgiven their one "sin" in return for joining sides with Christ and condemning the so-called Christians, more especially the Church of Rome, here in their turn called "dogs and swine"

Whose life laughs through and spits at their creed!
Who maintain Thee in word, and defy Thee in deed.[49]

Some of the Nonconformist preaching against the Scarlet Woman that Browning must have heard as a boy has crept into the Rabbi's invective here.

Browning's sympathy with the Jews is none the less very real, as he lists the infamies to which they have been subjected from age to age, culminating in the "summons to Christian fellowship". Once more the words are taken from the New Testament—

[46] "Holy-Cross Day", 91-6.
[47] Matthew xxvi. 40-3.
[48] Matthew, xxvi. 34.
[49] "Holy-Cross Day", 101-2.

> But I say, that the things which the Gentiles sacrifice, they
> sacrifice to devils, and not to God: and I would not that ye
> should have fellowship with devils.[50]

—and the Catholics who thus summon the Jews to partake of
their Mass are described in the same sentence of the poem as
"the Devil's crew". The context in Corinthians makes it clear
that the fellowship implied is that of the Communion:

> Ye cannot drink the cup of the Lord, and the cup of devils:
> ye cannot be partakers of the Lord's table, and of the table of
> devils.[51]

This whole question of religious segregation is typically
Nonconformist, underlying the refusal of so many similar sects
to intermingle. Nor do such sects consider it a virtue to mince
their words. Once more I am returning to the point that "the
Devil's crew" from its context in Corinthians springs from
Browning's own background and not from the Rabbi's. There
remains the possibility of "freedom" in translation: that is to
say that Browning may have introduced other Scriptural
phrases, this time New Testament, into his version of the
original Song of the Rabbi. Yet these references are so much
an integral part of the texture of the argument and the thread
of the reasoning as to make this hardly credible. Any such
translation, in a Jamesian phrase, would be of a freedom!

The poem finishes in a strange blending of all the elements
which went into its making, with the promise of the Jews to
vindicate the Name of Christ and to fight in it:

> A trophy to bear, as we march, thy band,
> South, East, and on to the Pleasant Land![52]

The passage is taken from Jeremiah in the Old Testament, but
by substituting "Christ's name" for "the name of the Lord"
Browning has greatly altered the meaning. The Lord in
Jeremiah was Jehovah, the God of Israel, whereas the promise
to fight in Christ's name can only mean a conversion to
Christianity. Rabbi Ben Ezra's Song of Death therefore

---

[50] I Corinthians x. 20.
[51] I Corinthians x. 21.
[52] "Holy-Cross Day", 119-20.

concludes in an invitation to the conversion of the Jews. If this fact had been stressed before, the question of the authenticity of the Song of Death could hardly have arisen. It is this that Browning, with typically Browningesque optimism, was looking forward to: the conversion of the whole Jewish race, not by "this bad business" of a forced sermon in a Catholic church, but by some miracle, bringing them among "the hosts of nations". The passage from Jeremiah is the following:

> At that time they shall call *Jerusalem* the *throne of the Lord*; and all the nations shall be gathered unto it, to *the name of the Lord*, to Jerusalem; neither shall they walk any more after the imagination of their evil heart. In those days the *house of Judah shall walk with the house of Israel*, and they shall come together out of the land of the north to the land that I have given for an inheritance unto your fathers. But I said, How shall I put thee among the children, and give thee *a pleasant land*, a goodly heritage of the hosts of nations?[53]

As at the beginning of the Rabbi's song the moment of the triumph of the Jews was the moment "When Judah beholds Jerusalem", so this last text from Jeremiah brings us back to the same point. The words and phrases in italics are those which Browning put straight into his poem.

Whereas in the prose introduction all the "hidden" texts, those written as it were in invisible ink between the lines, were concerned with the triumph of the Jews as victors and with an ultimate turning of the tables by which the "Gentiles" were to become the slaves of the Jews, Browning ends his poem on a different note, expressing his belief in a final unification of Jews and Christians in one band, marching, it is to be presumed, to the tune of "Onward Christian Soldiers". That he should force his source text to do so, introducing "Christ's name", as we have seen, into an Old Testament context is surprising, but his knowledge of his Bible is such that this can have been no slip but must have been deliberate. The change is not merely of a word but of a whole concept, and the explanation must, I believe, lie in the incorrigible optimism referred to before.

What does stand out clearly from an examination of the poem is that Browning was using the Jews above all as a stick

[53] Jeremiah III. 17-19.

with which to beat the Roman Catholics, and that this point of view was due to his early Congregationist training, the tenets of which, ever-present, underlie his later and more broad-minded reasoning.   His freedom of movement from text to text, with links now logical, now verbal, shows what a formidable understructure to his thought these doctrines were, and how freely he could use them for the purposes of dialectics.   Yet his technique was not that of the Schoolmen or the Divines but the closely argued reasoning he must so often have heard at his mother's side in the York Street chapel.[54]   Even a certain mixing or confusion of ideas originates from the same source: an appropriation of texts and freedom in their interpretation which comes naturally to exegetes who feel that they personally are working under the influence of divine inspiration.   Such were Browning's early teachers in such matters, and the poem shows how he had absorbed their lesson.

"Holy-Cross Day" is a disconcerting poem and not only for the youth or maiden postulated by the *Aberdeen Journal*.

What would have disconcerted the pious contemporary reader would be the keen and bitter irony, the assault against all the claptrap of religion (for the church-goer), the questioning of fundamental doctrines (for the chapel-goer), the doubt as to where the truth lies, and as to which is the best form of worship, a question raised repeatedly by Browning as a strictly personal problem, for at different periods of his life he went through a number of phases of chapel-going and church-going, and even of not going.

What disconcerts the reader today is different.   Having raised so many questions, having seen so clearly the sophistries and ironies underlying established beliefs and traditional interpretations of the Scriptures (noting, that is, that for the Jews the Christian texts could be read and interpreted in quite a different way, and one that would seem so much more to make sense), Browning lets the reader down wholly in the end.   We

---

[54] This chapel, which Browning attended with his mother, was by no means the Independent chapel described in *Christmas Eve*, but the religious position of the worshippers was the same, and it is interesting to note that in the poem of 1850, and in spite of his clear-sighted criticisms of this form of Christianity, it is the dissenting form of worship which Browning finally upholds against the splendour of Roman Catholicism and the aridity of German rationalism.

are brought up sharp against this inconsistency: that the clear-sighted Browning could so deliberately close his eyes to and turn his back on his own conclusions, to fix his gaze on that incongruous procession of converted Jews which has no meaning as a culmination to the poem, and is perhaps one of the main reasons why "Holy-Cross Day" has been left aside so often as unsatisfactory.

The flaw is not a failure of expression as in poor or weak poems. "Holy-Cross Day" on the contrary expressed and reflected all too faithfully a weakness and illogicality in Browning himself. But Browning's gift is not logical consistency, it is rather an ability to communicate with extraordinary vigour and freshness: this poem, because of its experimental nature, shows these qualities at their freest, so that besides being intensely readable it is intellectually stimulating. The reader may be no more anxious for the conversion of the Jews than was Marvell's coy mistress, but he will hardly refuse to share Browning's sympathy with them.

VI

Browning's Waste Land

THE waste land of " 'Childe Roland to the Dark Tower Came' " is the waste land of legend—it has been laid waste by a dragon. This monster never actually appears in the poem, but the atmosphere of horror and fear are the more convincing because we know that it is there. For the unseen is always more terrifying than the seen, and "Childe Roland" has many of the components of nightmare. Erdman, in the best single essay to be written about this much-discussed poem, realised this when he entitled his paper "Browning's Industrial Nightmare",[1] where he pointed out the main import of the poem as Browning's awareness of the evils of industrial competition, and showed how much it was influenced by Elizabeth Barrett's "The Cry of the Children". Everything which I have found in my reading of and around the poem supports this finding of Erdman's, not least a letter from Robert to Elizabeth postmarked 19 January 1846:

> . . . nightmare dreams have invariably been of *one* sort. I stand by (powerless to interpose by a word even) and see the infliction of tyranny on the unresisting man or beast (generally the last)— and I wake just in time not to die: . . . [2]

Cruelty to children, as expressed in sentimental terms by Elizabeth in "The Cry of the Children" and a sense of guilt for involvement in the system (the involvement guilt we feel today over the atom bomb) must underlie the factory-engine torture-tool images quoted by Erdman.

In his "conscious" poem on a factory child, *Pippa Passes*, written some thirteen years before "Childe Roland",

---

[1] See David V. Erdman, "Browning's Industrial Nightmare", pp. 417-35.
[2] *The Letters of Robert Browning and Elizabeth Barrett Barrett 1845-1846*, London 1899, I, 413.

Browning's approach was quite different. Pippa has the same genesis as Dickens' Bob Cratchit, there is the same optimistic idea of the goodness of the poor. Though slower in obtaining recognition, Pippa was nearly as popular as *A Christmas Carol*, and for the same reasons. Yet Dickens and Browning both knew well that extreme poverty brutalises, and the fact that Browning avoided saying so openly has made his hidden declaration so much the more intense.

To return to the invisible dragon. We find traces of its recent passage:

> What made those holes and rents
> In the dock's harsh swarth leaves, bruised as to baulk
> All hope of greenness? 't is a brute must walk
> Pashing their life out, with a brute's intents.[3]

Many of the details of this barren "romantic" landscape were unmistakably lifted, as DeVane has shown,[4] out of Gerard de Lairesse's *The Art of Painting in All its Branches*,[5] where they are given as examples of unpainterlike ugliness. There is nothing inconsistent in the fact that Browning should have found them in Lairesse with one connotation and utilised them with another. The indebtedness of Browning to Lairesse in "The Bishop Orders his Tomb"[6] goes to confirm DeVane's theory that the language and pictures of Lairesse were deeply imprinted on Browning's mind. Other images of horror emerge as we read the poem, and for some the source is more difficult to trace. It is interesting, and probably instructive, to note that they have appeared before in Browning's work. In stanza xxi the river of death forded by the Childe, into which suicidal willows throw themselves, contains corpses that are to be found in *Sordello*:

> how I feared
> To set my foot upon a dead man's cheek,
> Each step, or feel the spear I thrust to seek
> For hollows, tangled in his hair or beard!

---

[3] "Childe Roland", 69-72.
[4] DeVane, "The Landscape of Browning's *Childe Roland*", in *PMLA*, xl (1925), pp. 426-32.
[5] *Ibid.*
[6] See Chapter II, above, pp. 20-39.

> —It may have been a water-rat I speared,
> But, ugh! it sounded like a baby's shriek.[7]

In *Sordello* the baby is "a little skull with dazzling teeth" which is linked with one of Browning's most frequently repeated and effective symbols of horror, the mutilated limb:

> Stumbling upon a shrivelled hand nailed fast
> To the charred lintel of the doorway. . . .[8]

This charred flesh was to reappear in "The Heretic's Tragedy", where the burning is connected with the flames of Hell, and again in the expiation of M. Léonce Miranda in *Red Cotton Night-Cap Country*; and it is located in a background of "Childe Roland" vegetation:

> The thoroughfares were overrun with weed
> —Docks, quitchgrass, loathy mallows no man plants. . . .[9]

The feeling, as in "Childe Roland", is one of intense hatred:

> "May Boniface be duly damned for this!"
> —Howled some old Ghibellin. . . .
>
> "A boon, sweet Christ—let Salinguerra seethe
> To hell for ever, Christ, and let myself
> Be there to laugh at him!"—moaned some young Guelf.[10]

The linking of "Childe Roland" to *Sordello* would suggest another *motif* in Browning: his nightmare was not merely industrial, but was filled with war imagery. And there is a further link. Childe Roland, once across the river, asks

> Who were the strugglers, what war did they wage,
> Whose savage trample thus could pad the dank
> Soil to a plash? Toads in a poisoned tank,
> Or wild cats in a red-hot iron cage. . . .[11]

---

7 "Childe Roland", 121-6.
8 *Sordello*, IV, 19-20.
9 *Op. cit.*, IV. 22-3.
10 *Op. cit.*, IV. 12-13, 16-18.
11 "Childe Roland", 129-32.

In *Sordello* we have similar tanks, full of corpses:

> "The founts! God's bread, touch not a plank!
> A crawling hell of carrion—every tank
> Choke-full!"[12]

and a warrior sitting on the edge entangles the hair of his own
mother about his spur:

> Now both feet plough the ground, deeper each time,
> At last, *za, za* and up with a fierce kick
> Comes his own mother's face caught by the thick
> Grey hair about his spur![13]

Setting aside the Freudian implications, we have here an
intensely personal emotion, the horrors of warfare are those of
a nightmare, and there is clearly personal involvement. In
Colombe's Birthday too we have the threat of war to Juliers
expressed in these terms:

> You set your foot
> Upon a steaming bloody plash. . . .[14]

The trampled mud and plash are to be found once more in *The
Ring and the Book*, this time in a sexual connotation. Pompilia,
speaking of her real mother, the harlot, sees her as a "plashy
pool":

> every beast
> O' the field was wont to break that fountain-fence,
> Trample the silver into mud so murk
> Heaven could not find itself reflected there.[15]

This passage and the one from *Sordello* are, I feel, expansions of
the idea contained in "Childe Roland", stanzas xxi and xxii,
showing that all Browning's most intensely personal ideas of
horror were assembled behind and concentrated in these

---

[12] *Sordello*, IV. 89-91.
[13] *Op. cit.*, IV. 104-7.
[14] *Colombe's Birthday*, III. 257-8.
[15] *The Ring and the Book*, VII. 867-70.

stanzas: the horror of war,[16] the sense of social guilt, the horror of unchastity, and, above all, the horror of death. For "Tophet's tool", while it undoubtedly implies, as Erdman shows, industrial machinery.

> that horror fit to reel
> Men's bodies out like silk,

is taken from the Bible, where Tophet is symbolic of death, judgment and punishment:

> And I will make this city a horror, a thing to be hissed at . . .,
> Men shall bury in Tophet because there will be no place else
> to bury.[17]

Childe Roland is called upon to face everything which most filled Browning with horror: last and not least death itself.

Later, in stanza xxvi of the poem there is an interesting shift. The landscape, which had been laid waste by the forces of evil, or the dragon, is now seen as mere wanton creation, and a number of Browning's horror images converge at this point. There is the "palsied oak, a cleft in him" which appears in Lairesse, as does the split tomb with the corpse tumbling out. The two were intimately connected in Browning's mind, and his abnormal horror of such opening-up (which is linked to his love of privacy, as in "At the 'Mermaid'" or "House", or fear of "oozing through", as in "The Bishop Orders his Tomb") stands out in *The Ring and the Book* with the startling adjective "obscene tomb", significantly in juxtaposition with an "old malicious tower". Twenty-four years later Browning deliberately exploited the same idea, where Pacchiarotto the painter hides with a corpse in the tomb, but this scene is

---

[16] Cp. "Bishop Blougram's Apology", 455-62: "What's the vague good o' the world, for which you dare /With comfort to yourself blow millions up? /We neither of us see it! we do see /The blown-up millions—spatter of their brains /And writhing of their bowels and so forth, /In that bewildering entanglement /Of horrible eventualities /Past calculation to the end of time!" The reason Browning gives for voicing all these horrors is to be found in *Colombe's Birthday*, and is simply that he feels better afterwards, and that they seem less horrible once out in the open. It is interesting to note that he sees them as welling up from within. They are internal, not external, horrors. "Our best course is to say these hideous truths, /And see them, once said, grow endurable: /Like waters shuddering from their central bed, / Black with the midnight bowels of the earth, . . ." v. 107-10.

[17] Jeremiah, xix. 8, 11.

rendered less horrible by the very excess of macabre details, preventing us from taking it any more seriously than a horror film or a tale of terror.

The earth first created and then laid waste by a fool (a view Browning was later to examine more thoroughly in Caliban's questioning of Setebos) is followed in "Childe Roland" by disease imagery, where the soil

> Broke into moss or substances like boils[18]

—recalling the disease and disintegration symbolism he was to use later in *Fifine*. And finally we have the

> distorted mouth that splits its rim
> Gaping at death, and dies while it recoils.[19]

These lines (Eliot was to have recourse to similar imagery in the most barren section of his own *Waste Land*[20]) bring back the "split" tomb, but also the figure of horror, gaping at death, who is Louis XI and Don Juan, *alias* Browning, in *Fifine*.[21]

In this stanza of "Childe Roland", Browning had built up to a climax, assembling in fragmentary form key elements of what were to be his most intense horror images, all connected with death.

After this climax the poem changes: there is a shift in the scene of the nightmare. The plain dissolves, and Childe Roland finds himself ringed round by mountains, in a landscape reminiscent of Bunyan's. Besides the references to Lairesse and to ballad and fairy-tale literature (these literary sources have been studied very thoroughly in a basic contribution by Harold Golder),[22] and besides the influence of Elizabeth Barrett Browning and Browning's own suppressed sense of social guilt, the first part of the poem contains an even more personal reading.

[18] "Childe Roland", 153.
[19] *Op. cit.*, 155-6.
[20] "What the thunder said." See also, in connexion with Eliot's "Dead mountain mouth of carious teeth that cannot spit", the lines from "The Englishman in Italy" quoted below, n. 67.
[21] See below, pp. 172-4.
[22] Harold Golder, "Browning's 'Childe Roland'", in *PMLA*, xxxix (1924), pp. 963-78.

I

As DeVane has shown,[23] Browning had identified himself very closely with the Andromeda myth. His heroes were Perseus and the Christian equivalent, St George. Most of his poetry is written in the guise of Perseus, the poet of reason—but "Childe Roland" was a poem written by the monster. It is, essentially, a poem of hate. In *Pauline* we have the magnificent Andromeda passage, where Andromeda represents love:

> And one red beam, all the storm leaves in heaven,
> Resting upon her eyes and hair, such hair,
> As she awaits the snake on the wet beach. . . .[24]

The snake is the dragon or sea-monster, the monster which comes from the depths to claim its victims. A few lines earlier in *Pauline*, Browning had named this monster as "hatred", and had identified himself with it, acknowledging as his own this thing of darkness:

> But I begin to know what thing hate is—
> To sicken and to quiver and grow white—
> And I myself have furnished its first prey.[25]

In *Pauline* Browning portrays himself as falling a victim to this dragon, the monster which in "Childe Roland" was in complete possession. How this came about we can understand better if we consider the genesis of the poem. We have Browning's own authority for the fact that, on 1 January 1852 he made the resolution to write something every day.[26] He began by recording the dream poem, "Women and Roses".[27] On 2 January 1852 he wrote "Childe Roland", again a compulsive poem. On 3 January 1852 he wrote "Love among the Ruins",[28] this time a fully conscious poem. Significantly enough, on 4 January he was unable to keep up his resolution,

---

[23] DeVane, "The Virgin and the Dragon", pp. 33-46, reprinted in *Robert Browning: A Collection of Critical Essays*, ed. Philip Drew, London 1966, pp. 96-109.

[24] *Pauline*, 661-3.

[25] *Op. cit.*, 650-2. For another example of the sea-monster as an image of hatred, see *The Ring and the Book*, II. 1433-4: "Vengeance, you know, burst, like a mountain-wave /That holds a monster in it, o'er the house".

[26] DeVane, *Handbook*, p. 229.

[27] See Lilian Whiting, *The Brownings*, Boston 1917, p. 261.

[28] See below, n. 93.

for when he started writing consciously the immediacy broke down.

In 1852 he was a happily married man, living in Italy. He thought that he had set his house in order and the works written in the two or three years preceding show how preoccupied he had been with religious and metaphysical problems, and how convinced he was that he had solved them to his own satisfaction. This appears from "Cleon" and "An Epistle containing the Strange Medical Experiences of Karshish", which finally accept the existence of a supernatural power and also of basic Christianity, and further still from *Christmas Eve* and *Easter Day*, where the problem is debated at length and a solution offered, through the recognition of a divinity identified with Love.

What emerges from the dream poems seems instead to be the exact reverse of the conscious position assumed by Browning at the time in his public statements. In "Women and Roses", perhaps the most openly sexual of his poems, with the exception of those written towards the end of his life, Browning, the faithful husband, is discovered pursuing erotic dreams projected also into the past and future: dreams in which his imagination embraces statues, and where love has certainly nothing of the divine.

The second poem is "Childe Roland" with its theme of the quest. But the truth pursued in it is startlingly different from that pursued by Karshish, the physician, and Cleon, the philosopher. Throughout the poem, through visual and literary reminiscences, what is constantly stressed is the element of spite, utter repulsion, disgust, and, finally, hate. A hate which is irrational, which is as absolute as the divine love postulated in the conscious poetry of Browning. The cripple, the horse, the very landscape are all "hateful", "hated", "spiteful". Maimed, blinded, diseased, they make no claim on our sympathy—the one note sounded is that of vengeance and punishment. The horse[29] "must be wicked to deserve such

[29] A creature worthy to be set side by side with the horse in Baudelaire's "Une Gravure fantastique": "Sans éperons, sans fouet, il essouffle un cheval,/ Fantôme comme lui, rosse apocalyptique,/Qui bave des naseaux comme un épileptique." Both Browning and Baudelaire could have been using Poe's "Metzengerstein" as a source.

pain", the willows fling themselves suicidally into "the river which had done them all the wrong".

This hate, coupled with suicidal despair, for Childe Roland's turning-off toward the dark tower is a form of suicide, is the reversal and overturning of all the values which Browning accepted and in which he believed—it is the triumph of evil which we meet with in Poe's "Metzengerstein"[30] or in Shelley's *Zastrozzi*, and the triumph of despair. With Poe and Shelley we are at the opposite pole to the traditional Browning attitude. Many, probably most, readers have misunderstood the meaning of "Childe Roland" because of the need they felt to make it fit in with Browning's declared philosophy in poems like *Paracelsus*:

> No slow defeat, but a complete success:
> You will find all you seek, and perish so![31]

or "Prospice":

> Fear death? . . .
> No! let me taste the whole of it, fare like my peers
> The heroes of old. . . .[32]

Ignoring all the pointers of the imagery and the Lear title line from the most pessimistic of Shakespeare's plays, "Childe Roland", it is felt, must somehow conform to pattern and lead up to a final victory: anything else would be inconsistent. The most flagrant misuse of the poem was perpetrated in the last century by Thomas Wentworth Higginson,[33] who carried "Childe Roland" through "the then debatable ground between Kansas and Nebraska, in charge of an armed party of emigrants towards the besieged town of Lawrence". He marked, he tells us, the lines

> Fool, to be dozing at the very nonce,
> After a life spent training for the sight[34]

and commented "It shows that I carried it for a sort of elixir of life, and used it for that purpose". While other critics carry neither their convictions nor the poem to these lengths, there is a fairly general agreement that "Childe Roland" will win

---

[30] See Appendix C.   [31] *Paracelsus*, 1. 705-6.   [32] "Prospice", 17-18.
[33] T. W. Higginson, *Poet Lore*, Boston 1901, pp. 262-8.
[34] "Childe Roland", 179-80.

through at last. Charles R. Woodward couches this idea in modern terms by viewing the poem as a rebirth archetype.[35] Of the critics who have put forward negative interpretations, Gratz,[36] Erdman, and Betty Miller,[37] all follow Browning's own words and find failure evident, John Lindberg,[38] too, gives a negative interpretation of the poem, while Cohen seems to lean cautiously in this direction.[39] The variety of interpretations offered[40] reminds us forcibly of James Cowan's comment on the relations between literary criticism and "Childe Roland": that its ambiguity "serves as an unstructured stimulus for the projective interpretations of readers".[41]

The reasons Betty Miller gives for Childe Roland's defeat are very interesting indeed. She sees the nightmare, like Erdman, as the outcome of a sense of guilt, but finds the origin of this guilt to lie in:

> the corruption and sterility that must claim one who has failed, like many another "poor traitor" before him, to deliver to mankind the full burden of the message with which he has been entrusted.[42]

---

[35] Charles R. Woodward, "The Road to the Dark Tower: An Interpretation of Browning's 'Childe Roland' ", in *Tennessee Studies in Literature*, Knoxville 1961, pp. 93-9, following Maud Bodkin, "A Note on Browning's *Childe Roland*", in *Literature and Psychology*, x (1960), pp. 37. Maud Bodkin in her turn is following R. E. Hughes in his excellent detailed psychological study "Browning's 'Childe Roland' and the Broken Taboo", in *Literature and Psychology*, IX (1959), pp. 18-19. Hughes concludes: "Read from the standpoint of fantasy and symbol, 'Childe Roland' stands revealed, not as a comforting moral fable, but as a complex account of a strong emotional drive and consequent guilt feelings".

[36] See below, n. 59.

[37] Betty Miller, *Robert Browning*, p. 168.

[38] See John Lindberg, "Grail Themes in Browning's 'Childe Roland' ", *Victorian Newsletter*, XVI (Fall 1959), pp. 27-30. Childe Roland reverses the traditional motives of hope and salvation found in the Grail quest and embodies the anxieties of the Victorians about the evil in the world.

[39] J. M. Cohen, "The Young Robert Browning", in the *Cornhill Magazine*, 975 (1948), pp. 234-48, and *Robert Browning*, London 1952, pp. 78-82.

[40] An interesting early interpretation of "Childe Roland" was given to the Browning Society by J. Kirkman. See *Browning Society Papers*, I (1881-4), pp. 21-27. He concluded that it was an allegory of dying, thereby drawing down upon his head the wrath of other members, especially Furnivall. Mrs Orr quoted "Prospice" against him.

[41] James Cowan, "Literary Criticism and Projection", in the *Kansas Magazine* (1960), pp. 84-7.

[42] Betty Miller, *Robert Browning*, p. 168.

Betty Miller's interpretation fits in very well with one of
Browning's basic themes, the failed artist, such as Andrea del
Sarto: the man who has been content to give less than his
best, who has ceased to struggle. We can note in this connexion
that in *The Two Poets of Croisic*, a much later poem, Browning
uses the name "Roland" for the famous knight with whom his
poet, Maillard, is contrasted. Maillard is one of Browning's
many artistic failures who somehow succeed, who

> dream, strive to do, and agonize to do,
> And fail in doing,[43]

and Browning wrote of him

> I think it still more wondrous that you bared
> Your brow (my earlier image) as if praise
> Were gained by simple fighting nowadays![44]

For it is the aim of the poet and artist to win appraisal, that
drop of "pure gold", especially from his peers. Over and over
again in Browning's poetry the knight or artist, at the moment
of his trial, is surrounded by "watchers". These may be the
mountains themselves, as in "The Englishman in Italy", or the
giants at a hunting of "Childe Roland", cloud shapes, as in
Pauline, warriors as in *Luria*, the people as in *Sordello*:

> And round those three the People formed a ring,
> Of visionary judges whose award
> He recognized in full . . .
> > his first strife
> For their sake must not be ignobly fought. . . .[45]

and the "dead rivals" watching in *Paracelsus*. Perhaps the
quest of Paracelsus, where the watchers are poets, is the closest
parallel to "Childe Roland":

> As if all poets, God ever meant
> Should save the world, and therefore lent
> Great gifts to, but who, proud, refused
> To do his work, or lightly used
> Those gifts, or failed through weak endeavour,

---

[43] "Andrea del Sarto", 69-70.
[44] *The Two Poets of Croisic*, 734-6.
[45] *Sordello*, v. 456-8, 460-1.

So, mourn cast off by him for ever,— . . .
As if these leaned in airy ring
To take me; this the song they sing.
"Lost, lost! yet come,
With our wan troop make thy home . . .
And altogether we, thy peers,
Will pardon crave for thee, the last . . .
Yet we trusted thou shouldst speak
The message which our lips, too weak,
Refused to utter.[46]

If I have quoted at considerable length from *Paracelsus*, it is because the lost poets his peers, surrounding him in airy ring, with their undelivered message, seem to me to be the same as "the lost adventurers my peers" who stood ranged along the hillsides met to view the last of Childe Roland.[47]

Not that "Childe Roland" was a conscious allegory of an artist's progress, difficulties, and ultimate failure. Any such interpretation taken alone would leave unexplained much of the horror imagery and would fail to account for the disturbing effect of the poem as a whole. Much more is involved. Nevertheless Browning shows constant concern in his poetry with his task as poet and artist. He took this very seriously indeed, and much, if not most, of his work is indirectly concerned with it. A nightmare of failure and defeat would therefore imply for him defeat as a poet. There are, of course, two measures of success here: the one with which he was most concerned, the ultimate delivery of "the message", and the worldly success of public recognition. While he denies and refutes the validity of the latter, there are many hints in his work that he cared about it more than he would openly admit. The natural human wish for acknowledgment must have been strengthened in his case by his peculiar position as being the husband of a famous poetess, and financially dependent upon her. There was material for nightmare here. Probably the dead warriors of "Childe Roland" owe something, too, to the pageant of dead poets in Elizabeth's "A Vision of Poets".[48]

[46] *Paracelsus*, ii. 289-313.
[47] This connexion is also made by Harold Golder, "Browning's 'Childe Roland' ".
[48] This poem may also have suggested to Browning the three pools in *Pauline*.

In *Paracelsus* we find, beside the "dead adventurers"

> a fungous brood sickly and pale,
> Chill mushrooms coloured like a corpse's cheek[49]

—which fungus, we are told, supplies the place of his "dead aims". Read in conjunction with the "dead man's cheek" on which Childe Roland feared to set his foot, and with the sick vegetation, we can trace another element of the nightmare and of the guilt-feelings underlying it. The dead aims are those of an artist who has ceased to struggle, whose reach, in Andrea's words, no longer exceeds his grasp. There are many parallels between Childe Roland and Andrea, not least the felt need of an audience. Raphael is described as "pouring his soul, with Kings and Popes to see", while Andrea himself works best surrounded by Francis and his court:

> I painting proudly with his breath on me,
> All his court round him, seeing with his eyes,
> Such frank French eyes, and such a fire of souls
> Profuse, my hand kept plying by those hearts—[50]

and in the end, Andrea pleads for

> In heaven, perhaps, new chances, one more chance.[51]

This last chance Browning was never willing consciously to deny—we recall

> Sordello had one chance left, spite of all.[52]

But in the nightmare poem of "Childe Roland" the adventurer has reached the end. The celestial city, the new Jerusalem where Andrea hoped to find himself painting victoriously—

> Four great walls in the New Jerusalem,
> Meted on each side by the angel's reed,
> For Leonard, Rafael, Agnolo and me[53]

—is in ruins, is reduced to the dark tower. For the life-long quest of Childe Roland, the quest which he renounces at the

---

[49] *Paracelsus*, III. 542-3.   [50] "Andrea del Sarto", 158-61.
[51] *Op. cit.*, 260.   [52] *Sordello*, v. 325.   [53] "Andrea del Sarto", 261-4.

beginning of the poem when in utter weariness he consciously
turns into the wrong path, was the quest for the celestial city.

There is a frequent misunderstanding of the opening lines of
the poem. It is generally assumed that Childe Roland asks the
cripple the way to the dark tower, and that the cripple tells
him a lie, yet points out the right way. This has always been
hard to explain. If, instead, we assume that Childe Roland
has asked the way *to the celestial city*, and that he voluntarily
abandons the quest at this point out of sheer weariness, "unfit
to cope with that obstreperous joy success would bring", then
there is no contradiction.[54] He imagines the glee of the cripple

> If at his counsel I should turn aside
> Into that ominous tract which, all agree,
> Hides the Dark Tower. . . .[55]

but nevertheless he does so turn

> Yet acquiescingly
> I did turn as he pointed: neither pride
> Nor hope rekindling at the end descried,
> So much as gladness that some end might be.[56]

This acceptance of failure, as I said earlier, is practically a form
of suicide. Childe Roland is acting under the same kind of
compulsion that drives the young Baron Metzengerstein on to
his doom. It is echoed in the death-wish of the sick man in the

---

[54] The obstacle to this interpretation lies in stanzas vii and xxx. In stanza vii
Childe Roland says he has been writ "So many times among 'The Band'—to wit, /
The knights who to the Dark Tower's search addressed /Their steps—that just to
fail as they, seemed best, /And all the doubt was now—should I be fit?" This can
be read in the sense that he has at last accepted the failure which had often been
prophesied for him. The quest in which he had suffered in the first line of the
stanza is his original quest for the celestial city.

In stanza xxx Childe Roland fails to recognise his goal "after a life spent
training for the sight". This is understandable because, like Sordello at Goito
(see p. 136), he is taken by surprise at the change, finding only the ruin or dark
tower in the place of the celestial city. By accepting the apparent contradiction
that the two goals of *Childe Roland* are antithetical yet one and the same, as I hope
to substantiate, then all other contradictions disappear. For a concise statement
of the case for the opposition, see John W. Willoughby, "Browning's 'Childe
Roland to the Dark Tower Came' ", in *Victorian Poetry*, i, no. 4 (1963), pp. 291-9.

[55] "Childe Roland", 13-15.

[56] *Op. cit.*, 15-18.

odd borrowing from Donne in stanzas v and vi,[57] and in the very landscape where

> Drenched willows flung them headlong in a fit
> Of mute despair, a suicidal throng.[58]

This acceptance of failure, this pilgrimage in the direction of the dark tower instead of the celestial city, is the chief of many parallels between Browning's nightmare and Bunyan's dream. The two pilgrimages could be graphed as parallel lines running in opposite directions. I am grateful to Giorgio Melchiori for drawing my attention both to the importance of Bunyan in relation to "Childe Roland"[59] and to the links between the celestial city and the dark tower. *The Pilgrim's Progress* is "delivered under the Similitude of a Dream wherein is Discovered The manner of his setting out, His Dangerous Journey; And safe Arrival at the Desired Countrey".[60] Bunyan is evoked in Childe Roland by mention of the dragon-penned wings of

> A great black bird, Apollyon's bosom-friend.[61]

In Bunyan the wings are Apollyon's own:

> . . . now the Monster was hideous to behold, he was cloathed with scales like a Fish; (and they are his pride) he had Wings like a Dragon, feet like a Bear, and out of his belly came Fire and Smoak.[62]

Immediately after the passage of the bird, the landscape that surrounds the journey of Childe Roland changes by a dream-shift suddenly and surprisingly. It is no longer the flat waste

---

[57] See R. L. Lowe, "Browning and Donne", in *Notes and Queries*, Nov. 1953, pp. 491-2.

[58] "Childe Roland", 117-18.

[59] The connexion with Bunyan had already been noted by R. J. Gratz "The Journey of Childe Roland", *Poet Lore*, II (1890), pp. 578-9. Gratz also reads the poem pessimistically. He writes that Childe Roland finds himself "at last surrounded by the ugly heights of Doubting Castle, one more victim of Giant Despair. Indeed the *scenario* of the entire poem . . . vividly suggests the possibilities in detail of John Bunyan's By-Path Meadow leading from the stile, where sat the false shepherd, to Doubting Castle and the tombs of the lost pilgrims". He concludes: "Roland did what his predecessors failed to do. He so far separated himself from his miserable fate as to warn his fellow-travellers against it".

[60] From frontispiece of first edition, 1678.

[61] "Childe Roland", 160.

[62] John Bunyan, *The Pilgrim's Progress*, ed. J. B. Wharey, Oxford 1928, p. 56.

land. With a start, Roland, who had lifted his eyes following the passage of Apollyon's bird, realises that he is in a valley. Now, Christian's meeting and fight with Apollyon takes place in the Valley of Humiliation, and the landscape of *The Pilgrim's Progress* is a sequence of valleys, including the Valley of the Shadow of Death. From this point of the poem the influence of Bunyan is much more marked. It is at the end of the Valley of Humiliation that Christian meets two giants, Pagan and Pope (Childe Roland saw the hills as giants). Browning's own life reflected the struggle with these particular giants. In *Easter Day*, a poem on the theme of "how very hard it is to be a Christian" the celestial city towards which the pilgrim is making his way is shown to be a mirage. This scene follows close upon a nightmare of the end of the world and the last judgment, recalling "Childe Roland"—

> 'T is the Last Judgment's fire must cure this place,
> Calcine its clods and set my prisoners free.[63]

—with the same light of fire and storm, and the only mention outside "Childe Roland" of two words rare in Browning's work: "Tophet" and "calcine". Here, in *Easter Day*, the celestial city fades to a waste land:

> I saw . . . Oh brother, 'mid far sands
> The palm-tree-cinctured city stands,
> Bright-white beneath, as heaven, bright-blue,
> Leans o'er it . . .
>
> One morn,—the Arab staggers blind
> O'er a new tract of death, calcined
> To ashes, silence, nothingness . . .[64]

and there is much that echoes "Childe Roland" in:

> I have reached the goal—
> "Whereto does knowledge serve!" . . .
> The goal's a ruin like the rest![65]

Easter Day, however, was a daylight poem, not a nightmare, and ended on the usual waking note of optimism:

[63] "Childe Roland", 65-6.
[64] *Easter Day*, 624-7, 630-2.
[65] *Op. cit.*, 896-7, 901.

But Easter-Day breaks! But
Christ rises! Mercy every way
Is infinite—and who can say?[66]

It is the same optimistic note that we find in Bunyan. The
struggle of Childe Roland all the time is against despair, and
Christian and Hopeful were taken prisoners by Giant Despair.
The giant tries to break down Christian's resistance by showing
him the bones of those who had tried before him to reach the
celestial city, and had fallen victims, while Childe Roland
dwells on the thought of the "lost adventurers". Much of
Christian's journey is in the dark, day breaks only when he is
in view of the celestial city. In the same way Childe Roland's
journey takes place in a prolonged supernatural twilight, until
the last moment when he reaches the end of his journey.
Christian crosses a terrible river, the river of death, and faces
the last onslaught of Despair. Then, at a blast of trumpets, he
sees the golden celestial city of Revelation.

The last part of Roland's journey can be seen as a photo-
graphic negative of Christian's. What Roland finds at the end,
in the last flash of sinister light, is all that remains of the celestial
city, the "round squat turret, blind as a fool's heart". The
fool's heart is Browning's own.

This statement is supported by the shipwreck simile in
stanza xxi. The sudden seascape intrudes upon the mountain
scene, although we should remember that the dragon in
Browning's mind was intrinsically a sea-monster, the "wet
snake" of Andromeda.[67] Just after Childe Roland's first sight
of the dark tower, we are told

---

[66] *Op. cit.*, 1038-40.

[67] The same monster, dead and harmless, became part of the wild mountain
landscape of "The Englishman in Italy", 153-6, where the monster links the sea
to the mountains " 'Mid the rock-chasms and piles of loose stones /Like the loose
broken teeth /Of some monster which climbed there to die /From the ocean
beneath". It is curious also to note the connexion made in "Artemis Prologuizes",
45-46, where "from the gaping wave a monster flung /His obscene body in the
coursers' path". The monster coming from the sea, or the unconscious, is a usual
symbol in Browning, the equivalent of the monster that curled out of the man's
own heart in *The Ring and the Book*, I. 815, but the use of "obscene" reminds us of
the obscene tomb which has burst open. The gaping wave, like the open tomb, is
revealing those secrets which Browning considers it indecent to expose.

> The tempest's mocking elf
> Points to the shipman thus the unseen shelf
> He strikes on, only when the timbers start.[68]

It takes, I believe, a later poem of Browning's to help us to understand the inclusion of these lines here, but we need no such help to realise that they point away from any possibility of a final victory. The meaning of the "unseen shelf" on which the bark founders we learn from "With Francis Furini":

> and the dip began
> From safe and solid into that profound
> Of ignorance I tell you surges round
> *My rock-spit of self-knowledge.* Well and ill,
> Evil and good irreconcilable
> Above, beneath, about my every side,
> ... Evil there was good.[69]

This nightmare world of inverted values, with hatred substituted for love, the tower for the celestial city, is the waste land of "Childe Roland", and the moment of destruction is the moment of revelation.[70] Childe Roland calls himself "Dunce" and "Dotard" because the truth that is revealed to him, the "unseen shelf", is the truth of his own heart.[70a]

It is not uncommon in Browning's poetry to find glimpses of an awareness of suppressed evil underneath. One passage from "James Lee's Wife" has analogies with the shipwreck image of "Childe Roland":

> Love's voyage full-sail,—(now, gnash your teeth!)
> When planks start, open hell beneath
> Unawares?[71]

---

[68] "Childe Roland", 184-6.

[69] "With Francis Furini", 407-12, 417: my italics.

[70] Browning continues, in his imaginary conversation with Furini, 489-91, "Who proffers help of hand /To weak Andromeda exposed on strand /At mercy of the monster?"—showing how closely the image of Andromeda and the monster was bound up with Browning's idea of the conflict of good and evil.

[70a] See Patricia M. Ball's "Browning's Godot", in *Victorian Poetry*, III (1965), pp. 245-53. This came to my notice after I had written the present chapter, and it is interesting to find how completely our conclusions coincide. Miss Ball writes (p. 252): "The horn sounding, out of the horror of Roland's self-knowledge, into the dark and desolate landscape with its 'round squat turret, blind as the fool's heart', is Browning's fundamental vision transmuted into symbolic form . . .".

[71] "James Lee's Wife", 51-3.

and another passage is from *The Ring and the Book*:

> As when, in our Campagna, there is fired
> The nest-like work that overruns a hut;
> And, as the thatch burns here, there, everywhere, . . .

> There rises gradual, black amid the blaze,
> Some grim and unscathed nucleus of the nest,—
> Some old malicious tower, some obscene tomb
> They thought a temple in their ignorance,
> And clung about and thought to lean upon—
> There laughs it o'er their ravage.[72]

Here the evil takes the form of an old tower linked with an obscene tomb, and we recognise again the scene already set much earlier in *Sordello*, where the "one tower left" of a castle is connected with a broken tomb:

> a barrow burst
> And Alberic's huge skeleton unhearsed. . . .[73]

The frequent recurrence of the broken-tomb theme is, I believe, connected with the extreme need Browning felt to keep buried things buried, his dread of all exposure, which he repeatedly treats as a form of indecency.

In the key scene at the inn in *The Ring and the Book*, where, as DeVane expressed it, "the real conflict between the opposing forces takes place",[74] images from "Childe Roland" cluster thickly in the version given by Pompilia. Pompilia herself figures as Andromeda or the Christian martyr-maid (or again, in the Fisc's version, as Hesione):

> There stands Hesione thrust out by Troy,
> Her father's hand has chained her to a crag,
> Her mother's from the virgin plucked the vest,
> At a safe distance both distressful watch,
> While near and nearer comes the snorting orc.[75]

In *The Ring and the Book* the dragon finds his match in St George, who, as DeVane has shown,[76] is, together with Perseus,

---

[72] *The Ring and the Book*, x. 620-2, 625-30.   [73] *Sordello*, vi. 791-2.
[74] W. Clyde DeVane, "The Virgin and the Dragon", p. 42.
[75] *The Ring and the Book*, ix. 968-72.
[76] W. Clyde DeVane, "The Virgin and the Dragon", pp. 41-2.

one of the symbols for Caponsacchi, but Pompilia in her narration of the story uses words which recall the adventure of that other knight, Childe Roland:

> There's the journey: . . .
> How strange it was—there where the plain begins
> And the small river mitigates its flow—
> When eve was fading fast, and my soul sank, . . .
>
> So,—"This grey place was famous once," said he—
> And he began that legend of the place
> As if in answer to the unspoken fear,
> And told me all about a brave man dead, . . .[77]

So this key scene in *The Ring and the Book* is set on the same ground as "Childe Roland", and the story of his end is told. In "that tragical red eve" Pompilia describes her own feelings of defeat, and draws a picture of herself which reflects the situation of Childe Roland at this moment of trial:

> I saw the old boundary and wall o' the world
> Rise plain as ever round me, hard and cold,
> As if the broken circlet joined again,
> Tightened itself about me with no break,—
>
> . . . the friends my enemies,
> All ranged against me, not an avenue
> To try, but would be blocked and drive me back. . . .[78]

The red light of the scene stresses its apocalyptic quality, the magical return of day in "Childe Roland":

> why, day
> Came back again for that! before it left,
> The dying sunset kindled through a cleft . . .[79]

repeated in the threatening sunset in which the inn is first viewed in *The Ring and the Book*:

> Against the sudden bloody splendour poured
> Cursewise in day's departure by the sun . . .[80]

---

[77] *The Ring and the Book*, VII. 1528, 1532-4, 1538-41.
[78] *Op. cit.*, VII. 1546-9, 1551-3.
[79] "Childe Roland", 187-9.
[80] *The Ring and the Book*, I. 511-2.

and recalls an earlier key scene in *Sordello*, where instead it was
the prelude to victory and to Sordello's rescue of Palma:

> The hesitating sunset floated back,
> Rosily traversed in the wonted track
>
> . . . 't was day looped back night's pall;
> Sordello had a chance left spite of all.[81]

And in this supernatural light

> a sole grate showed the fiery West,
> As shows its corpse the world's end some split tomb—
> A gloom, a rift of fire, another gloom . . [82].

begins "Fate's second marvellous cycle". The specific reference
here to the end of the world, the moment at which the tomb will
split, and to the beginning of a new cycle, show the positive
elements of the vision, the vision which was to be reversed in
the "Childe Roland" nightmare where the ultimate trial takes
place in the same dramatic light, but where the end of the
world means Judgment Day.

The fear of death and the fear of Judgment Day are the two
inter-related elements operating in the final section of "Childe
Roland". The many details which add up to the sum of
Browning's sense of guilt are all subsidiary to the end of the
dream: the dark tower and the nightmare fear which it
embodies. Death for Browning often took the form of a
struggle. In *Pauline*, his first published poem, he had expressed
it in almost the same terms:

> For I seem, dying, as one going in the dark
> To fight a giant. . . .[83]

In *Pauline*, however, he is sure of victory:

> Know my last state is happy, free from doubt
> Or touch of fear.[84]

The fact that he felt the need to make this declaration suggests
an awareness of the state which came to the fore in "Childe

---

[81] *Sordello*, v. 317-18, 323-4.
[82] *Op. cit.*, v. 934-6.
[83] *Pauline*, 1026-7.
[84] *Op. cit.*, 1030-1.

Roland". The same image for death is used in his play, *Strafford*:

> I, soon to rush
> Alone upon a giant in the dark ![85]

and in "Prospice":

> I am nearing the place,
> The power of the night, the press of the storm,
>   The post of the foe;
> Where he stands, the Arch Fear in a visible form,
>   Yet the strong man must go . . .[86]

and in *Easter Day* we have a shipwreck, a trumpet blast, an awareness of what might have been done:

> Fool,
> To let the chance slip, linger cool
> When such adventure offered! Just
> A bridge to cross, a dwarf to thrust
> Aside, a wicked mage to stab. . . .[87]

There is, too, the fire of the storm and a destructive dragon:

> the earth was lit;
> As if a dragon's nostril split
> And all his famished ire o'erflowed . . .[88]

all leading up to Judgment Day:

> Leaving exposed the utmost walls
> Of time, about to tumble in
> And end the world. I felt begin
> The Judgement-Day.[89]

Browning is not usually regarded as an apocalyptic poet and yet there is much in his work that belongs to this stream. Judgment Day for him meant the risk of Hell, with very real punishments. The ancient torture instruments lying about on the plain in "Childe Roland" are reminders of this: they are the same instruments which constitute such an integral part of the

---

[85] *Strafford*, II. 155-6.   [86] "Prospice", 4-8.   [87] *Easter Day*, 483-7.
[88] *Op. cit.*, 535-7.   [89] *Op. cit.*, 544-7.

K

imagery of Guido's second book in *The Ring and the Book*.
Browning could write boldly in *Paracelsus*

> if he wake up
> The god of the place to ban and blast him there,
> Both well! What's failure or success to me?[90]

But "Childe Roland" shows us the underlying fear behind so
many brave declarations. This fear is concentrated in the
major symbol of the poem: the round, squat, blind tower.

The tower symbol was a constant throughout Browning's
work. It appears first in *Sordello* at Goito:

> just a castle built amid
> A few low mountains; . . .

> Some captured creature in a pound,
> Whose artless wonder quite precludes distress. . . .[91]

Yet this peaceful and innocent scene changes. Sordello,
wandering alone in the evening, comes upon it and finds it
ruined:

> 't was Goito's mountain-cup
> And castle. He had dropped through one defile
> He never dared explore. . . .

> Ah, the slim castle! dwindled of late years,
> But more mysterious; gone to ruin—trails
> Of vine through every loop-hole.[92]

But this is the tower of "Love among the Ruins", the poem that
Browning wrote the day after "Childe Roland",[93] and in which

---

[90] *Paracelsus*, II. 103-5.   [91] *Sordello*, I. 381-5.   [92] *Op. cit.*, II. 956-8, 978-80.

[93] See Johnstone Parr, "The Date of Composition of Browning's 'Love among
the Ruins' ", in *Philological Quarterly*, XXXII (Oct. 1953), pp. 443-6, in which he
argues for a later date of composition, and challenges the date accepted by Mrs Orr,
Griffin and Minchin, Betty Miller, and DeVane. See also John Huebenthal, "The
Dating of Browning's 'Love among the Ruins', 'Women and Roses', and 'Childe
Roland' ", in *Victorian Poetry*, IV (1966), pp. 51-4. Huebenthal traces the Griffin-
Minchin dating to a pamphlet of Furnivall's, and supports the order (1) "Love
among the Ruins", (2) "Women and Roses", (3) "Childe Roland". Arguing
against Erdman's reading of "Childe Roland", Huebenthal writes: "On the other
hand, if 'Childe Roland' is the last in the series, then perhaps it is not really a dark
poem at all, but a poem of hope, of success, since the course of Browning's mind is
usually an optimistic curve upwards . . .". While the external evidence remains
inconclusive, I think the internal evidence points to the DeVane dating. But
whether written first or last, "Childe Roland" reads pessimistically.

he consciously tried to re-establish his values, which the night-mare had destroyed. The mountain-cup and castle which had appeared so hideously in the nightmare are now tamed, harmless ruins:

> Now,—the single little turret that remains
>   On the plains,
> By the caper overrooted, by the gourd
>   Overscored, . . .
>
> Marks the basement whence a tower in ancient time
>   Sprang sublime. . . .[94]

And this is the setting of an idyllic love scene in a twilight purged of all its terror, till we come to the final affirmation "Love is best" with which he exorcises all the horror and hate of the picture he had drawn on the previous day. The tower is here specifically described as all that remains of a great city and the stress is laid on its harmlessness.[95] Nevertheless it is, we feel, the same ruined tower which appeared later so "maliciously" in the Roman *campagna* in *The Ring and the Book*. The sense of evil lingered on after "Love among the Ruins": it was never to be totally erased.

In "A Lovers' Quarrel" in 1853 the tower reappears, still further diminished

> I would laugh like the valiant Thumb
> Facing the castle glum
> And the giant's fee-faw-fum![96]

Together with Childe Roland, the castle has shrunk to insignificance, which was one way of meeting its challenge. For as early as *A Blot in the 'Scutcheon* (1840) the castle was present, as something which had ultimately to be faced:

---

[94] "Love among the Ruins", st. iv.

[95] See R. A. Law, "The Background of Browning's *Love among the Ruins*", in *Modern Language Notes*, xxxvii (1922), pp. 312-3. Law sees the city of "Love among the Ruins" as a composite picture of Babylon and Jerusalem. This fits in very well with my own view of it as the ruins of the celestial city, or new Jerusalem, which Browning had destroyed in his poem of the previous day, "Childe Roland".

[96] "A Lovers' Quarrel", 131-3.

> And the dim turret I have fled from, fronts
> Again my step; the very river put
> Its arm about me and conducted me
> To this detested spot.[97]

It was noted by Caponsacchi at Castelnuovo, the stopping place on the road to Rome where Guido catches up with the fleeing Pompilia—apparently innocent, yet holding menace, and may well be the tower from which Monsieur Léonce Miranda plunged to his death by suicide in *Red Cotton Night-Cap Country*:

> what means this Belvedere?
> This Tower, stuck like a fool's-cap on the roof—
> Do you intend to soar to heaven from thence?[98]

The fool's cap carries a faint echo of the "dunce" and "blind as a fool's heart" of "Childe Roland", but, whether or no, the tower is rightly seen as perilous. In *Fifine* Don Juan chooses the town "and not this tower apart", suggesting the isolation of the artist, and the dangers of introspection. Even so early as in *Pauline* Browning had broken out with the passionate cry "I'll look within no more", complaining

> ends
> Foul to be dreamed of, smiled at me as fixed
> And fair, while others changed from fair to foul.[99]

Childe Roland, foundering on "the rock-spit of self-knowledge" and substituting the dark tower for the celestial city, was giving a symbolic form to the situation Browning had already foreseen in *Pauline*. For "Childe Roland" was compulsive writing:

> The next day *Childe Roland* came upon me as a kind of dream. I had to write it, then and there, and I finished it the same day, I believe.[100]

This sets it in a class apart from the main body of Browning's work (although he wrote in this way more often than is generally

[97] *A Blot in the 'Scutcheon*, III. 1, 8-11.
[98] *Red Cotton Night-Cap Country*, 2228-30.
[99] *Pauline*, 943-5.
[100] See Lilian Whiting, *The Brownings*, p. 261, where these words are reported as addressed by Browning on 5 November 1887 to an anonymous caller.

believed). It has affinities with *The Ancient Mariner* and "Kubla Khan" (as Golder has noticed) or with Blake's *Prophetic Books*: that stream of visionary poetry that runs through English literature from Vaughan and Traherne to Dylan Thomas. Such poems, though enigmatic to their own authors, are at the same time most revealing inasmuch as they release ideas and feelings which, when he is in conscious control, the author hides from himself as well as others. Such poems also represent the accumulation of reading and memories of all kinds which emerge involuntarily yet mysteriously organised. Just as they embody a wide range of sources, both literary and personal, so they can bear a wide range of interpretation, in that each source brings with it new though related elements. I have tried to disentangle some of the threads by reference to other poems of Browning, written even long before and long after "Childe Roland", in which the same symbols, scenes, or even significant words recur, so that one passage can be read and interpreted in the light thrown by another.

The conclusion that I have reached, that "Childe Roland" is the poem of the monster, a poem of hate, of the thoughts Browning habitually fought and repressed, does not mean that it is to be regarded as a statement of what Browning really believed. It is one-sided. The quality of the best of Browning's poems lies in the constant struggle between what he professes and the dark monster inside. This struggle gives tension to his writing and adds to the ambiguity of much of his language. Our reading of his work is more rewarding if we are aware that behind the optimism and the accepted values Browning is holding in check a chaos of guilt and fear: fear of suffering, death, and judgment, fear of that most terrible of eternities, the Christian Hell as interpreted by the non-conformists. I have identified the dragon of his waste land with the wet snake of Andromeda, and we should do well to remember that the snake, for Browning, as for the Bible, was the Devil.

VII

Upon "Caliban Upon Setebos"

Wilde, when he declared that what fascinated Browning was not thought itself but rather the processes by which thought moves,[1] gave us a key to Browning's work which has since been too much neglected. The ultimate dissatisfaction one feels with so many of the critical books on Browning lies, I believe, in just this—that they are occupied too exclusively with Browning's thought, even with Browning's philosophy, while this early pointer of Wilde's has been too little followed. That Browning was a fine psychologist has always been noted in relation to the dramatic monologues, and to *The Ring and the Book*, but the extent to which he was discovering and applying psychoanalytical processes still remains to be investigated.[2] F. R. G. Duckworth, who set out to examine Browning thoroughly, came to the conclusion that "Browning, in spite of all appearances, does not as a rule probe deep", and adds "nor has he much to say of the part played by the unconscious in the working of the mind", although "a trace may be found, here and there".[3] This reasoned conclusion to a book which shows considerable understanding of both Browning's background and his poetry is hard indeed to understand, especially because Duckworth knew and quoted Swinburne's opinion that Browning had "an unique and incomparable genius for analysis". This much, indeed, Duckworth accepts, and even goes on to criticise Browning for the use he made of this gift:

[1] Oscar Wilde, "The Critic as an Artist", in *Selected Works*, ed. R. Aldington, London 1947, p. 69.

[2] Stewart W. Holmes, "Browning: Semantic Stutterer", in *PMLA*, LX (1945), pp. 231-55, attempts this approach to Browning. His examination of the inchoate constructions in the early poems is interesting, but his thesis that Browning cured himself is hardly tenable in view of later poems such as *Fifine*.

[3] F. R. G. Duckworth, *Browning: Background and Conflict*, London 1931, p. 124.

but he represents his characters as analysing themselves and expressing the results of their analysis with an insight and a delicacy and a thoroughness of which they were incapable.[4]

Browning's "Caliban upon Setebos; or, Natural Theology in the Island", written between 1859 and 1864, seems to lie open to this last criticism as no other poem, for the speaker of the monologue is a primitive man. This Caliban is the vehicle through which the complex and conflicting ideas of the thought of Browning's own time are filtered to us. C. R. Tracy has shown that the poem contains "an expression of Browning's own opinion on certain religious questions of considerable importance"[5] and that it reflects closely the ideas of the Unitarian, Theodore Parker: yet Caliban, as Paul de Reul wrote, "parle de lui-même à la troisième personne, comme un vrai sauvage".[6]

This "savage", none the less, comes to us already laden with a chain of literary associations; it is the Caliban of *The Tempest*,[7] the educated savage whose teacher was the mage Prospero himself. Prospero comments that his pains have all been lost, quite lost, and this, on a moral level, is true. Browning nevertheless has solved one of the major problems which his choice of subject raised: he has selected a primitive creature with a Shakespearian gift for expression and use of language. There is therefore no difficulty in communicating his thought in rich, even poetical words. It is when we consider the nature of his thought that we stand amazed at Browning's vision into the working of man's mind.

Two facts must be clearly remembered before we can fully

[4] F. R. G. Duckworth, *op. cit.*, p. 52.

[5] C. R. Tracy, " 'Caliban upon Setebos' ", in *Studies in Philology*, xxxv (1938), pp. 487-99.

[6] Paul de Reul, *L'Art et la pensée de Robert Browning*, Brussels 1929, p. 165. I find this simpler explanation more convincing than that given by E. K. Brown in "The First Person in 'Caliban upon Setebos' ", in *M.L.N.* (1951), pp. 392-5, which sets out to prove that "the shifts to the first person and back to the third enrich the characterization and heighten the drama." It would be interesting in this connexion to compare Caliban's monument of chalk and turf (ll. 192-9) with the Druid monument in *Fifine at the Fair*.

[7] See John Howard, "Caliban's Mind", in *Victorian Poetry*, i (1963), pp. 249-57, for a study of the characteristics of Caliban which Browning may have found in *The Tempest*.

appreciate this. "Caliban upon Setebos" was written when the publication of Darwin's *Origin of Species* was already giving rise to wide discussion, and some forty years before Freud's psycho-analytical work began. Stewart W. Holmes declares (italics mine) that Browning

> *never understood the theories behind Darwin's evolutionary hypothesis, apparently,* he was more interested in looking backward to certain people of importance in their day—who could not argue with him and who used terms in that good, old, easy, intentional, generalized way. He contorted [could this be a curious misprint for consorted?] with phantoms, human and linguistic.[8]

I wish to show in the following pages that "Caliban upon Setebos" was at least an inquiry into these theories of Darwin's, an attempt on Browning's part to understand and apply them, and that the short clear statement attributed to Huxley is the right interpretation of the poem: that Browning's aim was to present "a truly scientific representation of the development of religious ideas in primitive man".[9]

For Caliban is a primitive man—he has been defined as the "missing link"—who asks himself about the nature of God (Setebos). The poem is an examination of the thought-processes of this creature: Browning was using the poem to bring Darwin's theory of evolution to the test. The scientific evidence he accepts, the newt is there "turned to stone, shut up inside a stone" as part of the geological-historical evidence on which Darwin's theory is so largely based. But how, Browning asks himself, could thought grow and develop in evolved creatures? The question which the poem is debating is not, as has often been argued, as to whether Darwin's theory denies the existence of God. Browning asks instead: how did God evolve? And he answers the question by showing the thought processes by which a concept of God could, or would, come into being.

This does not mean that Browning accepts Darwin's

[8] S. W. Holmes, "Browning: Semantic Stutterer", p. 251.
[9] Quoted by Arthur W. Symons, *An Introduction to the Study of Browning*, p. 125.

theory, any more than he accepts Caliban's God:[10] as so often elsewhere, he begs the question by vague references to an over-God, called "the Quiet", which clearly covers a highly evolved concept, far beyond the Jehovah of the Old Testament and beyond any literal interpretation of the Trinity of the New, a name suggestive of philosophical meditation and a non-anthropomorphic deity, in no way concerned with the running of human affairs.

The starting-point of the poem is a text taken from Psalm L. 21: "Thou thoughtest that I was altogether such a one as thyself". This is the key Browning himself gives, and we should do well to read the Psalm. The stress throughout Psalm L is on the power of God. It opens with the words "the mighty God" and continues, in the second verse:

> Our God shall come, and shall not keep silence:[11]

> a fire shall devour before him,
> and it shall be very tempestuous round about him.

The God of the Old Testament, the Jehovah, who was, after all, the God of a fairly primitive people whose existence was largely tribal, is equated with Setebos coming in vengeance and tempest at the end of the poem. The last lines of the poem include two other references to a clearly Old Testament god— "His raven that has told Him all!", from the story of Elijah and the raven,[12] and the pillar of dust (in the Old Testament the pillar of cloud or fire meant God—here it is a pillar of dust, implying death).

More is taken from the psalm, as Browning meant his readers to realise when he affixed the motto, deliberately putting into our hands a key since grown rusty. Caliban thinks to appease Setebos with burnt offerings:

> Or of my three kid yearlings burn the best.[13]

---

[10] In a late poem, "Reverie", Browning definitely and characteristically refused to pronounce on the subject: "Do I seek how star, earth, beast, /Bird, worm, fly, gained their dower /For life's use, most and least? /Back from the search I cower".

[11] As such he is the opposite of "the Quiet".

[12] The raven is at the same time an attempt to find a Scriptural equivalent for Ariel, for in Shakespeare's *Tempest* it is Prospero and not Setebos who is the "god" with the supernatural powers of punishment.

[13] "Caliban upon Setebos", 272.

But in Psalm L. 8 God refuses burnt offerings:

> I will not reprove thee for thy sacrifices
>   or thy burnt offerings, to have been continually
>   before me.
> I will take no bullock out of thy house,
>   nor he goats out of thy fold.

The Old Testament God, that is to say, had evolved from the more primitive carnivorous God who accepted Abel's burnt offerings of flesh and refused Cain's garden produce at the very beginning of the story of creation. What the God at the time of King David requires in the place of burnt offerings (as Psalm L tells us) is "thanksgiving and vows"; he wants man to "call upon me in the day of trouble: I will deliver thee and thou shalt glorify me". That Browning remembered this is shown by his echo of it in Caliban's creation of a clay creature:

> I might hear his cry,
> And give the mankin three sound legs for one,
> Or pluck the other off, leave him like an egg,
> And lessoned he was mine and merely clay.[14]

The simile "like an egg" came to mind because it embodied the theory of Darwin as opposed to the theory of creation, for which the potter and the "clay" is a favourite Old Testament image. Even the concept of a god who breaks legs as well as making them is reflected from the psalm immediately following:

> Make me to hear joy and gladness,
>   that the bones that thou hast broken may rejoice.[15]

The God evolved in the mind of Caliban, that is to say, is not such an improbable being—he is the counterpart of the God evolved by the Jews at a certain stage of their development as a race—the God later adopted and adapted by the Christians. Browning is not afraid to face the inconsistencies in the figure of this creator-god which have puzzled so many orthodox Christians and Bible-readers, and he is attempting, in the light of Darwin's theory, to explain them.

Caliban, the primitive man, continues to see his god as

[14] *Op. cit.*, 91-4.   [15] Psalm LI. 8.

primitive, and to try to appease him with offerings and sacrifices. Threatened by the vengeance of Setebos at the end of the poem, he grovels—

> 'Lieth flat and loveth Setebos![16]

and makes the unwanted sacrifices—

> Will let those quails fly, will not eat this month
> One little mess of whelks, so he may 'scape![17]

The whole concept of sacrifice, so basic in primitive religions, is here raised—and we must remember that Browning was writing not only long before Freud, but long before Frazer's *Golden Bough*.[18] He had, that is, to solve the problems they were later to raise by doing his own field-work. If he argued at times too freely from analogy, yet he brought a retentive memory and a fine power of observation to bear. A further quality he shared with the scientists was his ability to look contrary evidence in the face and to attempt to explain it within his theory. As his theories were at times untenable, this led him to perform dialectic somersaults, often so spectacular as to draw all attention away from the serious groundwork he was doing.

Biblical quotation, as always in Browning's work, is used with a sense of the implications of the context. The psalm from which the motto is taken offers an interpretation of the poem as a whole which links up with its literary source in *The Tempest* and with Browning's own dilemma as a poet. The closing words of Psalm L are: "To him that ordereth his conversation aright will I show the salvation of God". The point of Browning's poem, both at the beginning and the end, is that it is Caliban's *speech*, rather than his actions, which vexes Setebos. At the beginning Caliban goes into hiding, in his grotto, for the express purpose of saying what he thinks:

[16] "Caliban upon Setebos", 292.

[17] *Op. cit.*, 294-5.

[18] This point has been noted by Leonard Burrows, in *Browning: An Introductory Essay, cit.*, p. 58: "Remembering that Browning wrote without the benefit of anthropology, one may find (as I do) that *Caliban* is persuasively plausible as a re-creation of a limited, earth-bound, egocentric anthropomorphism".

> And talks to his own self, howe'er he please,
> Touching that other, whom his dam called God.
> Because to talk about Him, vexes—ha,
> Could He but know! . . .

> Letting the rank tongue blossom into speech.[19]

This last line recalls Shakespeare's "You taught me language, and my profit on't/Is, I know how to curse". At the end of the poem Browning's Caliban returns to the theme of forbidden speech:

> If He caught me here,
> O'erheard this speech,

> It was fool's play, this prattling! . . .

> Fool to gibe at Him![20]

Caliban ends, crouching flat before the storm which bears the anger of his god, and the line

> 'Maketh his teeth meet through his upper lip[21]

shows how determined he is to hold his mouth firmly shut, to speak no more.

So the *sin* of Caliban against Setebos, as Browning sees it (and he finds support for this interpretation both in *The Tempest* and in Psalm L) lies in his speech. To this extent Browning is dealing with a personal problem. As a writer he was concerned with speech, and he must often have asked himself whether he was not offending God by some of the ideas he expressed. In Caliban's case the offence is followed by swift punishment, showing that what Browning unconsciously feared was divine wrath and the punishment of Hell.[22] As a child he had been taught to believe in this, and what his conscious reasoning could and did refute, his whole mind always dreaded. The

---

[19] "Caliban upon Setebos", 15-18, 23.

[20] *Op. cit.*, 269-70, 287, 291.

[21] *Op. cit.*, 293.

[22] C. R. Tracy, " 'Caliban upon Setebos' ", *cit.*, p. 494, writes: "His scorn of Calvinism remains, and also his rejection of the doctrine of eternal punishment". This refutation was conscious, but traces of the effect of this early teaching on his unconscious mind are frequent in his poems, especially "The Heretic's Tragedy" and *The Ring and the Book*.

introduction of Caliban's "dam" is significant here, for the teaching of this primitive creature has come from his mother

> Touching that other, whom his dam called God

and

> His dam held that the Quiet made all things
> Which Setebos vexed only. [Caliban] 'holds not so.[23]

In creating Caliban Browning had to search back into his own early or primitive experience, and what he found there was his own mother's early teaching, and his own first questioning of it, in the " 'holds not so!". What is striking is that in both the above quotations the child's god is shown as a creature who must not be "vexed" (the very word is childish), showing how closely the idea of punishment was connected with the simplest concept of a god. Later study has shown the general application of this, but it is remarkable to find Browning examining thought-processes so accurately as to observe and record the same phenomenon, realising its significance. Like Caliban he felt at the same time that such thoughts were dangerous, and could only be uttered in safety hidden away in a cave, and that even there God's raven might be eavesdropping. This poet's fear of offending God by his speech is, I think, the simplest reading of "Caliban upon Setebos", to which the opening quotation from the Psalms gives a clue.

The words of the quotation, of which so far we have only examined the background, "Thou thoughtest that I was altogether such a one as thyself", raise the question of the nature of God. Darwin's newly discovered theories had opened up a whole new interpretation of creation, it had become possible to conceive of God as imaginary, made by man in his own image. C. R. Tracy has shown how probable it is that Browning should have derived this idea from Theodore Parker, quoting Parker's own words:

> This is anthropomorphism. It is well in its place. Some rude men seem to require it. They must paint to themselves a deity with a form—the ancient of days; a venerable monarch seated on a throne, surrounded by troops of followers. But it must be

---

[23] "Caliban upon Setebos", 16, 170-1.

remembered all this is poetry; this personal and anthropo-
morphic conception is a phantom of the brain that has no
existence independent of ourselves.[24]

And again Tracy points out another passage from Parker which
may well have struck Browning and gone into Caliban's
conception of Setebos:

> A man rude in spirit must have a rude conception of God. He
> thinks the deity like himself. If a buffalo had a religion, his
> conception of deity would probably be a buffalo, fairer limbed,
> stronger, and swifter than himself, grazing in the fairest
> meadows of heaven.[25]

At a certain stage of man's development (which Browning
equates with the period of history related in the early books of
the Old Testament, where Jehovah seemed unjustly to favour
certain of his creatures, or to torment others) God would be
Setebos. So Setebos favours Prosper—"who knows why?"—
and torments Caliban, which is probably a protest of the poet's.
Throughout the poem Prosper and Miranda are asleep. Again
there may be sociological comment—they, the masters, sleep
while others work for them. But they have little importance
for the beast-man, whose relations are directly with Setebos.
True, Caliban imitates them, blinds a sea-creature to be his
Caliban, dresses up in the skin of a wild animal to resemble
Prosper, etc., but nothing much comes of it. His real personal
concern is with his God.

The body of the poem is concerned with Caliban's fantasy
of himself as a god, as the Lord of Creation, and the analogies
he draws between his own casual behaviour in awarding
rewards and punishments, and that of Setebos. How would
such a creature reason, how would he interpret the actions of
his god? This is the question before Browning, and his answers
are sometimes startling. It should be remembered that
Darwin's theory was based on the physical life cycle: creation
through procreation. The poem is chock-full of sexual symbolism, much of which Browning uses elsewhere, but much

[24] Theodore Parker, *A Discourse of Matters pertaining to Religion*, Boston 1907,
pp. 146-7, quoted by C. R. Tracy, " 'Caliban upon Setebos' ", p. 496.
[25] T. Parker, *op. cit.*, pp. 120-1, quoted by C. R. Tracy, " 'Caliban upon
Setebos' ", p. 497.

also new. The fullest possible use is made of plants and animals —images which would come naturally to Caliban, but at the same time which are relevant also to Darwin. And reading the symbolism we find that the reason given for Setebos' creation of both men and animals is simply so that they can supply the faculty of reproduction which the god does not possess.

Caliban argues by analogy. He wishes that he had been born a bird:

> Put case, unable to be what I wish,
> I yet could make a live bird out of clay:
> Would not I take clay, pinch my Caliban
> Able to fly?—for, there, see, he hath wings,[26]

therefore, if he creates a clay Caliban, he will fashion it with wings. Leaving aside the Freudian symbolism of wings in this context, I suggest we follow Caliban's own argument:

> He, [Setebos] could not, Himself, make a second self
> To be His mate . . .
> But did, in envy, listlessness or sport,
> Make what Himself would fain, in a manner, be—
> Weaker in most points, stronger in a few. . . .[27]

Having so created them, Setebos envies and plagues them:

> And envieth that, so helped, such things do more
> Than He who made them.[28]

The power given by Setebos to his creatures, the power he envies them for, is just the power of procreation on which the theory of evolution depends. For Setebos lacks this "warmth"[29] —the power with which the Greeks and Romans so generously endowed their gods:

---

[26] "Caliban upon Setebos", 75-8.

[27] *Op. cit.*, 57-8, 61-3.

[28] *Op. cit.*, 113-14.

[29] In *The Ring and the Book*, VII, 792-3, "warmth" is used with a sexual connotation in lines spoken by the Archbishop commanding Pompilia to yield her virginity to Guido: "The earth requires that warmth reach everywhere:/What, must your patch of snow be saved forsooth?" The same connotation was current as early as Dryden's "Absalom and Achitophel", 7-9: "Then, Israel's Monarch, after Heaven's own heart,/His vigorous warmth did, variously impart/To Wives and Slaves . . .".

> it came of being ill at ease:
> He hated that He cannot change His cold,
> Nor cure its ache.[30]

To explain what this "ache" was, Caliban has recourse to a simile of a fresh-water fish attracted and repulsed by the warm sea-water, a simile which would have little meaning were it not for the strongly marked sexual symbolism it contains. The icy fish attempting to

> thaw herself within the lukewarm brine
> O' the lazy sea her stream thrusts far amid,
> A crystal spike 'twixt two warm walls of wave, . . .[31]

but who

> ever sickened, found repulse . . .

> Flounced back from bliss she was not born to breathe,[32]

reflects the despair of Setebos at his physical limitations. So, as Caliban makes his image with wings, Setebos endows *his* with the powers of reproduction:

> Weaker in most points, stronger in a few.

Over and over again the symbolism of the poem echoes this theme of sexual potency. In the second sentence we have "a flower drops with a bee inside";[33] Caliban makes himself drunk with a "gourd-fruit" to which he adds "honeycomb and pods" which "bite like finches when they bill and kiss", the "froth rises bladdery", and Caliban says he will

> throw me on my back i' the seeded thyme,
> And wanton.[34]

What Browning is openly describing in these lines is the effect of drink, but the words chosen ("bill and kiss", "bladdery",

---

[30] "Caliban upon Setebos", 31-3.

[31] *Op. cit.*, 35-7.

[32] *Op. cit.*, 38, 41.

[33] *Op. cit.*, 10. Browning often uses the same symbol of the flower and the bee with sexual overtones. The most obvious examples are in "Women and Roses" and "Popularity", but in "Porphyria's Lover" and *The Ring and the Book* the sexual implication of the symbol, although not openly stated, is none the less present, as I believe it to be in the above lines from "Caliban upon Setebos".

[34] "Caliban upon Setebos", 73-4.

"seeded", "wanton") indicate the further meaning of the passage. This meaning is more basic to the sense than Caliban's drunkenness, which is a literary echo from Shakespeare. The preoccupation with the process of reproduction is further hinted at in the introduction of the swimming creatures,

> Yon otter, sleek-wet, black, lithe as a leech,[35]

and the badger, and again by

> the pie with the long tongue
> That pricks deep into oakwarts for a worm. . . .[36]

The creatures themselves betray the underlying theme: they are poetic symbols, not scientific specimens, and are far from being engaged in overt sexual activities. The primly Victorian billing and kissing of the finches is indeed the nearest approach to anything of the kind.

The underlying concern with the processes of reproduction is offset by another series of images, all concerned with mutilation, in the castration symbolism Browning had used elsewhere,[37] and which emphasise the predicament of Setebos. The first victims are the grass-hoppers, for the Caliban bird is commanded to begin to live and to

> Fly to yon rock-top, nip me off the horns
> Of grigs high up that make the merry din. . . .[38]

The bird, however, soon falls a victim himself with

> His leg snapped, brittle clay,[39]

and his Caliban creator amuses himself either with removing the remaining leg or in giving him four. This may contain a passing reference to the evolutionary process with its development through sports and rejects. Soon after, we have the line of crabs, and the one with purple spots gets "one pincer twisted off". After this we have the odd image of the broken pipe, which is used later in *Fifine* to suggest impotence. This pipe is a

[35] *Op. cit.*, 46.   [36] *Op. cit.*, 50-1.
[37] See his letters to Elizabeth, some of *The Ring and the Book*, *Fifine at the Fair*, and above all, *Red Cotton Night-Cap Country*.
[38] "Caliban upon Setebos", 82-3.
[39] *Op. cit.*, 85.

L

thing "created" by Caliban as a bird-whistle, but should the
pipe declare

> I make the cry my maker cannot make
> With his great round mouth; he must blow through
>   mine![40]

then, Caliban declares

> Would not I smash it with my foot? So He [Setebos].[41]

Once again the god is seen as jealous of his creature's powers of
reproduction, and the punishment implied by the imagery is
castration.   These mutilations, occurring to the various
creatures in the poem, are nevertheless symbolic of the central
situation of the god who creates but does not procreate.   The
worst vengeance, the final impotence, awaits Darwin's newt,
a creature Setebos

> may have envied once
> And turned to stone, shut up inside a stone.[42]

The newt is a central symbol here and its presence has an
interesting history.   For even before being Darwin's, the newt
was Browning's own.   In a letter written to Elizabeth on
5 January 1846, a letter she describes as "all alive as it is with
crawling buzzing wriggling cold-blooded warm-blooded creatures", he writes of Horne's question to him "for what do you
know about newts?"   Browning, as he proceeds to show, has
spent a long time in observation of newts or water-efts:

> What a fine fellow our English water-eft is; "Triton paludis
> Linnaei"—*e come guizza* (*that* you can't say in any other
> language; cannot preserve the little in-and-out motion along
> with the straightforwardness!)—I always loved all those wild
> creatures God "*sets up for themselves*" so independently of us, so
> successfully. . . .[43]

But what is more interesting is the way in which he relates the
creature to Elizabeth herself, and the suppressed eroticism of
his final invocation.   His injunction to her to "*walk*, move,

---

[40] *Op. cit.*, 124-5.   [41] *Op. cit.*, 126.   [42] *Op. cit.*, 214-15.
[43] Robert to Elizabeth, postmarked 5 Jan. 1846, in *The Letters of Robert Browning
and Elizabeth Barrett Barrett, 1845-1846.*

guizza, anima mia dolce" shows the stress of these months when he was trying to convince her to find the strength to escape with him, and using every means in his power:

> "I may change"—too true; yet, you see, as an eft was to me at the beginning so it continues—I *may* take up stones and pelt the next I see—but—do you much fear that?—Now, *walk*, move, *guizza, anima mia dolce.* Shall I not know one day how far your mouth will be from mine as we walk?[44]

That the newt so full of life here is the same newt we find imprisoned in the fossil is shown by the repetition in the poem of the argument of the letter, the idea that he may take up stones and pelt the next he sees. Caliban, speaking of the crabs, says he will

> Let twenty pass, and stone the twenty-first,
> Loving not, hating not, just choosing so.[45]

Browning, that is to say, when he was writing "Caliban upon Setebos" recalled the letter written to Elizabeth some four to eight years earlier, or perhaps rather than the letter itself he recalled the mood and suppressed emotions which lay behind. A personal emotional state, which had left a deep mark on him, has entered, utterly transmuted, into the material of the poem. This assertion finds further support from another passage in the same letter, which contains mutilation imagery of exactly the same sort we find in the poem:

> But never try and catch a speckled gray lizard when we are in Italy, love, and you see his tail hang out of the chink of a wall, his winter-house—because the strange tail will snap off, drop from him and stay in your fingers—and though you afterwards learn that there is more desperation in it and glorious determination to be free, than positive pain (so people say who have no tails to be twisted off)—and though, moreover, the tail grows again after a sort—*yet* . . . don't do it, for it will give you a thrill![46]

Browning was writing here with a frankness few lovers would risk today. The "thrill" he speaks of can only be related to a

[44] *Ibid.*   [45] "Caliban upon Setebos", 103-4.
[46] Robert to Elizabeth, postmarked 5 Jan. 1846, in *The Letters of Robert Browning and Elizabeth Barrett Barrett 1845-1846.*

situation which he outlines in an earlier letter of 18 September 1845:

> ... for at, and after the writing of *that first letter*, on my first visit, I believed—through some silly or misapprehended talk, collected at second hand too—that your complaint was of quite another nature—a spinal injury irremediable in the nature of it. Had it been *so*—now speak for *me*, for what you hope I am, and say how *that* should affect or neutralize what you *were*, what I wished to associate with myself in you?[47]

The extraordinary situation of a man who for a time was uninformed as to the "nature" of the complaint of the woman he wished to marry, his ignorance confessedly extending to an uncertainty as to whether physical union would at any time be possible, explains his unusual preoccupation with mutilations and impotence, a preoccupation noticeable in many of his poems, but nowhere more than in "Caliban upon Setebos".

That this interpretation of the thought-processes of Caliban, who sees god as jealous of his creatures, and furnishes this odd explanation of the cause of his jealousy, is not fantastical, is further shown by the nonsense song in which Caliban from his hiding place dares to taunt the god:

> What I hate, be consecrate
> To celebrate Thee and Thy state, no mate
> For Thee; what see for envy in poor me?[48]

Like Antiochus' riddle in *Pericles*, the nonsense song is used by Caliban for the purpose of concealing-revealing the truth which cannot openly be uttered. It is the clue to the whole poem. For in it Caliban dares, from his hiding place, to mock at Setebos. He consecrates to him only what he hates, and mocks him for being without a mate, for being forced to envy his own creature, even such a creature as Caliban knows himself to be.

Yet the god hears him; or rather hears through his messenger the raven, and the punishment begins, with the storm and the moving pillar of dust. And here we have a further echo from the Old Testament. The last lines of the poem, where Caliban offers a sacrifice of appeasement

[47] Robert to Elizabeth, 18 Sep. 1845, *op. cit.*
[48] "Caliban upon Setebos", 276-8.

> Will let those quails fly, will not eat this month
> One little mess of whelks, so he may 'scape![49]

echoes Numbers XI. 29-35, which is a description of God's punishment on the Israelites because they lusted after flesh. The wrath of the Lord was kindled, and

> there went forth a wind from the Lord and brought quails from the sea and let them fall by the camp.

The surfeit of quails is too much for the Israelites, weary of their diet of manna, and "there they buried the people that lusted . . .".

Caliban, seeing the approaching storm, first rebukes himself

> Fool to gibe at Him[50]

(so the song *was* intended in mockery), then tries the old line of appeasement

> Lo! 'Lieth flat and loveth Setebos![51]

This failing in effect, he makes what amounts to a vow of abstinence, hoping thereby to appease the "envious" god. The flesh after which the Israelites lusted had for Browning, I believe, a further meaning more in keeping with the New Testament teaching of St Paul:

> This I say then, Walk in Spirit, and ye shall not fulfil the lust of the flesh[52]

which links, in turn, back to the underlying concept of the poem, the physical pleasure in reproduction, arousing the jealousy of a god deprived of the capacity enjoyed by his creatures. A daring thought, but Browning's mind was often daring.

Darwin's theory of evolution seemed to undermine the whole of Christianity or of any other theology. What need for a creator god if man was self-created or evolved? For this reason many theologians simply refused to consider Darwin's evidence, and it was only later that some Churches came to terms with evolution as the "method" of creation employed by

---

[49] *Op. cit.*, 294-5.
[51] *Op. cit.*, 292.
[50] *Op. cit.*, 291.
[52] Galatians, v. 16.

God, or more often settled down in an uneasy truce until the scientists should find all the missing links. To many thinking people Darwin's discovery seemed to strike right at the heart of accepted beliefs, and Browning, who was always interested in ideas, and who had already written "An Epistle containing the Strange Medical Experiences of Karshish", inevitably turned them over in his mind. Postulating, in order to work out Darwin's theory in full, the idea of a god *evolved* in the mind of man, Browning has to explain the relationship between "creator" and "creature". Taking the fairly primitive concept of god as exemplified in the Jehovah of the early books of the Old Testament, he struggles to find a convincing psychological explanation of why a primitive man should conceive of a creator and how he would motivate the creator's interest in him. The solution he finds, that of an impotent god deriving a somewhat vicarious satisfaction by creating creatures capable of physical reproduction, and then provoked to petty acts of spite and vengeance through jealousy, is a subtle attempt to penetrate primitive thought-processes, documented as best he might with the material that lay closest at hand, the early history of the Jews as recounted in the Old Testament, and his own childish reasoning. His exposition is not scientific, but poetic; nevertheless it is a poem in which he was attempting to work in full conscious control of his material and to allow his character to express himself through psychologically convincing images[53]—the gift Shakespeare possessed so supremely, in which Browning from time to time reached up to touch him.

"Caliban upon Setebos" is neither an acceptance nor a refutation of Darwin's theory of evolution: it is an experiment in the application and development of new ideas. "Thou thoughtest I was altogether such a one as thyself" is a clear statement of this approach to the subject, and Browning's own theological beliefs are quite outside this discussion, fluctuating between his early training, which left the idea of Heaven and Hell indelibly printed on his mind, and the more philosophical, more evolved concept of "the Quiet". What remains most

---

[53] An even better example of this psychological realism is the use of torture imagery by the condemned Guido in *The Ring and the Book*.

striking in this poem is, not so much the rather doubtful conclusion reached concerning the hypothetical reasoning of primitive man, but rather the modernity of Browning's approach: that almost immediately after the publication of *The Origin of Species* he grasped that it opened the way to great discoveries in the field of psychoanalysis and that such study should go hand in hand with anthropological research. His investigation in 1864 of natural theology in the island was pioneer work in research which only the twentieth century was to see developed. That it is also poetry is greatly to his credit. However complex and even confused the ideas discussed, even a cursory reading leaves us with the newt

> turned to stone, shut up inside a stone[54]

—a symbol as beautiful and significant in its way as was Keats's Grecian urn, and no less durable.

[54] "Caliban upon Setebos", 215.

VIII

Browning's Don Juan

A VICTORIAN poem on Don Juan seems almost a contradiction in terms—Don Juan for the English reader must always remain Byron's magnificent romantic hero, the cynical amoralist, the anarchist, the satirist who demolishes accepted standards of behaviour, law, and religion. Yet it was just such a contradiction which could offer a challenge to Browning, a challenge which, in the years 1871-2, when *Fifine at the Fair* was written, he found peculiarly acceptable. For this was right in the middle of his casuistic period, after the composition of *The Ring and the Book*, years in which he was even more argumentative than usual, a period in reference to which the word "puzzling" appears ever more frequently in the comments of his critics and exegetists. *Fifine* is prefaced by a long quotation from Molière's *Don Juan* opening with the words of Donna Elvira:

> Vous plaît-il, don Juan, nous éclaircir ces beaux mystères?

and it was with delight that Browning plunged into "this fine mysteriousness" and pulled out a poem which he himself defined, as Domett notes in his diary, as "the most metaphysical and boldest he had written since Sordello".[1]

The interest aroused by the poem has always been considerable, for it is a work in which Browning discusses, or rather rediscusses, a great many of his basic theories on art and life. Its interest is therefore to a large extent autobiographical, and here lies the central puzzle, already seen and expressed very clearly in 1885 by Mrs Orr: the difficulty of distinguishing

---

[1] W. Hall Griffin and H. Minchin, *The Life of Robert Browning*, p. 248.

"where Mr. Browning ends and where Don Juan begins".[2] The battle has raged, at times hotly, backwards and forwards. In 1895 Hugh Walker wrote:

> ... the argument of *Fifine at the Fair* is, not in a mere turn of phrase or casual expression of opinion, but vitally and almost everywhere Browning's own. The Don Juan of the piece is a mere shadow. ...[3]

The opposite argument is stated perhaps most clearly and fully by Hall Griffin and Minchin, in their *Life*, first published in 1910:

> To understand the poem it is necessary to remember, once more, Browning's fondness for putting a case, and his proneness to write "dramatically". If some reviewers and readers, as did happen, attributed to the poet the opinions upon love which he has put into the mouth of the Don Juan of *Fifine*, the mistake arose from their ignoring these methods of his. ... Yet the mistake was made; and this, too, though *Fifine* was introduced and closed by two short poems which breathe a passion of faithful remembrance, whose application, in the light of his own past history, cannot by any possibility be misconstrued.[4]

Griffin and Minchin overlook here the fact that it is just this deliberate introduction of an obviously personal prologue and epilogue which first awakens the reader's suspicion that Don Juan is not another "creation" comparable with Andrea del Sarto, Fra Lippo, or even Mr Sludge. The indignation of the apologists is aroused chiefly by the idea that Browning's respectability should in any way suffer from an even partial identification with his protagonist, that his moral reputation should be besmirched or that any shadow should be cast on his almost legendary marriage.

[2] Mrs Sutherland Orr, *A Handbook to the Works of Robert Browning*, London 1913, p. 150. Here I wish to add that the arguments against restricting the interpretation of *Fifine at the Fair* to this autobiographical reading are well expressed in Philip Drew's reply to my essay, "Another View of *Fifine at the Fair*, in *Essays in Criticism*, XVII (1967), pp. 244-5. In this paper he comes to the defence of the metaphysical parts of the poem, which I have ignored as "grey wastes of casuistry". It would nevertheless be a mistake to play down the sexual elements in a poem about Don Juan, a poem in which the imagery is more obviously sexual than anywhere else in Browning. The two readings are complementary.

[3] Hugh Walker, *The Greater Victorian Poets*, London 1895, p. 168.

[4] W. Hall Griffin and H. Minchin, *The Life of Robert Browning*, p. 248.

For Browning, in writing *Fifine at the Fair*, was setting out quite deliberately to be franker than usual. Byron's *Don Juan* even more than Molière's or Mozart's was in his mind, a dramatised self-portrait, larger than life, a romantic figure. The problem Browning set himself in his own poem was the creation of a Victorian Don Juan. How would Don Juan behave in the mid-nineteenth century? What would his temptations be? How would he react? What, too, would Elvire, his Victorian wife, be like? Instead of the romantic hero, Browning wanted to create a contemporary bourgeois hero.[5] By great intuition and intellectual honesty he nearly succeeds: Don Juan has nothing heroic about him, he has become mean, his twists and turns of argument are no nobler than those of Mr Sludge, his only greatness lies in his humanity, which, as one of Miss Compton Burnett's characters remarks of those who are "only human", is not much. Nor, till the very end of the poem, is there any infidelity: it is a repressed Don Juan trying to justify himself *first* to an accusing wife. It is a story of temptation, but not of temptation nobly resisted. The passages in praise of the nobler, spiritual love for the wife are at times degraded into mere flattery. Marriage is presented in some passages much as it was seen by Guido Franceschini in *The Ring and the Book*, as a trap, that aspect of the Victorian marriage which was so energetically expressed by Samuel Butler in *The Way of All Flesh*:

> —But a voice kept ringing in his ears which said: "You CAN'T, CAN'T, CAN'T".
> "CAN'T I?" screamed the unhappy creature to himself.
> "No," said the remorseless voice, "YOU CAN'T. YOU ARE A MARRIED MAN".[6]

Browning has deliberately placed Byron's foot-loose hero in an undignified position. With his wife leaning reproachfully on his arm he lusts after the "pert" circus girl, but if his feet are

---

[5] In his *The Hero in Eclipse in Victorian Fiction*, London 1956, Mario Praz has made a detailed study of the decline of the heroic in the novels of the Victorian period, and Browning's Don Juan seems to me to be a further example of the same phenomenon.

[6] Samuel Butler, *The Way of All Flesh*, Oxford 1944, p. 59.

chained, his mind is free to roam.[7] In the attempt to explain, justify and excuse his desires, he ranges far and wide over Browning's whole world of ideas.

DeVane[8] traces a literary source which a number of verbal echoes makes very convincing. Raymond,[9] while accepting DeVane's theory that Rossetti's "Jenny", and the whole controversy stirred up by Buchanan's attack on the Fleshly School of Poetry, were a probable influence, apart from the given starting-point of the actual recollection of a gypsy girl seen at the fair of St Gille in Pornic, finds that the origin of the poem lies in Browning's feeling of guilt for having been unfaithful to the memory of his dead wife, in that it is known that just in the year of the poem's composition he proposed marriage to, and was refused by, Lady Ashburton. This theory, too, which fits in with DeVane's, and is strongly supported by the sandwiching of the poem between a Prologue and Epilogue both concerned with Browning's feelings about his dead wife, seems to me wholly convincing.

I believe, however, that even more that was personal went into the poem, that *Fifine at the Fair* is one of the most truly autobiographical of the works of this most reticent of poets. In a letter to the Storys, complaining of the publication of one of his letters, Browning had written:

> There's nothing in my letter I care about except the indecent nature of the exposure—it's just as if, being at my toilette, some clownish person chose to throw the bedroom door wide.[10]

I would suggest that, in *Fifine*, Browning took less care than usual to close this door properly behind him. On the intellectual plane, where arguments are concerned, it is very difficult, as all critics have pointed out, to disentangle Robert Browning from Don Juan. But on the level of imagery, the Don Juan figure can no longer provide adequate cover for his

[7] The mood of rebellion is much the same as in Tennyson's outburst in *Locksley Hall*: "There the passions cramp'd no longer shall have scope and breathing space /I will take some savage woman, she shall rear my dusky race".

[8] W. Clyde DeVane, "The Harlot and the Thoughtful Young Man: A Study of the Relation between Rossetti's *Jenny* and Browning's *Fifine at the Fair*", in *Studies in Philology*, xxix (1932), pp. 463-84.

[9] William O. Raymond, *The Infinite Moment*, Toronto 1950, pp. 105-28.

[10] Quoted by Betty Miller, in *Robert Browning*, p. 108.

creator, especially as the same themes run through from the clearly autobiographical Prologue into the poem proper. And the symbolism underlying much of the imagery is clearly sexual. A sensitive early critic, Stopford A. Brooke, felt something odd at times in the nature descriptions of this poem, though he failed to discover why. Of a description of a sunset he writes:

> Nevertheless, in *Fifine at the Fair* there are several intercalated illustrations from Nature, all of which are interesting and some beautiful. . . . There is also that magnificent description of a sunset which I have already quoted. It is drawn to illustrate some remote point in the argument, and is far too magnificent for the thing it illustrates.[11]

There is something here which did not meet the eye in 1902, but which in 1968 seems almost too obvious.

An examination of this symbolism entails a detailed reading of at least parts of the poem. For an understanding of the whole structure of the poem, and for an excellent prose rendering, J. T. Nettleship's essay, published in 1890,[12] remains fundamental, as does much of his interpretation. On the intellectual level he is invaluable as a guide, but poetry operates also on the emotional level, and communicates even more subtly than through the subtlest of arguments, and this is the level which I propose to investigate.

The poem opens with a lyrical Prologue in which the poet swims out alone in the sea. Over his head flies a butterfly. He toys with the fancy that it is his dead wife:

> What if a certain soul
> Which early slipped its sheath,
> And has for its home the whole
> Of heaven, thus look beneath,
>
> Thus watch one who, in the world,
> Both lives and likes life's way,
> Nor wishes the wings unfurled
> That sleep in the worm, they say?[13]

---

[11] Stopford A. Brooke, *The Poetry of Robert Browning*, London 1902, p. 107.
[12] J. T. Nettleship, *Robert Browning: Essays and Thoughts*, London 1895, pp. 221-67.
[13] "*Fifine at the Fair*", Prologue, sts. ix-x.

His wife is in another, spirit world, unable to touch his. Nor does the poet even desire to unfold his wings, he prefers to remain a grub or worm. It is essential for the full under-standing of this Prologue, and indeed for the poem as a whole, to remember that the sea is one of the basic symbols for the unconscious, so that what Browning is really stating at the outset is that he has immersed himself in this element.[14] Raymond, reading the same lines, interprets them as showing Browning's sense of guilt in that he lives in the world and "likes life's way"—that is to say that he does not long to die and be reunited with the spirit of his dead wife, but is happy to go on living in this world.[15] This, I think, is true. What I wish to stress is the multisignificance of the passage, the plurality of levels of meaning, the verbal pregnancy which makes it poetry. Browning himself gives the lines an "intel-lectual" interpretation, reading the sea as art, or poetry; thereby equating poetic inspiration with the unconscious:

> Emancipate through passion
>   And thought, with sea for sky,
> We substitute, in a fashion,
>   For heaven—poetry:
>
> Which sea, to all intent,
>   Gives flesh such noon-disport. . . .[16]

Again at the end of this long and formless poem, after much wandering through grey wastes of casuistry, long inconclusive divagations into metaphysical questions, a strangely unbeautiful yet haunting Venetian dream-sequence, and passages of ex-traordinarily naïve self-revelation, some light breaks through, and Browning cries out indignantly:

> . . . All these word-bubbles came
> O' the sea, and bite like salt. The unlucky bath's to
>   blame.[17]

---

[14] In physical terms, the unconscious is represented by the waters of the womb, and the poet, in referring to himself as a grub or a worm, is associating himself with the foetus. This implies a Christian concept of death as a second birth, for which the poet feels himself unready, which links up with Raymond's reading.

[15] It was this aspect of Browning which interested James in his tale "The Private Life".

[16] *Fifine*, Prologue, sts. xiv-xv.   [17] *Op. cit.*, cxxxi (2315-16).

The poet is giving expression to a whole flood of emotions which the swim, real or imaginary, has let loose. The breadth of his psychological insight, shown by his creation of a wide variety of credible characters, has often been praised, but the above lines show that he was also capable of a depth of intuition in self-analysis coupled with a saving humour, as expressed in the half-rueful "unlucky". His equation of the sea (the unconscious) with poetic inspiration is especially revealing in an intellectual poet, in one of his most casuistic poems. Behind and underlying all the argument, all the reasoning, we have the force which makes it (for passages at least) into poetry; something beyond ratiocination, something in which ambiguities have full play. What I wish to suggest is not that all poetry is necessarily written in this way, but that some at least of Browning's poetry is, and that here he reveals his method most openly and comes closest to an awareness of it himself, although he fails to draw all the conclusions.

To appreciate his method fully, we must look extremely closely at the text. The sea theme is treated at length, not only in the Prologue, which gives the key to the whole poem, but also in stanzas lxiv-lxix (swimming) and lxxxi-lxxxix (sailing), as well as in the Venetian setting for the day-dream sequence; but we shall come to that in time.

The poem proper opens with a description of the entry of a circus troupe into the French village of Pornic, and this description includes the striking line, very much out of context,

'T was not for every Gawain to gaze upon the Grail![18]

—apparently choosing this odd way of saying that it was difficult to catch a glimpse of the performers before the show began. It has been suggested to me that Browning had the Gawain of Tennyson's *Holy Grail* in mind, the knight who failed to see the Grail, and who described his failure in the following words:

> For I was much awearied of the Quest:
> But found a silk pavilion in a field
> With merry maidens in it. . . .[19]

---

[18] *Op. cit.,* iv (28).
[19] *The Poetical Works of Alfred Lord Tennyson,* London (Macmillan) 1907, p. 430.

The *Holy Grail* volume was published only three years before *Fifine*, so Browning may well have had Tennyson's poem in mind during the composition of his own, the "silk pavilion in a field" linking up with the "airy structure" of the circus tent, and the "merry maidens" with the "baladines" of the troupe. More important is the Grail itself, which brings the reader sharply to a pause, for it signals the annunciation of the chastity theme, the key theme of the poem. Browning's Don Juan protagonist, like Tennyson's Gawain, sins against chastity, and may at the same time reflect Browning's preoccupation with his own "sin" against the memory of Elizabeth in his proposal of marriage to Lady Ashburton, though I see this proposal as indicative of a wider state of sexual restlessness, and not, with Raymond, as the cause of this restlessness. Besides symbolising chastity, the Grail had Christian implications, linking it up with the communion cup. Lastly, the Grail is a recognised female sexual symbol (as opposed to Gawain's lance) and is the equivalent of the flower chalice of which Browning was so fond. While Browning would be aware of the literary borrowing from Tennyson, and of the religious significance of the Grail, he may well have been unaware of this last association, but the fact that it was present in his mind is shown by its re-emergence only six lines later, where Fifine is described in the following words:

> . . . so shyly-sheathed, began
> To broaden out the bud which, bursting unaware,
> Now takes away our breath, queen-tulip of the Fair![20]

The same male-female sexual symbolism continues even in the background, with the male *tower* of the village, and the female *dome* of the circus tent:

> . . . 'neath the tower, 'twixt tree and tree appeared
> An airy structure; how the pennon from its dome,
> Frenetic to be free, makes one red stretch for home![21]

Below lies the sea, the dominant background feature of the whole poem:

> . . . ocean-idleness, sky-blue and millpond-smooth. . . . [22]

---

[20] *Fifine*, iv (32-4).   [21] *Op. cit.*, v (36-8).   [22] *Op. cit.*, v (42).

These are the backcloth against which the action takes place, the dominant symbols which might have been placed there by a modern stage-designer.

The return of the same symbols later in the poem is extremely interesting. They reappear when the poet settles down after his bathe to dream at an open window, and where he returns, in pensive mood, to his cigar:

> I smoked. The webs o' the weed,
> With many a break i' the mesh, were floating to re-form
> Cupola-wise above. . . .[23]

Recollecting his previous emotion in tranquillity, he arrives, much closer than many of his critics have done, at its source. He sits watching

> One loose long creeper-branch, tremblingly sensitive
> To risks which blooms and leaves,—each leaf tongue-
>   broad, each bloom
> Mid-finger-deep,—must run by prying in the room
> Of one who loves and grasps and spoils and speculates.[24]

The sensitive plant seems to be the poet's own mind, feeling the way back, back to the moment of generation, to what he himself calls, four lines later,

> . . . fancies manifold
> From this four-cornered world, the memories new and
>   old,
> The antenatal prime experience—what know I?—
> The initiatory love preparing us to die—[25]

The "what know I?" is a disarming attempt to disown the truth that he has dared to grasp, and a few lines later he attempts to escape from it again by a conscious evasion through music. His mind

> resolved to shift
> Its burthen to the back of some musician dead

---

[23] *Op. cit.*, lxxxix (1540-2).
[24] *Op. cit.*, lxxxix (1552-5).
[25] *Op. cit.*, lxxxix (1559-62).

And gone, who feeling once what I feel now, instead
Of words, sought sounds, and saved for ever, in the
    same,
Truth that escapes prose,—nay, puts poetry to shame.[26]

Undoubtedly this instinct was wise; sounds were safer as an
outlet for emotion than words. But the music brings us back to

a tent whence the red pennon made
Its vivid reach for home and ocean-idleness—[27]

Browning's own conscious interpretation of the flag was the call
to lawlessness:

And, do you know, there beats
Something within my breast, as sensitive?—repeats
The fever of the flag? My heart makes just the same
Passionate stretch, fires up for lawlessness . . .[28]

by which he means the lawlessness of the gypsies, the freedom
of the roads. Nevertheless the symbolism of these lines lies open
to a more strictly sexual interpretation, implying another sort of
freedom.

Raymond sees Fifine as exemplifying the world, and the
temptations of the world, which came between Browning and
the memory of Elizabeth, who had been dead ten years at the
time this poem was written. He writes:

In moments of spiritual depression, the world must have
presented itself to him in the guise of a beguiling but treacherous
gipsy, "an enemy sly and serpentine", dazzling his eyes with
tinselled show, and seeking to wean him from the cherished
past.[29]

Yet the basic sexual imagery of the poem seems to me to show
that Browning was struggling with another enemy: it was the
flesh rather than the world or the Devil that he had in mind.

That Fifine is as definitely a "harlot" as Rossetti's Jenny
is made quite clear when the father of Fifine, the circus
manager, is described as "selling" the gypsy girl:

[26] *Op. cit.*, xc (1568-72).
[27] *Op. cit.*, xci (1594-5).
[28] *Op. cit.*, vi (43-6).
[29] William O. Raymond, *The Infinite Moment*, p. 115.

M

> his daughter that he sells
> Each rustic for five sous.[30]

Surface respectability is preserved by the fact that what is being sold is the right to gaze:

> fie, the fairy!—how she flees
> O'er all those heads thrust back,—mouths, eyes, one
>   gape and stare,—
> No scrap of skirt impedes free passage through the air,
> Till, plumb on the other side, she lights and laughs again,
> That fairy-form, whereof each muscle, nay, each vein
> The curious may inspect. . . .[31]

But the imagery betrays the underlying meaning, without subtlety, but rather with the vulgarity which the sordid transaction seems to warrant:

> are you worth the cost of a cigar?
> Go boldly, enter booth, disburse the coin at bar
> Of doorway. . . .[32]

The phallic symbol chosen suggests that Browning was unsuspicious of any such implication, although the disbursing of the coin may probably have meant more to him, in that he elsewhere made use of the image of Danae and the golden shower.

Within the booth stand a recognisable group, Madame to the fore:

> And forthwith you survey his Graces in a group,
> Live Pictures, picturesque no doubt and close to life:
> His sisters, right and left; the Grace in front, his wife.[33]

Don Juan's choice falls on Fifine, for she it is who

> performs the feat of the Trapeze?
> Lo, she is launched . . .[34]

—the trapeze suggesting a sexual rhythm which elsewhere, most notably in "The Last Ride Together", is referred to quite unequivocally in terms of equitation:[35] while "launched",

---

[30] *Fifine*, xi (120-1).   [31] *Op. cit.*, xi (115-20).   [32] *Op. cit.*, xi (108-10).
[33] *Op. cit.*, xi (111-13).   [34] *Op. cit.*, xi (114-15).
[35] See Russell M. Goldfarb, "Sexual Meaning in 'The Last Ride Together' ", in *Victorian Poetry*, III (1965), pp. 255-61.

traced back to its basic meaning of a ship sliding down into the sea, is comparable with the more traditional erotic image of the ship entering port, as in Carew's "A Rapture".

The wife notes her husband's obvious interest with anxiety, and Don Juan, forestalling her protest—

> the flesh that claimed
> Unduly my regard, she thought, the taste, she blamed
> In me, for things extern[36]

—hastens to reassure her. He suggests that the male costume unsexes Fifine, and that therefore Elvire is "lunging at a phantom", at a "sexless and bloodless sprite", an exotic lily. The details of the ensuing flower imagery are however far from reassuring. They revert to the overweighted flower-and-insect symbolism of Browning's earlier "Women and Roses", revealing that the emotions inspired by the gypsy were by no means sexless:

> I' the chalice, so, about each pistil, spice is packed,—
> Deliriously-drugged scent. . . .
>
> I ask, is she in fault who guards such golden gloom,
> Such dear and damning scent, by who cares what
>   devices,
> And takes the idle life of insects she entices
> When, drowned to heart's desire, they satiate the inside
> O' the lily . . . ?[37]

The spice-packed chalice into which the "insects" penetrate till they are "drowned to heart's desire" reads not only woman but whore; in the earlier poem the flower was entered by the singular "bee" and the implications were of pleasure, not danger. Here the moralist is at work and Fifine is described as a

> . . . gorgeous poison-plague, on thee no hearts
>   are set![38]

with the conclusion intended at least to be reassuring:

> We gather daisy meek, or maiden violet:
> I think it is Elvire we love, and not Fifine.[39]

---

[36] *Fifine*, xxviii (332-4). [37] *Op. cit.*, xvii (178-9, 183-7).
[38] *Op. cit.*, xviii (196). [39] *Op. cit.*, xviii (197-8).

This, through countless twists and turns of argument, is what
Don Juan sets out to prove, while image after image goes to
show the real trend of his thought. Fifine in his imagination is
made to proffer a "cup of witchcraft", and tempts him to "sup
of my sorcery", an image which is fully worked out in the
wine-press, where she challenges him:

> ". . . He knows
> "Nothing of how I pack my wine-press, turn its winch
> "Three-times-three, all the time to song and dance, nor
> flinch
> "From charming on and on, till at the last I squeeze
> "Out the exhaustive drop that leaves behind mere lees
> "And dregs. . . ."[40]

And there is a *cri du cœur* in the provoking challenge:

> ". . . You die, nor understand
> "What bliss might be in life: you ate the grapes, but
> knew
> "Never the taste of wine, such vintage as I brew! . . ."[41]

Is this intended only for Don Juan, or is it not rather turned by
Browning against himself? He was sixty years old when *Fifine*
was published, his wife whom he had dearly loved was dead,
from what we know of his biography it seems probable that he
had led a chaste youth—and now he is tormented by the
mocking words of the harlot:

> "Where is the plenitude of passion which endures
> "Comparison with that, I ask of amateurs? . . ."[42]

The last word, incidentally, is a curious example of verbal
concentration. While the surface meaning is that of *dilettante*,
the word contains a pun arising from its Latin origin in *amator*,
"lover", and at the same time evokes its opposite, "pro-
fessional", equated with prostitute.

Arm in arm, husband and wife together watch the gypsy
rope-dancer, and some of the tension built up by the over-
loading of sexual symbolism is relieved by touches of humour.

[40] *Op. cit.*, xxxii (437-42).
[41] *Op. cit.*, xxxii (445-7).
[42] *Op. cit.*, xxxii (460-1).

In obviously bad faith Don Juan sets out to justify the life led by Fifine, who, like Rossetti's Jenny, was

> An infant born perchance as sensitive and nice
> As any soul of you, proud dames,[43]

and who, he suggests, was driven perhaps to "the ignoble trade" to preserve the innocence of a younger sister:

> . . . You draw back skirts from filth like her
> Who, possibly, braves scorn, if, scorned, she minister
> To age, want, and disease of parents one or both;
> Nay, peradventure, stoops to degradation, loth
> That some just-budding sister, the dew yet on the rose,
> Should have to share in turn the ignoble trade,—who knows?[44]

The "parents one or both" has a saving grace about it which suggests that Browning puts forward this argument for exactly what it is worth, in open satire of such moral reading as was then current, and of the heroines who culminate in the pathetic little circus girl of *A Peep behind the Scenes*.[45] It is surprising, therefore, to find Nettleship, and some later critics following him, accepting as valid this justification of Fifine.[46]

Other touches of humour are to be found in the comment on mid-Victorian swathing, to which Fifine offers such a refreshing contrast:

> nor let your womankind appear
> Without as multiplied a coating as protects
> An onion from the eye![47]

And the comment by the statue of the Saint on Pornic church at the sight of the naked charms of Cleopatra is in much the same vein:

> though, sure,
> She must have stripped herself only to clothe the poor.[48]

---

[43] *Op. cit.*, xxiv (275-6).
[44] *Op. cit.*, xxiv (278-83).
[45] Mrs O. F. Walton, *A Peep Behind the Scenes*, London 1877.
[46] J. T. Nettleship, *Robert Browning: Essays and Thoughts*, p. 258.
[47] *Fifine*, xii (131-3).
[48] *Op. cit.*, xx (244-5).

These last lines are taken from the Pageant sequence, stanzas
xix-xxii, a brief and somewhat abortive attempt, not very well
assimilated into the body of the poem, to set the figures of
Elvire and Fifine in a line of historical beauties.   What should
have been a long line, Browning's dream of fair women, breaks
down after Helen, Cleopatra, and the Saint on Pornic church.
Helen is seen as the moon breaking through clouds, an idea
much more fully developed in Browning's later "Pan and
Luna", laying stress on her nakedness, while Cleopatra stands
"bared, the entire and sinuous wealth/O' the shining shape",
but both fail to come alive, and it is only Fifine, ending the
masque with "curtsey, smile and pout,/Submissive-mutinous"
who catches the eye as she "Points toe, imposes haunch, and
pleads with tambourine"; the tambourine in which Don Juan
places coins (with a return to the sexual symbolism, an image
which is more fully developed in the assignation passage at the
end of the poem).   What is most curious about this Pageant is
its introduction:

> Suppose, an age and time long past
> Renew for our behoof one pageant more, the last
> O' the kind, sick Louis liked to see defile between
> Him and the yawning grave, its passage served to screen.
> With eye as grey as lead, with cheek as brown as bronze,
> Here where we stand, shall sit and suffer Louis Onze. . . .[49]

The dying Louis XI strikes us as being as oddly out of context as
was Gawain a few stanzas earlier.   What had fascinated
Browning was the fact that the sick king made use of these
masques to beguile his thoughts away from death—they shut
out the sight of the "yawning grave".[50]   The *lead* of his eye
and *bronze* of his cheek, besides being the physical signs of his
mortal sickness, are words belonging to his death itself, as
symbols of the coffin, and the masque is at the same time a

---

[49] *Op. cit.*, xix (200-5).
[50] In "Numpholeptos", 31-5, there is the theme of physical love intervening
and forcing death back: ". . . sting awake the palsied limb, /Bid with life's ecstasy
sense overbrim /And suck back death in the resurging joy— /Love, the love whole
and sole without alloy! /Vainly! the promise withers!"   The situation is exactly
that of *Fifine*, including the equation "impotence = death".

forewarning of his funeral procession—"One pageant more, the last".[51]

Why, we may wonder, should Browning be concerned with this somewhat macabre figure in a poem ostensibly dealing with sexual temptation and marital infidelity? Many critics have concerned themselves with *Fifine*, but it has generally been assumed that Louis XI is simply another of Browning's odd literary and historical references. Yet Browning is a great poet, and the more closely we look at his work, the more such figures are seen to be an integral part of it. Louis XI is the first statement we have of one of the poem's major themes: the fear of approaching death, and its sexual implications and repercussions. A few stanzas later, xlv-xlix, the same theme is brought further to the fore in a striking passage, where Don Juan bends down and with the end of a fisherman's broken pipe traces three faces in the sand

> —Smooth slab whereon I draw, no matter with what skill,
> A face, and yet another, and yet another still.
> There lie my three prime types of beauty![52]

The relevance of this passage to its context is very slight, but it has a deeper significance which is essential to the interpretation of the whole poem. For while one is the face of Fifine, and one the face of Elvire, the first face of the trio which he draws, and which should represent Don Juan himself, is described in these words:

> observe how brow recedes,
> Head shudders back on spine, as if one haled the hair,
> Would have the full-face front what pin-point eye's
>   sharp stare

---

[51] The *Lettres* of Philippe de Comines (to which Browning refers in *Red Cotton Night-Cap Country*) describe Louis's fear of death and the excesses to which this led him, but they make no mention of these pageants: the only pageant which Comines describes is one which welcomed the King into the city on his coronation. The *Biographie universelle*, a favourite source of Browning's, gives a striking picture of the terror of the King as death approached: "et les approches de la mort, ajoutant à son caractère inquiet et soupçonneux, il ne s'occupait plus que de ses terreurs. . . . Ne voulant pas paraître si près de sa fin, et craignant de faire connaître l'altération de son visage, le roi ne se montrait plus au public que de très loin et magnifiquement habillé; ce qui contrastait singulièrement avec sa simplicité habituelle. . . . Une seconde attaque étant venue augmenter ses terreurs, sa défiance devint extrême. . . ." This may have added the detail as to the change in the King's face, but neither Comines nor the *Biographie* are sources for the pageant.

[52] *Fifine*, xlv (698-700).

Announces; mouth agape to drink the flowing fate,
While chin protrudes to meet the burst o' the wave: elate
Almost, spurred on to brave necessity, expend
All life left, in one flash, as fire does at its end.
Retrenchment and addition effect a masterpiece,
Not change i' the motive: here diminish, there increase—
And who wants Horror, has it.[53]

It is a portrait, in Gérôme's melodramatic style, of a dying man, and his death is horrible. As if haled by the hair (recalling religious paintings where the damned are dragged by the hair down to Hell,[54] or the same subject treated in literature—in stanza lxx he refers to "all Descents to Hell whereof I ever read") he gazes in terror at what is before him "what pin-point-eye's sharp stare/Announces", a man fully conscious of the death which awaits him. And the title of the picture is Horror. Now why should Browning, who had set out to trace in the sand "my three prime types of beauty", substitute this gruesome picture for what should have been Don Juan's self-portrait?

There may easily be a visual source for the drawing (probably a painting by Gérôme himself, although as yet I have been unable to trace it). But, even so, why should it be here at all? I believe that it is an interesting example of the surfacing of the underlying theme of the whole: the fear of death. The man who is debating between the two women is a man who is afraid to die—terrified of death. Gone is the earlier bravery of "Prospice", gone even the desperate challenge of "Childe Roland". Browning saw death before him, invested with all the terror it would hold for a man who, as a child, had listened to the Hell-fire sermons which inspired his "Heretic's Tragedy". The threat of impotence, which comes out more fully in the Venice dream sequence (a first hint of this may be traced in the fisherman's broken pipe with which Don Juan makes his drawing in the sand)[55] brought the thought of death

---

[53] *Op. cit.*, xlvii (709-18).

[54] The Victorian Don Juan is so conditioned that as soon as he feels temptation to commit a sin, the thought of Hell comes forcibly to his mind.

[55] Cp. "The Flight of the Duchess", 412, 415-16: "Her usual presents were forthcoming . . ./(Just a sea-shore stone holding a dozen fine pebbles,)/Or a porcelain mouth-piece to screw on a pipe end . . .". Here the gypsy is offering the unbroken pipe mouthpiece to the Duke, who has no use for it and refuses it impatiently. He needs no sexual awakening, but sends the gypsy instead to his wife, who requires "weaning".

suddenly much nearer: and with a consciousness of failing powers he grasped at life and youth as embodied in Fifine. The gypsy girl, awakening his desire, seemed to ward off the threat, to offer new hope, and to stand between him and the horror.

The sexual attraction of Fifine, earlier underscored by the trapeze and flower imagery, is later related more closely to the unconscious and almost wholly expressed in terms of the sea. Many central stanzas of the poem (lxiv-lxxxiv) are a return to the bathe of the Prologue. But it is the sailing passages and the ship simile, built up elaborately through stanzas lxxxi-lxxxiv, which are most revealing. In this extended simile Elvire is "yon superior ship", safe in port,

> moored, with not a breath to flap
> The yards of her, no lift of ripple to o'erlap
> Keel, much less prow.[56]

While regretting that this ship cannot see him safely through the voyage of life

> I would there were one voyage, and then no more to do . . .
>
> I would the steady voyage, and not the fitful trip,—
> Elvire, and not Fifine,—might test our seamanship.[57]

Yet Don Juan
> accepts all fact,
> Discards all fiction—steers Fifine, and cries, i' the act,
> Thou art so bad, and yet so delicate a brown![58]

The pleasure of "the act" is intensified by the woman's very badness, an interesting outcome of Victorian repression which Browning was quick to note. It was only a step from this to the relation of beauty to evil. Here, in the "cockleshell, Fifine", lies a voyage of excitement, after the safety and staleness of his marriage experience:

> Elvire is true, as truth, honesty's self, alack!
> The worse! too safe the ship, the transport there and back
> Too certain! . . .

---

[56] *Fifine*, lxxxi (1392-3).
[57] *Op. cit.*, lxxxii (1399, 1404-5).
[58] *Op. cit.*, lxxxii (1416-18).

> How can I but suspect, the true feat were to slip
> Down side, transfer myself to cockle-shell from ship. . . .[59]

> The rakish craft could slip her moorings in the tent,
> And, hoisting every stitch of spangled canvas, steer
> Through divers rocks and shoals,—in fine, deposit here
> Your Virgil of a spouse, in Attica. . . .[60]

Browning quite deliberately employs this long-drawn-out simile of the two ships, the wife Elvire and the gypsy Fifine, as a mode of expressing Don Juan's constant hankering after marital infidelity. The adventurous voyage in the cockleshell "through divers rocks and shoals" in which the "impious vessels leap across and tempt a thing they should not touch—the deep" is quite open sexual symbolism which Browning felt to be justified by the nature of his protagonist, Don Juan. But the following stanza suggests a closer identification with his hero than Browning probably intended to reveal. Reaching harbour safe, Don Juan turns to his wife with the reassuring, though somewhat insulting words:

> Elvire, I'm back with you!
> Share in the memories![61]

Insulting, that is to say, if we pay attention to the sad *post-coitum* under-reading of the following lines, which open with the grim threat

> How quickly night comes!

—for night in this poem, as the dream sequence shows, means death. Fifine, like the masque of Louis XI, has served for only a little time to block out the sight of the grave. The physical details here are stark and tragic:

> . . . overcrept by grey, the plains expand,
> Assume significance; *while ocean dwindles, shrinks
> Into a pettier bound*: its plash and plaint, methinks,
> Six *steps away*, how *both retire, as if their part
> Were played*, another force were free to prove her art,

---

[59] *Op. cit.*, lxxxii (1422-4, 1428-9).
[60] *Op. cit.*, lxxxiii (1443-6).
[61] *Op. cit.*, lxxxiii (1457-8).

Protagonist in turn! Are you unterrified?
All false, all fleeting too! And nowhere things abide,
And everywhere we strain that things should stay,—the one
Truth, that ourselves are true![62]

The italics are mine, to stress not so much the key words, which
stand out clearly enough, as to draw attention to the extraordinary effect of counterpoint which is produced by bringing
forward the under-reading.[63] "Steps" shifts plausibly enough
from noun to verb, and "the one" can be read with the foregoing words as the desire (strain) to maintain the achieved
sexual unity or oneness, with its inevitable failure and disillu-
sion. The words "Are you unterrified?" ostensibly addressed
to the wife with reference to the increasing darkness, can be
read, too, as addressed to Fifine in the under-reading, with
something of the gentleness of words exchanged between
lovers. They have besides a further and still deeper meaning
as a question asked by the speaker to himself—he and Fifine
have played their parts, and a new force has taken the stage, the
power of night and death. Once more he is brought face to face
with his fear.

It is important, however, not to overlook the fact that the
whole of the ship voyage and the sad reflexions which follow it
take place in the imagination, not only of Browning, but even of
Don Juan. Nothing at all has happened. He has stood, with
Elvire on his arm, watching the trapeze artist perform, and
afterwards has strolled out along the darkening beach, arm-in-
arm with his wife. The very intensity of his emotion is due to
its repression. The arch-philanderer continues to behave with
full Victorian respectability, notwithstanding the inner chaos
which the imagery betrays. Not until the final assignation is
there any love-making, even for Don Juan. Indeed, what he
tries to prove to himself, as well as to his wife, is that all he

---

[62] *Op. cit.*, lxxxiv (1463-71): my italics.

[63] Such secondary readings, making no direct appeal to the intellect which is
occupied with grasping the "sense" of the poem (and in Browning the intellect is
often kept very busy indeed) have an incalculable effect on the value of the poem
as a whole. If we want to understand the emotional impact of a poem, such
"hidden persuaders" cannot be ignored, although such an understanding is
wholly unrelated to the appreciation of the poem, as their effect is more likely to be
diminished than increased by intellectual apprehension.

required of Fifine was one of those "flashes struck from mid-nights" which Browning frequently evoked in his poetry. At this point the reader feels that there is a very close identification between Don Juan and his creator. Fifine, dressing for the show in a corner of the tent, is described as

> some girl by fate reserved
> To give me once again the electric snap and spark
> Which prove, when finger finds out finger in the dark
> O' the world, there's fire and life and truth there, link
> but hands
> And pass the secret on.[64]

Browning the romantic declares that all he needs, whether from Fifine or Queen Cristina, is an exchanged glance of the eyes, or a little hand-holding, which he is willing to share with all the world, in a sort of spiritual *La Ronde*:

> Lo, link by link, expands
> The circle, lengthens out the chain, till one embrace
> Of high with low is found uniting the whole race,
> Not simply you and me and our Fifine, but all
> The world: the Fair expands into the Carnival,
> The Carnival again to . . . ah, but that's my dream![65]

With the Carnival we are in Venice, in the long dream sequence, where much that before is only hinted at is made clear in the imagery of this curious passage in which Browning seems voluntarily, even voluptuously, to have stretched himself out on a literary psychiatrist's couch where he disemburdens himself of the daydream of Venice, that sea-city where the themes of love and death have so often tangled together in literature.

The dream opens with Don Juan looking down from the heights of the Campanile. Oddly enough, he uses the same phrase "however I got there" which, with slight modification, is found in that subtler dream poem, "Childe Roland". Browning notes, that is to say, some mysterious process at work: he is unable to trace the logical links of thought which place him alone so high in the Campanile tower. Yet the Venetian

---

[64] *Fifine*, xci (1602-6).
[65] *Op. cit.*, xci (1606-11).

Campanile links up, dream fashion, with the tower of St Gille, and at the end of *Fifine* he returns to the tower overlooking the sea—the tower which is the dominant symbol of the whole poem—only to determine to leave it for good:

> I stickle for the town,
> And not this tower apart; because, though, half-way
>   down,
> Its mullions wink o'erwebbed with bloomy greenness, yet
> Who mounts to staircase top may tempt the parapet,
> And sudden there's the sea![66]

From this "tower apart" (situated not unlike Joyce's martello tower) Browning deliberately tries to escape, because its windows "o'er-webbed with bloomy greenness" are an insufficient contact with the world; he wants instead to take refuge in the town, away from the sea, because the town has "no memories to arouse, no fancies to delude!"—no "antenatal prime experience" to stir up, he might well have added. In the same way the high tower of his dream in St Mark's Square signifies his isolation, and it is true that this tall, pencil-slim structure, standing alone, off-centre, cut off from all other buildings, near the junction of the two squares, the great Piazza and the smaller Piazzetta, with its wide view over city and sea across to the mountains of the mainland, gives a greater sense of isolation than many much higher edifices. At the same time Browning is picking up the earlier "backcloth" sexual symbols: the campanile tower and St Mark's dome carrying on the basic visual symbolism with which the poem opened. This plurisignificance of symbols, which is characteristic of dreams, is by no means rare in poetry. The isolation theme is meanwhile introduced and discussed on the intellectual level by Browning. The sexual symbolism remains hidden from both author and reader, but makes a subliminal impact which is no less relevant and important to the development of the poem.

From the tower he looks down on the masked crowd, but the masks are not those of the traditional Venetian Carnival, the concealing masks of the figures of a Longhi painting. They are instead designed to reveal

[66] *Op. cit.*, cxxxi (2321-5).

> the face, an evidence
> O' the soul at work inside; and, all the more intense,
> So much the more grotesque.[67]

Yet the explanation of this grotesqueness lies, Browning finds, in his own separation, for when he "pitches" into the square and looks closer, the faces seem less horrible, less monstrous. He finds in all "some deviation" from "God's prime purpose", but the moral which he draws in some eighty lines on the same theme is that of a conscious moralist. He is no longer dreaming his dream but interpreting it in accordance with his waking theories, treating his field full of folk as an allegory to be explained and expounded in religious and sociological terms, so that it loses much of its poetic significance.

When he returns to the dream the interest shifts from the masked crowds to the buildings themselves, and a number of frustration elements appear. We come to what Stopford Brooke had referred to as "that magnificent description of a sunset. . . . It is drawn to illustrate some remote point in the argument, and is far too magnificent for the thing it illustrates".[68] That is to say that once again we have what is practically an interpolated passage, like the Louis XI pageant and the three portraits. It is a passage that Browning felt to be so relevant that he did not take the trouble to link it logically with the rest of the poem, except in the loosest and most unconvincing way. Yet these, and other passages like them are, I suspect, the reason why Swinburne wrote of *Fifine*:

[67] *Op. cit.*, xcvi (1719-21). In his essay "Wordsworth, Tennyson and Browning, or, Pure, Ornate and Grotesque Art in English Poetry", in *Literary Studies* (1895), Walter Bagehot has described Browning as the poet of the grotesque. The carnival crowds seem to me to fit in well with this definition and to be in the tradition of Hogarth and Dickens. Other examples in the same vein of descriptive grotesque are to be found in "Holy-Cross Day". Bagehot, like his contemporaries, used the term "grotesque" with a derogatory connotation: for a more objective view, considering the "grotesque" as the most valid form of artistic expression of "that estrangement and alienation which grips mankind when belief in a perfect and protective natural order is weakened or destroyed", see W. Kayser, *The Grotesque in Art and Literature*, Bloomington 1963. There could be no clearer emblem of the feeling of estrangement than this dream of the man on the tower. For an examination of the grotesque in *Fifine*, see John M. Hitner, "Browning's Grotesque Period", in *Victorian Poetry*, IV (1966), pp. 1-13. This essay, which unfortunately came to my notice only recently, throws valuable light on this period of Browning's work.

[68] Stopford A. Brooke, *The Poetry of Robert Browning*, p. 107.

"This is far better than anything Browning has yet written. Here is his true province".[69] For with the description of a stormy sunset, Browning returns to the theme of death and impotence:

> [The sun] plays, pre-eminently gold, gilds vapour, crag
>   and crest
> Which bend in rapt suspense above the act and deed
> They cluster round and keep their very own, nor heed
> The world at watch; while we, breathlessly at the base
> O' the castellated bulk, note momently the mace
> Of night fall here, fall there, bring change with every blow,
> Alike to sharpened shaft and broadened portico
> I' the structure: heights and depths, beneath the leaden
>   stress,
> Crumble and melt and mix together, coälesce,
> Re-form, but sadder still, subdued yet more and more
> By every fresh defeat. . . .[70]

Stanzas cvi-cxi are an extraordinarily faithful recording of dream technique, and in writing Browning has clearly let his mind run on in a fantasy. The dream contains two descriptions of dissolution: the first, which is a cloud structure, can still be explained logically as a poetical sunset scene, the second which follows a few lines later, is no longer logically coherent. The crumbling temples in both passages are dream buildings, and if we are to make anything of this sequence of the poem it must be read and analysed as a dream. Only then can its relevance to the context be seen and understood, and only then can we appreciate Browning's rare skill, his scientific accuracy, in recording this dream process. A full analysis would go beyond the scope of this chapter, so the conclusions may seem arbitrary, but I wish to stress their relevance to the theme of the poem, and that only by admitting the underlying psychological interpretation does a very puzzling poem make sense *as a whole*.

Briefly I read the dream as a symbolic statement of the state of mental and physical depression in which the poet found himself when the stimulus of a fresh sexual attraction seemed to hold out new hope to him, the hope which Fifine represented for

[69] Quoted by Hall Griffin and Minchin, *The Life of Robert Browning*, p. 258.
[70] *Fifine*, cvi (1831-41).

Don Juan. If his emotional reaction seems excessive, it is essential to remember that in pushing back the threat of impotence, he is pushing back the threat of death:

> till, lo, a second birth,
> And the veil broke away because of something new
> Inside, that pushed to gain an outlet. . . .[71]

Salvation seems to him to lie, in stanza cxxv where his dream ends, in Fifine herself:

> What through the dark and drear
> Brought comfort to the Titan? Emerging from the lymph,
> "God, man, or mixture" proved only to be a nymph . . .[72]

the "sea nymph, called Fifine". Once more, with her emergence, all is well with the dreamer, he hears

> the clink on clink of metal (money, judged
> Abundant in my purse)[73]

The dream is over, but it has served its purpose:

> Awaking so,
> What if we, homeward-bound, all peace and some fatigue,
> Trudge,[74]

As before in the sensitive-plant passage, Browning shows remarkable sensitivity to the underlying meaning. He sees life for a moment not in terms of moral theory but as a physical cycle:

> We end where we began: that consequence is clear.
> All peace and some fatigue, wherever we were nursed
> To life, we bosom us on death, find last is first
> And thenceforth final too.[75]

His dream release has left him for the moment relaxed, un-demanding, ready to accept the cycle of birth and death, of which the sexual act is both a symbol and a part, ready for a moment to see it as self-sufficient, for he arrives at the startling

[71] *Op. cit.*, cx (1899-1901).
[73] *Op. cit.*, cxxv (2217-18).
[75] *Op. cit.*, cxxvii (2242-5).
[72] *Op. cit.*, cxxv (2214-16).
[74] *Op. cit.*, cxxvii (2238-40).

conclusion of "thenceforth final". Naturally enough his whole
Christian concept of life springs to its feet at this point, and
the next stanza opens with a startled cry: "Why final?", but
this does nothing to invalidate the conclusion which he had
instinctively reached. The dream, by bringing out his fear of
impotence and death, has pointed to the solution of acceptance
of the natural cycle, bringing with it a feeling, as he repeats
twice, of "all peace and some fatigue".

A problem remains. The dream may have reached a
satisfactory conclusion, but the poem as yet has not. Don Juan,
if only for historical verisimilitude, must be allowed his assignation. Yet here, too, there are some curious elements: he
remains a Victorian figure. Instead of playing the part of male
hunter, as is proper to the legend, the assignation is thrust
upon him. Walking along the sea-shore, one hand open behind
his back, he is *attacked*!

> . . . you do not use to apprehend attack!
> No doubt, the way I march, one idle arm, thrown slack
> Behind me, leaves the open hand defenceless at the
>   back. . . .[76]

Into this open hand is slipped the letter of assignation. This
ending is read by Raymond and others as cynical, in that Don
Juan, despite all his promises to his wife, here slips away to
meet the gypsy girl. Yet it is at the same time pathetic. This
assignation, made *behind his own back*, is the only kind that such
a Victorian hero dared to conceive. Of course Don Juan had
deliberately provoked it, placing in the gypsy's tambourine not
the five sous of the yokels, or even "the largesse of a franc"
against which Elvire had protested, but a gold coin. There is
an interesting inversion and doubling of symbols at this point,
for it is the male who places the egg in the female nest

> to better help the blank
> O' the nest, her tambourine, and, laying egg, persuade
> A family to follow, the nest-egg that I laid
> May have contained,—but just to foil suspicious folk,—
> Between two silver whites a yellow double yolk![77]

---

[76] *Op. cit.*, cxxxii (2341-3).
[77] *Op. cit.*, cxxxii (2347-51).

N

But the silver whites and double yolk of the egg are coins,[78] with promise of more to follow, so that we are back with Danae and her shower.

So, unheroically, the hero slips away to the assignation, and Browning closes the poem with an unattractive lyrical epilogue, in a personal tone, called "The Householder".[79] Ugly as it is, being one of those half-facetious half-serious poems, a *genre* which Browning often attempted, but in which he rarely succeeded, it cannot be ignored, for it brings us back to the figure of the wife, the butterfly Elizabeth of the prologue and the Elvire of the poem proper. Ostensibly Elvire is the betrayed wife of Victorian fiction; she is virtue personified, a walking conscience, a sore trial to her flesh-and-blood husband. Her character suffers in the poem, as has been pointed out, from the fact that all her words reach us through her husband's monologue: they are the words and thoughts which Don Juan attributes to her. Browning makes no real attempt to personify her—all that interests him is her husband's view of her. This in so far as the wife is Elvire and the husband Don Juan.

There are a number of passages instead where Browning has slipped into the persona of his protagonist and where Elvire simultaneously becomes Elizabeth Barrett. It seems never to have been noted that not only in the personal Prologue and Epilogue, but also at times in the text of the poem itself, Elvire is spoken of, or to, as dead.

The first time this occurs is at the end of the pageant scene, in stanza xxxviii:

> 'T is not fit your phantom leave the stage. . . .[80]

---

[78] The yellow double yolk of l. 2351 must be a double *louis d'or*, which Browning found so profusely in the Pornic legend used in "Gold Hair". The "double" yolk suggests that Browning was thinking of two gold coins hidden between the silver francs. In fact a double *louis d'or* is recorded in Littré as the name of a single coin.

[79] William Lyon Phelps, *Robert Browning: How to Know Him*, London 1915, p. 88, felt quite differently about this epilogue, to which he refers in the following terms: "One of the most original and powerful of Browning's lyrical pieces comes just where we should least expect it, at the end of that dark, dreary, and all but impenetrable wilderness of verse, *Fifine at the Fair*. It serves as an *Epilogue*, but it would be difficult and unprofitable to attempt to discover its connexion with the poem to which it is appended. Its metre is unique in Browning, and stirs the heart with inexpressible force. In music it most closely resembles the swift thrilling roll of a snare drum, and can be read aloud in exact accord with that instrument."

[80] *Fifine*, xxxviii (580).

The phantom is ostensibly the imaginary projection of Elvire whom Don Juan has placed in the pageant, but the whole of this and the following stanza reveal that the woman in Browning's mind is his dead wife:

> How ravishingly pure you stand in pale constraint!
> My new-created shape, without or touch or taint,
> Inviolate of life and worldliness and sin . . .[81]

and he goes on to describe her in words which might very well be a recollection of his last sight of Elizabeth, as she lay in her coffin,

> the dress
> Deep swathed about with folds and flowings virginal,
> Up to the pleated breasts, rebellious 'neath their pall,
> As if the vesture's snow were moulding sleep not death, . .

> And what shall now divert me, once the sweet face revealed,
> From all I loved so long, so lingeringly left?[82]

Browning seems quite to have forgotten that Don Juan is speaking to a living wife, who is leaning on his arm. Here it seems clear that these lines were meant for Elizabeth, and that Browning had laid aside for the moment his mask and was speaking in his own person.

The same thing happens again, though less unequivocally, in the ship simile. The "good Elvire" moored in the safe harbour seems to me to fit the dead Elizabeth even better than the wife of Don Juan, and the lines

> I would there were one voyage, and then no more to do . . .

and

> I would the steady voyage, and not the fitful trip,—
> Elvire, and not Fifine,—might test our seamanship . . .[83]

can be read as regret for the loss of his wife and the end of the safe voyage of his marriage, although they can be interpreted in their context as uttered in bad faith by Don Juan to placate Elvire. Lastly, at the end of the poem, the lines

[81] *Op. cit.*, xxxviii (586-8).
[82] *Op. cit.*, xxxviii (601-4, 607-8).
[83] *Op. cit.*, lxxxii (1399, 1404-5).

> How pallidly you pause o' the threshold! Hardly night,[84]
>
> Which drapes you, ought to make real flesh and blood so
>   white!
> Touch me, and so appear alive to all intents!
> Will the saint vanish from the sinner that repents?
> Suppose you are a ghost! A memory, a hope,
> A fear, a conscience! Quick! Give back the hand I grope
> I' the dusk for![85]

serve as a deliberate connecting link between the live Elvire of
the poem and the dead Elizabeth of the Epilogue, and are
important in support of Raymond's theory that the whole poem
was written in remorse after Browning had been unfaithful to
the memory of his dead wife in proposing marriage to Louisa,
Lady Ashburton. The Epilogue is openly addressed to Elizabeth, even containing, in stanza ii, a strictly private half-
jocular reference to his wife's belief in spiritualism, which had
so aroused Browning's anger during her lifetime:

> Quick, in its corners ere certain shapes arouse!
>   Let them—every devil of the night—lay claim,
> Make and mend, or rap and rend, for me! Good-bye!
>   God be their guard from disturbance at their glee. . . .[86]

The lyric ends in the joint composition by husband and wife of
his epitaph, the last words being those of Elizabeth:

> "Love is all and Death is nought"! quoth She.[87]

Browning, that is to say, deliberately rounds off his poem with
a Christian moral concept, that "perfect love casteth out fear"
—the love of husband and wife. Re-united to the memory of
Elizabeth, Browning has landed safely back in a Florentine
cemetery, after his rash immersion in the waters of the unconscious. His epitaph treats of love and death in accepted terms
—its very ugliness shows a wish to accept the ordinary. He has
pushed back all thought of the "unlucky bath" and the train of
"fancies manifold" that it started, in order to accept death in

---

[84] Night, throughout this poem, symbolises death.
[85] *Fifine*, cxxx (2306-12).
[86] *Op. cit.*, Epilogue, st. ii.
[87] *Op. cit.*, Epilogue, st. iv.

the most traditional fashion by regarding it as the spiritual reunion with his wife. He has left the "tower apart" by the sea to be "duly domiciled" in the town.

It is, he chooses that it shall be, as if he had never mounted "to staircase top to tempt the parapet", had never viewed from thence the sea, and had no knowledge of

> The antenatal prime experience,—what know I?—
> The initiatory love preparing us to die—[88]

which need not surprise us, for Browning was always turning his back on his own conclusions, when they seemed to contradict or in any way to conflict with the view of life which he had willed to accept.[89]

[88] *Op. cit.*, lxxxix (1561-62).

[89] Cp. Philip Drew, "Henry Jones on Browning's Optimism", in *Victorian Poetry*, ii (1964), p. 38: It is true to say that a quality in which Browning is deficient is the determination to follow his reason steadfastly even when it is in conflict with all he most values".

IX

The Poetry of Reticence

A POET like Browning invites exploration rather than conclusions. This may be because, in spite of the excellent instrument which DeVane has provided in his *Handbook*, Browning studies are not yet so far advanced as to justify any serious and general summing-up. Certainly I am in no position to attempt any such critical synthesis. In the foregoing chapters I have taken a few single poems for detailed analysis of the imaginative process which went into their making. The selection of these rather than other poems was made for no better reason than that I liked them and felt curious about them. At other times I have followed recurring themes throughout his work as a whole, one or two of the innumerable possible themes, chosen again because they stirred my curiosity. But others, and not least his use of torture imagery and symbolism, and that morbid streak which lay beneath the poetry of every good Victorian, I have left uninvestigated.

The approaches to Browning in this book have all been attempts at catching the essential nature of an art which seems to be particularly evasive. Browning is an explorer of the world of words and of the infinite ways of incorporating them into new and original structures. My enquiry, however fragmentary, should have been sufficient to establish one or two points. The "philosophical" or ideological conceptions behind the poems, the content of thought, has a fairly limited range: but then Browning was a poet and not a philosopher. Not that he accepted without question the ideas of his own time:

Browning's method was to question everything, and this gives his thought a peculiarly modern tone which is often misleading, because Browning remained shackled, above all in his conclusions, to the Victorian age, and over and over again the logical processes in his poetry break down as he forces the argument back through loops and arabesques of fantastical reasoning to a pre-established conclusion. While it is difficult to trace the point at which the fallacies intervene, we are left today with a sense that somewhere, somehow, he has begged the question.

Yet what gives his thought poetical variety and scope is an inexhaustible curiosity focused on details: the idea followed up in all its ramifications becomes metaphor and image explored in its minutest realistic particulars (whether in "Caliban upon Setebos" or in "Andrea del Sarto"). The capacity for effective representation of this kind at times takes over completely, particularly in some of Browning's best work, giving the impression of a proneness to digression and, on the intellectual level, evasion. It is this evasiveness that permitted the apparently contrasting attitudes of Browning's admirers and critics in the nineteenth century: the admirers seeing in it unsounded depths from which they extracted essential notions in order to set him up as a great moral and even religious teacher; the critics seeing only obscurity and grotesqueness. It is this same evasiveness which caused the decline of his reputation in the present century, when his dramatic monologues were considered only as clever but substantially shallow experiments in psychology. When William Empson sweeps Browning aside with Oscar Wilde's *bon mot*,[1] the reason must lie here. Had Empson looked closer, the *Seven Types of Ambiguity* might well have had a further chapter, for Browning's poetry is rich in verbal ambiguities.

One essential aspect of Browning's poetry strictly connected with the evasive quality of his writing has been generally overlooked: this is an instinctive and at the same time deliberate reticence in apparent contrast with the diffuseness, the

---

[1] W. Empson, *Seven Types of Ambiguity*, London 1930, p. 20: "Browning and Meredith, who did write from the world they lived in, affect me as novel writers of merit, with no lyrical inspiration at all".

seemingly uncontrolled flow of his verse.[2] This is why I have
repeatedly tried to get behind his guard, taking advantage of
Browning's compulsive accumulations of words and images and
playing them against his instinct for personal reticence. I feel
at times that his ramblings, his lengthy comparisons and elaborate similes are deceptive. They should by rights illustrate and
graphically develop the ideas and feelings expressed in a poem,
but Browning uses them instead as a further defence in order
to complicate the issue to the point of obscuring it. They are
used as camouflage, and under the pretext of generalising the
idea or feeling involved they protect and hide its private value.
But such defences are in their turn unavailing, and they may
reveal more clearly what they are meant to conceal. Not
because they can be seen through, but because of the materials
which went into their making. Necessarily a poet draws them
from the very same world of private images and associations
which is the essence of his personality. Inasmuch as these
defences are "figures" and not rational ideas, they belong to an
even more private and secret part of the mind. They belong
to the poet himself and not to the rational man who deliberately
puts on the mask of this or that character.

It may well be objected that such revealing images are more
relative to the study of psychology than aesthetics. And this is
true. But with a poet like Browning how can we draw a firm
line between the two? His dramatic monologues are deliberate
though indirect explorations of psychological processes. His
analyses are complicated by the notion of the presence of a real
or imaginary audience for the speaker of the monologues.
This, as has frequently been remarked, conditions the speaker,
who is forced to assume a stance or mask according to the effect
that he wants to make on the listener. Browning's ability as an

[2] In an almost forgotten essay in *The London Mercury*, XII (1925), pp. 180-9,
which came to my notice only because Mario Praz republished it in his *Prospettiva
della Letteratura Inglese*, Milan 1946, Edward Shanks puts forward the same
theory regarding Browning's poetry that I have tried to illustrate throughout the
present book. Shanks writes (p. 182): "Within his heart an immensely strong
instinct of reticence was at war with his natural exuberance of self-expression.
He feared always that he might too much expose himself to the gaze of the public
and to this fear, I believe, eventually most of his obscurity and strangeness may be
traced. The labyrinth of his poetry is a labyrinth he made so that he might hide
himself in it".

explorer of psychology is that of revealing in full the true nature of the character in spite of the mask assumed for the imaginary audience. Some of his best poetry is born out of these enquiries into the mental processes of characters placed in the position of deliberately hiding part of their true nature, which is revealed instead by the very images they use, and the mental associations from which these spring. Is it unreasonable, therefore, to apply the same method to Browning himself, since his own mind as a poet was working along these lines? Browning hid himself behind the masks of his characters, which he tried to objectify in order to remain himself impersonal. It seems legitimate to analyse the associations of Browning's poetic images in order to arrive, as he did himself with the characters he created, at his own nature behind the mask assumed for the sake of that prying audience of readers of which he seems so conscious. What I wish to suggest is that in so doing we are getting an insight not so much into Browning the man and his private life as into Browning the maker of poems, because we are applying the method he used while composing some of his best work.

The application of the method I have just described is very far from being an exhaustive treatment of Browning's poetry, but it throws light on one essential aspect of his creative process and it helps us to understand the poems and passages under analysis more thoroughly. I think it reveals, too, another strictly poetical characteristic of his writing. Poetry is born of tension, and tension in Browning is born of his constant impulse to explore with the utmost finesse the inner nature of human beings, their motivations and secret thoughts, while on the other hand such an investigation of his own nature was an excruciating exposure, a profanation. The conflicting impulses to reveal and conceal, in which all Browning's attention is concentrated on reticence, so that revelation takes its revenge by being fuller and deeper and more personal than in most other poetry, introduce an extremely modern element into his art. For parallels we find ourselves looking at the work of Henry James and of Yeats, and not to Browning's contemporaries. For his reticence is reflected in his technique, expressive and exploratory, which looks forward to that of the modern novel and of modern poetry. One form which this evasion takes is that

Browning's thought seeks cover in metaphorical images which become symbols, in such titles as *The Ring and the Book, Bells and Pomegranates, Turf and Towers*. Giorgio Melchiori has pointed out how later these metaphorical titles passed from poetry to prose in the work of Henry James.[3] Browning, at a time when titles were still largely descriptive, found in his later poetry this form of revealing and concealing increasingly attractive.

From his reticence, too, derives one of the main and most characteristic motifs of his work: the uncertainty as to truth. With *The Ring and the Book* and the multiple view of truth Browning was taking an important step in the direction of the novel, he was bringing the two arts of poetry and the novel very near together—for which he has never been forgiven. One of the things which I regret not having done in the present book is showing how well he did this, how he continued to use legitimate poetical techniques, how he sacrificed nothing of poetry except the *mystique* which we can so well do without, and found a Victorian form to replace the epic (which none of his contemporaries did successfully though many of them attempted it) and wrote the only satisfactory long poem since Byron's *Don Juan*. Browning's approach to the long poem is another demonstration of his consciousness of his own time, his awareness of being a writer of the nineteenth century: in the same way as his Don Juan in *Fifine* becomes an introverted Victorian husband, so the epic tradition, the narration of events of heroic proportions, becomes the close analysis of a single sordid event, and the method used is once again that of the monologue, revealing and hiding the psychology of the speaker and providing a series of versions of the same story, each of which is presented as biased, and which are not necessarily true even for the speakers themselves, who are taking into account their potential audience and the effect they wish to make on them. The subject is more appropriate to a novel, a historical novel, than to an epic, but the treatment it receives is connected with

[3] G. Melchiori, "Cups of gold for the Sacred Fount", in *The Critical Quarterly*, VII (1965), p. 301. I owe many of the ideas in this chapter to Giorgio Melchiori, particularly those concerning Browning's influence on twentieth-century prose and poetry. Fuller treatment of them can be found in his book, *The Tightrope Walkers*, London 1956, pp. 49-52, 104-6, and in "Browning e Henry James", *Friendship's Garland, Essays presented to Mario Praz*, ed. V. Gabrieli, Rome 1966, II. 143-80.

neither. With *The Ring and the Book* Browning not only demonstrates that a certain form of poetry will no longer serve, but he suggests to the novelists to what lengths the trend toward the interiorisation of the narrative could be taken. Henry James was right in considering *The Ring and the Book* as a novel, but this recognition came half a century later, when indeed the novel had taken the road pointed out by Browning's poem.[4] In the eighteen-sixties such concentration on the inner exploration of character and motive was inconceivable in prose, while poetry could deal with the subtler and more evasive shades of feeling. So it is appropriate that Browning should have written in verse the first modern novel, while later novelists like James, Conrad, Ford, Joyce, Virginia Woolf, and Henry Green wrote in a prose approaching nearer and nearer to verse techniques. Browning by carrying to its logical extreme the dramatic monologue established the technique of the point of view.

One qualification is necessary at this point: though the point-of-view structure is modern, the advance for Browning is rather in technique than in thought. For the poem is, after all, an epic of relativism, and it links up with the relativism of the Victorian age. It is based on Victorian morality, in the conclusion that Pompilia is innocent, a point as to which Browning leaves no doubt. But though the conclusion is Victorian, the structure allows for the plurality or even non-existence of truth. This is revolutionary in relation not only to poetry but also to narrative. Henry James, who read and thought much about Browning, and whose story "The Private Life" is equally important for an understanding of Browning and of James himself, followed in Browning's steps with the theory of the multiple point of view, a theory which reaches a further limit in the art of Pirandello, where truth can no longer be known. In *Così è (se vi pare)* we have a deliberate statement at the end by a veiled figure (today a face would seem more expressive and more hopelessly negative, but we can see that both Browning and James were leading up to just such a veiled

---

[4] See H. Sykes Davies, *Browning and the Modern Novel*, St John's College, Cambridge Lecture, Hull 1962; and E. Lucie-Smith's introduction to *A Choice of Browning's Verse*, London 1967.

revelation), a statement that both the conflicting and contradictory theories around which the play is woven are true, a statement made to an audience in which the awareness has been growing throughout the drama that truth can lie with neither. Nor had Pirandello taken the last step along the road of the point of view and the ambiguity of truth. James Joyce in *Finnegans Wake* muffles up the answer and even the questions in a cloak of words which Browning could only have envied. This, too, was a technique which he had begun to explore, yet another technique that springs from his reticence, giving rise to endless ambiguities. In *Sordello* words are used to conceal as much as to reveal, and we know that Browning took refuge in this technique quite deliberately after he had suffered intensely from the criticisms of the personal revelations he had made in his earlier and more Shelleyan *Pauline*. Sordello is Browning himself, but so wrapped in a mantle of words as to defy recognition, to discourage all prying and to defeat interpretation.

In his attempt at what I have called camouflage, Browning finds that the traditional literary media, neatly classified as lyric, epic, narrative, etc., will not serve, and he is forced to cut across the divisions and find more inclusive forms of poetical expression. The importance of Browning in breaking down the barriers of literary *genres* cannot be overrated. Though apparently working in the opposite direction to the aesthetics of art for art's sake, he succeeded in bypassing them to arrive at the same conclusions to which they had been leading, an attitude towards poetry and art which is concerned with processes, developments, relations rather than with finality and completeness. What matters is no longer the end of the story but a series of revelations of its inner meanings at different moments of its development. This is probably what Browning was trying to communicate when he wrote of alchemy, a metaphor for poetry:

> The prize is in the process: knowledge means
> Ever-renewed assurance by defeat
> That victory is somehow still to reach . . .[5]

lines not to be brushed aside as an expression of facile optimism but read as referring to a whole method of work. In the same

[5] "A Pillar at Sebzevar", 17-24.

way for Browning the short poem does not aim at defining once and for all a particular feeling, but at catching a fleeting state of mind with no sense of permanence or of finality. It is an attitude which was to be taken up and expressed as theory by the writers of the present century, not only by the novelists I have mentioned before, but also by the poets: Ezra Pound, who acknowledged his debt to Browning (and who gave the title of *Personae* to one of his earliest and best volumes of verse), and Eliot, whose major early works are dramatic monologues, although he was less willing to acknowledge his debt than Pound, possibly because Browning's reputation was at such a low ebb at the time. In Eliot, the listener is less identified than in Browning for Eliot combined Browning's dramatic monologue technique with that of the French symbolists. The very method of presentation by Pound and Eliot, their exclusion of logical links, of open statements is, to alter Pope's formula, reticence methodised. Browning's poetry of reticence, born as a personal defence, is transformed by them into a technique of expression.

In each of the essays in the present book I have laid the stress on Browning's reticence, examining its causes, which has inevitably led me to trespass into the field of psychology, terrain on which the literary critic ventures at his peril, and its results, which are the poetry proper. It is with this, with Browning's personal, at times peculiar, but none the less valid, kind of poetry that I have been concerned. In 1965 Geoffrey Tillotson wrote[6] one of the most useful modern essays on Browning, in which he does little more than select passages of the poetry and say to the student "Read this for yourself and see how good it is". Browning has been most notoriously abused, and most unfortunately ticketed and labelled, his poetry has repeatedly been called prose, and such uninviting words as "difficult" and "didactic" have continued to keep readers at a distance. A multiplicity of messages have been attributed to him, none of them having much meaning for the reader today, although the fashion of message-hunting dies hard.

[6] G. and K. Tillotson, *Mid-Victorian Studies*, "A Word for Browning", London 1965, pp. 110-17.

The idea that he is an artist, a great artist whose work can provide full and complete aesthetic enjoyment, has been put forward by only a few of the writers who have been concerned with his work. It comes across most fully I believe in the writings of William Clyde DeVane, and in the essays which W. O. Raymond collected under the title *The Infinite Moment*. I should like to think that the present essays add something to an understanding of this art, showing the use he made of his sources, his experiments, and his constant preoccupation with the art of writing, and that this analysis has not obscured the pleasure to be felt in reading Browning's poetry.

APPENDICES

A FRENCH SOURCE OF "ANDREA DEL SARTO"
IN DE MUSSET

As William Clyde DeVane pointed out in his *Handbook*[1] and in his *Browning's Parleyings*,[2] the principal source of Browning's monologue "Andrea del Sarto" was Vasari's *Le Vite dei più Eccellenti Pittori, Scultori, e Architetti*. There seems to be no doubt that Browning knew and used both the first edition of these *Lives* and the much modified and re-written second edition. A further Italian source, as DeVane points out again, was probably Filippo Baldinucci's *Notizie de' Professori del Disegno*, a book with which Browning was undoubtedly familiar.

These facts are generally known and accepted by Browning scholars, but I believe that no one has drawn attention to Alfred de Musset's play *André del Sarto*, which was first published in 1833 in *Un Spectacle dans un fauteuil*. This play, like Browning's poem, was based on Vasari's *Life* of Andrea. Either De Musset had read Vasari in the original, or, more probably, was familiar only with an abbreviated French version "les notices abrégées qui accompagnent les gravures du musée Filhol", which was, according to the anonymous editor of the *Mercure* edition (Paris 1910), "un des livres qu'il aimait le plus et qu'il feuilletait sans cesse". What I should like to suggest here is that Browning, who was living with his wife in Paris from September 1851 to November 1852, had the opportunity of seeing De Musset's play, which was re-written for performance in 1848, and staged again in 1850, 1851, 1853, and 1856. Even if he did not actually attend a performance, moving as he did in a literary society, he was probably stimulated to read the play.

A letter from Elizabeth Barrett Browning to Henrietta dated Paris, 1 April 1852 shows that Robert Browning and De Musset were moving in the same circles, although they did not, as far as our records go, touch:

> Robert went with our dear friend M. Milsand (noble and excellent he is) to the house of M. Buloz, the great man of the

---

[1] W. Clyde DeVane, *A Browning Handbook*, pp. 244-48.
[2] W. Clyde DeVane, *Browning's Parleyings*, pp. 173-76.

Revue des deux Mondes, where the Parisian literati of the first order are apt to congregate, last Saturday evening, by especial invitation, and was received with great cordiality, and much interested by what he saw and heard. Alfred De Musset who passes with some, as the first living French poet, was to have been there to meet him, but was hindered—another night, he says, he will do it.[3]

With George Sand the Brownings were more successful, as an enthusiastic letter, again from Elizabeth to Henrietta, dated 3 March 1852, shows:

Oh Henrietta—you will never guess what I am going to do tonight. I am going (by invitation) with Robert to see the first representation of George Sand's new play at the Gymnase. She wrote me the kindest note possible three days since. . . .[4]

DeVane is inclined to date Browning's poem early in 1853:

It is possible that *Andrea* may have been among those poems upon art and music which Browning describes himself as engaged upon, in his letter to Milsand on February 24, 1853. From a letter of Mrs. Browning's dated April 13, 1853, we know that Browning was deep in his study of Vasari at this time.[5]

When the definitive edition of the Brownings' correspondence is published, we may have conclusive evidence that Browning had read or seen De Musset's *André*. As it is, I should like to point out a few parallel passages between *André* and "Andrea" which are more easily explicable as direct borrowings than by reference to the common source of Vasari's *Life*.

De Musset's main contribution to the theme lies in his invention of the character of Cordiani, the lover of Lucrèce. Neither Vasari nor Baldinucci mention any such figure. Vasari speaks of Andrea as suffering from jealousy, but tells us nothing as to whether Lucrezia gave him any cause. The whole point of De Musset's melodramatic play turns, instead, on the triangle so created; and in Browning, too, the figure of the "cousin" is vitally important. Lucrezia is so occupied with the thought of the waiting "cousin" that only the wish to obtain money for him keeps her sitting still throughout her husband's monologue, to which she lends but half an ear, as her interpolation "What he?" in l. 199 shows. And throughout the

---

[3] Elizabeth Barrett Browning, *Letters to her Sister, 1846-59*, pp. 158-9.
[4] *Op. cit.*, p. 155.
[5] W. Clyde DeVane, *A Browning Handbook*, p. 245.

monologue the figure of the "cousin" is as present to Andrea as to his wife—he, too, is waiting for, and hears, the repeated whistle which calls her away from him.

But apart from the basic situation, which De Musset develops quite differently in the end (in the place of Andrea's resigned acceptance we have in *André* the stock duel of melodrama), there are a number of striking verbal echoes:

> ANDRÉ [*à* LUCRÈCE] Réponds-moi; qui t'amène à cette heure?
> As-tu une querelle? faut-il te servir de second? As-tu
> perdu au jeu? Veux-tu ma bourse?
> *Il lui prend la main.*[6]

> Must you go?
> That Cousin here again? he waits outside?
> Must see you—you, and not with me? Those loans?
> More gaming debts to pay?[7]

The gaming debts are transferred in Browning to the lover instead of the wife, but Vasari makes no mention of gaming, suggesting only that the French King's money was dissipated in "Murare e darsi piacere"—building and pleasure.

Then in both De Musset and Browning there is a passage, following immediately after the moment when the situation between the husband, wife and "friend" has been made clear, which is filled with the same tone of regret and longing:

> ANDRÉ: Les moments que nous passons ensemble sont si rares!
> et ils me sont si chers! Vous seule au monde, Lucrèce, me
> consolez de tous les chagrins qui m'obsèdent. Ah! si je
> vous perdais! Tout mon courage, toute ma philosophie
> est dans vos yeux.[8]

> Only let me sit
> The grey remainder of the evening out,
> Idle, you call it, and muse perfectly. . . .[9]

lines which echo the earlier

> should you let me sit
> Here by the window with your hand in mine
> And look a half-hour forth on Fiesole,

---

[6] A. de Musset, *André del Sarto*, I, III. This and all subsequent quotations from De Musset's plays are taken from his *Oeuvres*, Paris 1876, Vol. III.
[7] "Andrea del Sarto", 219-22.
[8] A. de Musset, *André del Sarto*, I, III.   [9] "Andrea del Sarto", 226-8.

Both of one mind, as married people use,
Quietly, quietly the evening through. . . .[10]

The identity of the situation is remarkable. Both husbands are trying, at any price, to retain their wives by their side. Neither has any illusions about the wife's real character, yet both are weak men afraid of losing Lucrezia and unable to face life without her. This timidity of character was hinted at in Vasari, where it is proffered as a reason for Andrea's failure to achieve greatness as a painter, but it is De Musset who develops the muted mood which keeps Browning's Andrea musing "quietly, quietly the evening through":

Ne me juge pas, mon ami, comme tu pourrais faire un autre
homme. Je suis un homme sans caractère, vois-tu?
J'étais né pour vivre tranquille.[11]

It is in this conception of the character of the painter, in a certain meekness and timidity, both pitiable and blamable, that I find the closest analogy between Browning's and De Musset's treatment of the subject. There are, however, some other points of similarity. Browning's Andrea declares that

I dared not, do you know, leave home all day,
For fear of chancing on the Paris lords.[12]

which echoes De Musset's

ANDRÉ: Point d'argent de ce juif! des supplications sans fin, et
point d'argent! Que dirai-je quand les envoyés du roi de
France. . . . Ah! André, pauvre André.[13]

Both authors may here be embroidering on Vasari's lines:

The King was so disgusted that it was a long time before he
would look kindly upon any Florentine painter, and he swore
that if he ever got Andrea into his power he would cause him
more pain than pleasure. . . .[14]

In Vasari, however, the "Paris lords" are wanting, while in De Musset they are present.

---

[10] *Op. cit.*, 13-17.
[11] A. de Musset, *André del Sarto*, III, II.
[12] "Andrea del Sarto", 145-6.
[13] A. de Musset, *André del Sarto*, I, II.
[14] G. Vasari, Life of Andrea del Sarto. I am quoting from the 1568 edition of Vasari, *Le Vite dei più Eccellenti Pittori, Scultori, e Architetti*. The English translation of this and subsequent quotations from Vasari is my own.

Again, Vasari gives a description of Andrea's life in the French court:

> When at last they reached the court, they were welcomed by the King with great kindness, and before a day had passed Andrea tasted of the liberality and courtesy of that munificent monarch, receiving gifts both of money and of rich and noble apparel. Soon afterwards he began to work and was appreciated by the king and by the whole court, and so much honoured by all, that his fate seemed to have led him from the depths of despair to the highest felicity.

But he does not define the length of Andrea's stay. De Musset instead writes, in a passage modelled on Vasari, of "une année de richesse et de bonheur"[15] which may easily have furnished Browning with that magnificent line

> And that long festal year at Fontainebleau![16]

Again, Andrea, weakly selling himself for the smiles of Lucrezia— "Well, let smiles buy me"—echoes De Musset's more conventional lines:

> La vie m'était moins chère que l'honneur, et l'honneur que l'amour de Lucrèce; que dis-je? qu'un sourire de ses lèvres, qu'un rayon de joie dans ses yeux. . . .[17]

The evening mood of the Fiesole scene, embracing as it does Andrea's very art

> A common greyness silvers everything . . .[18]

and

> My youth, my hope, my art, being all toned down
> To yonder sober pleasant Fiesole . . .[19]

seems again to be caught rather from De Musset than from Vasari:

> Je lutte en vain contre les ténèbres; le flambeau sacré s'éteint dans ma main.[20]

---

[15] A. de Musset, *André del Sarto*, II. I.
[16] "Andrea del Sarto", 150.
[17] A. de Musset, *André del Sarto*, II. I.
[18] "Andrea del Sarto", 35.
[19] *Op. cit.*, 39-40.
[20] A. de Musset, *André del Sarto*, II. I.

and the symbol of the sacred torch may have been in Browning's mind when he wrote

> There burns a truer light of God in them . . .[21]

and

> When the young man was flaming out his thoughts
> Upon a palace-wall for Rome to see. . . .[22]

The passages I have quoted, though providing no conclusive evidence, seem to me to suggest direct borrowing by Browning from De Musset, although De Musset's play as a whole is much more conventional and less subtle than Browning's monologue. It might easily, nevertheless, have touched off Browning's interest in the subject of Andrea in the first place, so that when he returned to Florence from Paris at the end of 1852 he looked with renewed interest at the paintings of Andrea del Sarto, and reopened his Vasari.

---

[21] "Andrea del Sarto", 79. [22] *Op. cit.*, 186-7.

Appendix B

THE PORTRAIT OF LUCREZIA

The reason Browning gave for writing "Andrea del Sarto" is that his friend John Kenyon desired a reproduction of a painting in the Pitti gallery depicting Andrea del Sarto and his wife. Unable to obtain a copy, Browning sent this pen-portrait instead.[1] The painting in question is probably No. 118 in the Pitti catalogue entitled *Il Pittore e sua Moglie* (*The Painter and his Wife*). There is considerable doubt as to whether it was, in fact, a self-portrait. It is generally thought today to be the work of a follower and not of Andrea himself, and although the title remains *The Painter and his Wife*, the commentator to the Pitti catalogue judges that the subject, too, is mistakenly ascribed. From the point of view of the poem, the important fact is that Browning and Kenyon did regard this as a self-portrait of the artist and his wife, but for the purpose of completeness I will list here other self-portraits of Andrea in Florence which Browning had certainly seen. There is a self-portrait, an "affresco staccato", at the Uffizi. At the Pitti (catalogue No. 191), there is an *Ascension of the Madonna* which contains a self-portrait, in the Apostle who is seen from the back, but who turns his face towards the viewer.

As for the portraits of Lucrezia, Browning makes a point in his poem of Andrea's frequent use of his wife:

> you must serve
> For each of the five pictures we require:
> It saves a model.[2]

It is probable that this was impressed on his mind by noticing the repetition of the same face in Andrea's paintings. Vasari, in the second edition of his *Life*, had likewise noted these repetitions:

> Two figures are kneeling in the foreground, a Magdalene with rich clothing, whose face is the portrait of his wife, for he nowhere portrayed a woman who was not modelled on her,

---

[1] This incident is related by Hall Griffin and Minchin, in *The Life of Robert Browning*, p. 20.

[2] "Andrea del Sarto", 23-5.

205

and even when it happened that sometimes he took another model, yet because he was so used to gazing at his wife, and had drawn her so many times, and even more, because she was so impressed on his mind, the result was that almost all the women's heads he painted resembled her.[3]

It seems probable that Browning, put on the track of this by Vasari, had enjoyed verifying it for himself in the Florentine galleries. The subtlety of "it saves a model", a direct appeal to Lucrezia's meanness, is his own.

It is curious, though perhaps fruitless, to wonder whether the fact, recorded by Vasari, that Andrea painted his wife as Mary Magdalene, may have provided a hint of Lucrezia's unfaithfulness to Browning and to De Musset before him; the unfaithfulness which has no historical basis. The painting in question is the *Disputation of the Trinity*, and the lower portion showing the figure of Mary Magdalene was considerably damaged by the flooding of the Arno in 1555, so that any influence it had on Browning probably came straight from the literary source of Vasari, and not from the painting directly, although as it is in the Pitti gallery, he would certainly have seen it.[4] But what mattered for Browning as source material was always the words of the art-historian or biographer, whether Vasari, Baldinucci, or Gerard de Lairesse: he was interested in paintings and looked at them carefully and in detail, but what comes out in his work is either the subject-matter (the story in the painting) or the life of the artist himself (the story behind the painting). Certainly in his "Andrea del Sarto" Browning makes no mention of Lucrezia posing for Mary Magdalene—he lays the stress quite the other way

> But still the other's [Andrea's] Virgin was his wife. . . .[5]

This would be psychologically in keeping with Andrea's attitude in the monologue: his refusal to face up to the situation of what his wife really is, which is suggested but not stated in such lines as

> Love, does that please you? Ah, but what does he,
> The Cousin! what does he to please you more?[6]

---

[3] See Appendix A, n. 14.

[4] Browning's insistence on Lucrezia's hair connects her with the figure of Mary Magdalene as represented in literature and the arts.

[5] "Andrea del Sarto", 179.

[6] *Op. cit.*, 242-3.

and in his musing on what he might have achieved as a painter had she been otherwise. The Andrea created by Browning would take pleasure in painting his wife as the Virgin, clothed even vicariously in the chastity he so desired in her. For the same reason he would be quite unable to portray her as Mary Magdalene. The historical and less sensitive Andrea could and did so portray her.

In writing the preceding line ("The Roman's [Raphael's Virgin] is the better when you pray"), Browning either ignores or overlooks the fact that Raphael's model for one of his celebrated Virgins (the Dresden Madonna of San Sisto) was his mistress, La Fornarina!

THE TAPESTRY HORSE

Against the consciously romantic background of "Childe Roland"
a landscape in which the sublime and horrible meet, stands the
gaunt and ominous figure of a horse:

> One stiff blind horse, his every bone a-stare,
> Stood stupified, however he came there. . . .[1]

Browning was unable, when writing the poem, to account for this
apparition, "However he came there", although later, when
questioned, he connected it with a horse in a tapestry in his own
drawing-room.[2]

I wish to suggest that before this domesticated animal entered
the poem it had been fused, by one of those strange tricks of a poet's
memory, with a more fearsome creature out of the stables of the
Count Berlifitzing in Poe's tale "Metzengerstein". A little the worse
for wear, old now, and blind, "Thrust out past service from the
devil's stud", he is the wreck of one of the most dramatic horses in
romantic fiction.

> Alive? he might be dead for aught I know,
> With that red gaunt and colloped neck a-strain,
> And shut eyes underneath the rusty mane;
> Seldom went such grotesqueness with such woe;
> I never saw a brute I hated so;
> He must be wicked to deserve such pain.[3]

Childe Roland, meeting with this wholly pitiable creature, is
filled with an irrational hatred, so irrational that Browning feels the
need for justification, and decides, improbably enough on the
surface, that "he must be wicked to deserve such pain". We have
to turn to Poe's "Metzengerstein" to understand the horror aroused

---

[1] "Childe Roland", 76-7.

[2] Cp. Mrs Sutherland Orr, *A Handbook to the Works of Robert Browning*, p. 274:
"I may venture to state that these picturesque materials included a tower which
Mr. Browning once saw in the Carrara mountains, a painting which caught his
eye years later in Paris; and the figure of a horse in the tapestry of his own drawing
room".

[3] "Childe Roland", 79-84.

by the horse in "Childe Roland", a horror so vivid for Browning
that he expects the reader to take it on trust.   There is little doubt
that Browning was familiar with "Metzengerstein".   The 1845
edition of Poe's poems bore a handsome dedication to Elizabeth
Barrett; and in their 1845-6 correspondence Elizabeth and Robert
Browning repeatedly mention and discuss not only Poe's poems but
also his tales.

The horse in Poe is first seen through the eyes of the Baron
Metzengerstein:

> his eyes were turned unwittingly to the figure of an enormous
> and unnaturally colored horse, represented in the tapestry as
> belonging to a Saracen ancestor of the family of his rival.   The
> horse itself, in the foreground of the design, stood motionless
> and statue-like—while, farther back, its discomfited rider
> perished by the dagger of a Metzengerstein. . . . The longer
> he gazed the more absorbing became the spell—the more
> impossible did it appear that he could ever withdraw his
> glance from the fascination of that tapestry.[4]

The attention of the Baron is, however, momentarily distracted by
the tumult from the blazing stables of his enemy Berlifitzing, which
had been set on fire.   Looking back at the tapestry

> To his extreme horror and astonishment, the head of the
> gigantic steed had, in the meantime, altered its position.   The
> neck of the animal, before arched, as if in compassion, over the
> prostrate body of its lord, was now extended, at full length, in
> the direction of the Baron.   The eyes, before invisible, now
> wore an energetic and human expression, while they gleamed
> with a fiery and unusual red; and the distended lips of the
> apparently enraged horse left in full view his sepulchral and
> disgusting teeth.[5]

Badly shaken, the Baron rushes out for air, to be met by his
servants "restraining the convulsive plunges of a gigantic and fiery
colored horse", and he "became instantly aware that the mysterious
steed in the tapestried chamber was the very counterpart of the
furious animal before his eyes".   A page runs out to inform him at
the same moment that a small portion of the tapestry has dis-
appeared.   The horse has W.V.B. (Wilhelm Von Berlifitzing)

---

[4] Edgar Allan Poe, *The Complete Tales and Poems*, Modern Library, New York
1938, p. 674.
[5] *Ibid.*

branded on its forehead. Another messenger hurries up to inform
the Baron that his enemy Berlifitzing has perished miserably in the
flames in the attempt to rescue a part of his hunting stud. The
Baron at this point is "slowly and deliberately impressed with the
truth of some exciting idea".[6] Nor has the reader any difficulty in
following him, for Poe has prefaced his tale with a brief discussion
of what he calls "the Hungarian superstition of Metempsychosis".
There are some points, Poe tells us, "which were fast verging to
absurdity": the soul *"ne demeure qu'une seule fois dans un corps sensible:
au reste—un cheval, un chien, un homme même, n'est que la resemblance peu
tangible de ces animaux"*.[7] This is the "absurdity" which he sets out to
illustrate in his tale—the diabolic horse is a reincarnation of the
Count Berlifitzing after his violent death in the burning stables,
taking the semblance of the tapestry horse: "the devil from the
stables of Berlifitzing", recalled in Browning as "from the devil's
stud".[8]

The purpose underlying this reincarnation is one of vengeance.
The horse, first seen in the original tapestry as arching its neck as
though in compassion over the prostrate body of its lord, has now
become a creature wholly given to evil—and it is in this position,
with neck a-strain, that Browning recalls it. Nor is it vengeance for
a single deed, but, as in "Childe Roland", there is a long history of
deaths to be avenged. Here the vengeance takes place within the
framework of the hereditary hatred of the two families, Berlifitzing
and Metzengerstein: "Never before were two houses so illustrious,
mutually embittered by hostility so deadly".[9] The vengeance is
dramatically achieved. The fiery horse, of which the "ferocious and
demon-like propensities" are constantly stressed, took possession of
the young Baron Metzengerstein, who fell completely under his
influence. No one doubted the affection of the young nobleman
"for the fiery qualities of his horse" except a "misshapen little page"
(who perhaps puts in a brief appearance as the "hateful cripple" of
"Childe Roland") asserting that

> his master never vaulted into the saddle without an unaccount-
> able and imperceptible shudder; and that, upon his return from
> every long-continued and habitual ride, an expression of
> triumphant malignity distorted every muscle of his counten-
> ance.[10]

So the struggle between man and beast goes on, until the climax
of the final vengeance. Returning from a night ride "the stupendous

---

[6] *Op. cit.*, p. 676.   [7] *Op. cit.*, p. 672.   [8] "Childe Roland", 78.
[9] E. A. Poe, *Complete Tales and Poems*, p. 672.   [10] *Op. cit.*, p. 677.

and magnificent battlements of the Palace Metzengerstein, were discovered crackling and rocking to their very foundation, under the influence of a dense and livid mass of ungovernable fire". Up the tottering staircases of the palace the steed bears its helpless rider into "the whirlwind of chaotic fire".

> The fury of the tempest immediately died away, and a dead calm sullenly succeeded. A white flame still enveloped the building like a shroud, and, streaming far away into the quiet atmosphere, shot forth a glare of preternatural light; while a cloud of smoke settled heavily over the battlements in the distinct colossal figure of—*a horse*.[11]

What were the elements that attracted Browning to this, one of the most memorable of Poe's tales, and enabled it to take such a hold on his imagination? In the first place, possibly Poe's own introduction, his scientific investigation of the theory of the supernatural. It was the kind of approach Browning himself found attractive. He was to write "An Epistle containing the Strange Medical Experience of Karshish", and "Mr Sludge, 'The Medium' ", both showing his interest in the occult. But what he took from Poe's tale is not the subject-matter, but rather the atmosphere. There is the sense of hatred: the only living creatures that Childe Roland meets are the "hateful cripple" and the horse that he "hated so", besides the black bird "Apollyon's bosom friend". The atmosphere and the sense of supernatural terror—then—but even more than these there are the pictorial effects: "the sheet of flame" with which "Childe Roland" ends has something of the same violent drama as the "white flame" and "glare of preternatural light" of the final scene in "Metzengerstein". Above all there is the visual impact of the figure of the tapestry horse itself "with that red gaunt and colloped neck a-strain", the neck that in Poe is "extended, at full length, in the direction of the Baron". The horse is first seen in Poe in "the glare of ruddy light" of the blazing stables, and in Browning in the "grim red leer" of the sunset.

This passage shows, too, an odd verbal recollection. Browning writes in "Childe Roland":

> All the day
> Had been a dreary one at best, and dim
> Was settling to its close, yet shot one grim
> Red leer to see the plain catch its estray.[12]

---

11 *Op. cit.*, p. 678.
12 "Childe Roland", 45-8.

"Estray" is rather a rare word, not in common usage in English, so rare, indeed, that such popular dictionaries as the *Pocket Oxford Dictionary* or *Everyman's* do not list it at all. Webster instead gives this definition: "*in law*: any valuable animal, not wild, found wandering from its owner"; and as a second meaning "anything out of its normal place, *v.i.* to stray". And this is the sense in which Browning uses it. It is a person straying, the estray is Childe Roland himself, and the plain catches or closes in around him. The same word is used in "Metzengerstein" in its first or legal sense. The groom who finds the horse after the fire, leads him up to the Baron, saying

> He is your own property, sire . . . at least he is claimed by no other owner. We caught him flying, all smoking and foaming with rage, from the burning stables of the Castle Berlifitzing. Supposing him to have belonged to the old Count's stud of foreign horses we led him back as an estray.[13]

Browning was a poet who always made use of a very wide vocabulary. His supposed obscurity is in part due simply to this, to his use of technical terminology, often out of the expected context, or with insufficient explanation. It was only natural that a word like "estray" should have remained in his mind and should have come back to him when he was recalling the horse, and it confirmed the link between the threat in the red light of the sunset—"one grim red leer"—and the glare of the blazing stables of Berlifitzing, preparing the way for the entrance of Metzengerstein's horse.

The stiff blind horse evoked in Browning's mind all the fear and terror of the fiery horse in Poe, whether this horse had been torn straight out of the tapestry in Baron Metzengerstein's apartment, or whether it had also been torn from Browning's own drawing-room, as Mrs Orr tells us. In Poe's tapestry the horse stands "motionless and statue-like", in Browning's "stiff" and "stupified", he "might be dead for aught I know", stressing both that he is part of the picture and reminding us of the theory which gave him birth, that the soul "*ne demeure qu'une seule fois dans un corps sensible*".

In "Childe Roland" the description of the horse occupies only nine lines in a poem of two hundred and four lines; and the horse does not take any "active" part in the weird story. Technically it is simply a part of the landscape description, unlike, for example, the "hoary cripple with malicious eye", who serves instead to point the

---

[13] E. A. Poe, *Complete Tales and Poems*, p. 675.

way. The function of the horse is simply to introduce all the fear and horror that Poe, who was a master in the *genre* of the horrific, had been able to confer on the animal in one of his most impressive tales. It was not necessary for either Browning or the reader to make the conscious connexion, it is enough that the poem is enriched by the association.

THE COURTSHIP OF ROBERT BROWNING AND THE MUTILATION OF MONSIEUR LÉONCE MIRANDA

Several elements in Robert Browning's strange tale *Red Cotton Night-Cap Country* seem to contain recollections of his courtship with Elizabeth Barrett twenty-six years earlier, but one curious link has remained, I believe, unobserved. This is the self-mutilation of the goldsmith who, after the decision to separate from his mistress, re-reads her old love letters:

> Monsieur Léonce Miranda, one by one,
> Had read the letters and the love they held,
> And, that task finished, had required his soul
> To answer frankly what the prospect seemed
> Of his own love's departure—pledged to part![1]

In the poem the result of this re-perusal is dramatic, for he burns the letters and with them his own hands off at the wrists:

> Then, answer being unmistakable,
> He had replaced the letters quietly,
> Shut coffer, and so, grasping either side
> By its convenient handle, plunged the whole—
> Letters and coffer and both hands to boot,
> Into the burning grate and held them there.[2]

This mutilation has a historical basis in the madness of a certain Antonio Mellerio (see DeVane's *Handbook*), but as a choice of material for poetry it has always remained puzzling. I should like to suggest that it had a more personal meaning for Browning.

Read in conjunction with some extraordinary mutilation images in Browning's early letters to Elizabeth (26 May 1845 and 25 September 1845), letters written at a difficult stage in his courtship, when she was refusing to consider marriage, this gesture of Miranda may well be seen as castration symbolism. The relevant passages in the letters, written when it seemed to Browning that he

---

[1] *Red Cotton Night-Cap Country*, 2579-83.   [2] *Op. cit.*, 2584-90.

would have to content himself with a life-long *friendship* with the poetess, are the following:

> since the offering to cut off one's right-hand to save anybody a headache, is in vile taste . . . how much worse to really make the ugly chop, and afterwards come sheepishly in, one's arm in a black sling, and find that the delectable gift had changed aching to nausea![3]

and (the inset quotations are present in the original, and are passages from her letters to which he is replying):

> Chop off your legs, you will never go astray; stifle your reason altogether and you will find it difficult to reason ill. "It is hard to make these sacrifices!"—not so hard as to lose the reward or incur the penalty of an Eternity to come; "hard to effect them, then, and go through with them"—*not* hard, when the leg is to be *cut off*,—that it is rather harder to keep it quiet on a stool I know very well.[4]

This letter ends: "I would be no more than one of your brothers." Clearly they were difficult months for the poet, and must have left a deep impression on him. The castration images which have slipped into the letters probably did so because of the freedom and lack of control with which he was confessedly writing, for the second letter contains the admission:

> I fling these hasty rough words over the paper, fast as they will fall—knowing to whom I cast them, and that any sense they may contain or point to, will be caught and understood, and presented in a better light.[5]

It is interesting to speculate how far "any sense they may contain or point to" was really "caught and understood" by Elizabeth. Enough, at least, to allow her in time to be over-persuaded.

---

[3] *The Letters of Robert Browning and Elizabeth Barrett Barrett.*
[4] *Op. cit.*   [5] *Op. cit.*

PERSONAL INVOLVEMENT IN
"THE FLIGHT OF THE DUCHESS"

J. M. Cohen defined "The Flight of the Duchess" as a fantasy:

> For the poem was, in essence, the product of an unnoticed day-dream, that twice required the stimulus of a magic and suggestive phrase to bring it to consciousness, and such fantasy can, at times, speak more truly of a man's deep experience than do tales or reasonings that have undergone a more vigorous intellectual sifting.[1]

I have already drawn attention to the dream-change undergone by the gypsy; and I fully agree with Cohen's reading of the poem as a day-dream. It is even curious to note the number of verbal echoes from another dream poem, "Kubla Khan", especially in

> And the very tresses shared in the pleasure,
> Moving to the mystic measure,
> Bounding as the bosom bounded. . . .

> . . . left them midway in the world

> Breathless, half in trance.

The trend which this particular fantasy of Browning's took is intimately connected with the time when the poem was written. Stanzas x-xvii were written during Browning's difficult courtship. The theory that the poem was deliberately written and utilised by Browning as part of his courtship has been put forward by Fred Manning Smith[2] and accepted by DeVane. Edward Snyder and Frederic Palmer have examined the changes in the text of "The Flight of the Duchess" proposed by Elizabeth Barrett in her letter to Browning of July 1845. They believe that Browning wished her

---

[1] J. M. Cohen, *Robert Browning*, p. 40.

[2] See W. Clyde DeVane, *A Browning Handbook*, pp. 171-6; and Fred Manning Smith, "Elizabeth Barrett and Browning's *Flight of the Duchess*" and "More light on Elizabeth Barrett and Browning's *Flight of the Duchess*", both in *Studies in Philology*, XXXIX (1942), pp. 102-17, 693-5.

to study the poem with especial care because it contains the message that "a brilliant, vital woman withering in her home under the deadening influence of her own family does well to cut all ties and seek salvation in a new life . . .".[3]

While the biographical interest of the poem is thus agreed on, no comment has been made on its marked sexual motivation, although Cohen, in the passage I have quoted, comes closest to sensing a hidden stimulus.

The dawn landscape passage with which the fantasy section opens in stanza x (the preceding stanzas were written at an earlier date and in quite another key),[4] seems to me to set, in an undertone, the whole mood for the dramatic changes which ensue in the quiet life of the Duchess:

> When the stag had to break with his foot, of a morning,
> A drinking-hole out of the fresh tender ice
> That covered the pond till the sun, in a trice,
> Loosening it, let out a ripple of gold,
> And another and another, and faster and faster,
> Till, dimpling to blindness, the wide water rolled. . . .[5]

The image of the stag's foot breaking the ice, the thawing warmth of the sun (a common symbol for sexual awakening) the adjective "tender" which fits the under-reading better than the surface one, add up to a statement of the basic theme of the poem. The source of the scene described, the frosty morning and the stag, were a reminiscence of a visit paid by Browning to Sir John Hanmer at Bettisfield Park. The surface connexion would be sufficient justification for its inclusion in the poem: the stag on the autumn morning was an introduction of the hunting theme. But the under-reading to which I am here drawing attention tells us more. The images in the descriptive passage were more closely linked with the basic meaning of the poem: the sexual awakening of the young Duchess.

In these lines the loss of virginity is seen as a natural process, as something gentle, tender, and beautiful, in no way terrifying to the tiny Duchess, "the smallest lady alive", who had married out of a convent. Such, the poem suggests, should have been her initiation, but instead the Duke prepares a ruder awakening. We have here a situation not unlike that of Pompilia in the later *The Ring and the*

---

[3] E. Snyder and F. Palmer, "New Light on the Brownings", in *The Quarterly Review*, 269 (1937), pp. 48-63.

[4] W. Clyde DeVane, *A Browning Handbook*, p. 174.

[5] "The Flight of the Duchess", 217-22.

Book, a child bride for a time left alone by her husband, wife only in name, and with a similar horror of that husband. All this is explained openly in *The Ring and the Book*, but here the same story is told only through the imagery. Yet the meaning of the hunt prepared by the Duke is unmistakable;[6] indeed, with all due solemnity he makes

> the announcement with proper unction
> That he had discovered the lady's function. . . .[7]

The naïveté of these words would suggest that Browning was unaware of the full meaning of what he was writing. However, the lady's function, as indicated by medieval hunting usage, is simply to take her rightful place in the marriage bed, to serve her lordship's pleasure:

> When horns wind a mort and the deer is at siege,
> Let the dame of the castle prick forth on her jennet,
> And, with water to wash the hands of her liege
> In a clean ewer with a fair toweling,
> Let her preside at the disemboweling.[8]

Not only have we the horn, death, riding, and ewer symbols, but the marriage sheets are suggested by the "fair toweling" while "disemboweling" is a basic traditional literary symbol for the sexual act. Browning may even have had in mind Donne's lines:

> And at the Bridegroomes wish'd approach doth lye,
> Like an appointed lambe, when tenderly
> The priest comes on his knees t'embowell her.[9]

Like Pompilia, the young Duchess, affrighted "thanking him, declined the hunting", but unlike Pompilia she makes her escape in time. The plea of the lady is on the grounds of health

> But spoke of her health, if her health were worth aught,
> Of the weight by day and the watch by night,
> And much wrong now that used to be right. . . .[10]

---

[6] In *The Ring and the Book*, vi, 1286, a hunting image is used of Pompilia fleeing from Guido, again with obvious sexual overtones. Her terror at her husband's approach is expressed in terms of a hunted fawn threatened by a "probing spear": ". . . like the fawn's /Tired to death in the thicket, when she feels /The probing spear o' the huntsman".

[7] "The Flight of the Duchess", 260-1.   [8] *Op. cit.*, 263-7.

[9] John Donne, "Epithalamion made at Lincolnes Inne", 88-90.

[10] "The Flight of the Duchess", 287-9.

which links the poem with Browning's own situation, in his wooing of a sick woman. That the whole poem is impregnated with sexual imagery can be seen from a passage near the end, where the old retainer, telling the story, uses the following words:

> What's a man's age? He must hurry more, that's all;
> Cram in a day, what his youth took a year to hold:
> When we mind labour, then only, we're too old—
> What age had Methusalem when he begat Saul?
> And at last, as its haven some buffeted ship sees,
> (Come all the way from the north-parts with sperm oil)
> I hope to get safely out of the turmoil
> And arrive one day at the land of the Gipsies,
> And find my lady. . . .[11]

This is not part of the story, but simply the meditations of the narrator: what need, we may well ask, had Browning to employ the image of the ship entering harbour, or to mention the begetting of Saul (Elizabeth's age was one of her chief pleas against the proposed marriage, and the "hurry more" reasoning may have been an answer to this), and why should the ship in question be carrying the un-poetical cargo of sperm-oil? The explanation lies simply in the fact that the underlying meaning was forcing itself, clumsily enough, to the surface: "The Flight of the Duchess" is a poem concerning the sexual awakening of the girl from the convent, and reflecting Browning's preoccupation with his own emotional situation at the time of his courtship, as he tried, in the words of the folk-song, to persuade Elizabeth to leave her house and gold and goose-feather bed to lead a less protected life with him. It is important to recognise this to see how, when he picked up the Old Yellow Book, Browning found "a subject made to *his* hand", for the basic situation was one which he had already gone a long way towards imagining and interpreting. A full analysis of "The Flight of the Duchess" would undoubtedly yield very much more, but I am interested here in pointing out that Browning's personal involvement with the theme, which has already been acknowledged on the conscious level, runs through the whole web of the poem's imagery.

---

[11] *Op. cit.*, 881-9.

Bibliography

I. WORKS BY ROBERT BROWNING

The Works of Robert Browning, ed. F. G. Kenyon. Centenary edn, 10 vols. London 1912.
The Poetical Works of Robert Browning, ed. A. Birrell. New edn, 2 vols. London 1929.
A Choice of Browning's Verse, ed. Edward Lucie-Smith. London 1967.
The Letters of Robert Browning and Elizabeth Barrett Barrett. 2 vols. London 1899.
Browning to his American Friends, ed. Gertrude Reese Hudson. London 1965.

II. WORKS ABOUT ROBERT BROWNING

1. BOOKS

BENZIGER, JAMES. *Images of Eternity.* Carbondale 1963.
BERLIN-LIEBERMAN, JUDITH. *Robert Browning and Hebraism. A study of the poems of Browning which are based on Rabbinical writings and other sources in Jewish Literature.* Jerusalem. 1934.
BROOKE, STOPFORD A. *The Poetry of Robert Browning.* London 1902.
BROWNING, ELIZABETH BARRETT. *Letters to her Sister 1846-59,* ed. Leonard Huxley. London 1929.
BURROWS, LEONARD. *Browning, an Introductory Essay.* Perth (Australia) 1952.
CHESTERTON, GILBERT KEITH. *Robert Browning.* London 1903.
COHEN, J. M. *Robert Browning.* London 1952.
CROWELL, NORTON B. *The Triple Soul, Browning's Theory of Knowledge.* Albuquerque 1963.
DAVIES, HUGH SYKES. *Browning and the Modern Novel.* St John's College, Cambridge Lecture, 1961-2. Hull 1962.
DEVANE, W. CLYDE. *Browning's Parleyings: The Autobiography of a Mind.* New Haven 1927.
——. *A Browning Handbook.* 2nd edn. New York 1955.
DREW, PHILIP. See *Robert Browning, a Collection of Critical Essays.*
DUCKWORTH, F. R. G. *Browning: Background and Conflict.* London 1931.
DUFFIN, HENRY CHARLES. *Amphibian, a Reconsideration of Browning.* London 1956.

FOAKES, R. A. *The Romantic Assertion.* London 1958.
GRIFFIN, W. HALL, AND HARRY CHRISTOPHER MINCHIN. *The Life of Robert Browning.* London 1938.
HONAN, PARK. *Browning's Characters, a Study in Poetic Technique.* New Haven 1961.
HOVELACQUE, HENRI-LÉON. *La Jeunesse de Robert Browning.* Paris 1932.
HUTTON, JOHN A. *Guidance from Robert Browning in Matters of Faith.* Edinburgh 1903.
KING, ROMA A. *The Bow and the Lyre: The Art of Robert Browning.* Ann Arbor 1957.
LANGBAUM, ROBERT. *The Poetry of Experience: The Dramatic Monologue in Modern Literary Tradition.* London 1957.
MACHEN, MINNIE GRESHAM. *The Bible in Browning.* New York 1903.
MILLER, BETTY. *Robert Browning, a Portrait.* London 1952.
MILLER, J. HILLIS. *Of the Disappearance of God: Five Nineteenth-Century Writers.* Cambridge (Mass.) 1963.
NETTLESHIP, J. T. *Robert Browning: Essays and Thoughts.* London 1895.
ORR, MRS SUTHERLAND. *A Handbook to the Works of Robert Browning.* London 1913.
PHELPS, WILLIAM LYON. *Robert Browning: How to Know Him.* London 1915.
RAYMOND, WILLIAM O. *The Infinite Moment and Other Essays in Robert Browning.* Toronto 1950.
REUL, PAUL DE. *L'Art et la pensée de Robert Browning.* Brussels 1929.
Robert Browning, a Collection of Critical Essays, ed. Philip Drew. London 1966.
SYMONS, ARTHUR W. *An Introduction to the Study of Browning.* New edn. London 1906.
WALKER, HUGH. *The Greater Victorian Poets.* London 1895.

2. ARTICLES AND ESSAYS

BAGEHOT, WALTER. "Wordsworth, Tennyson and Browning, or, Pure, Ornate and Grotesque Art in English Poetry", in *Literary Studies,* vol. 2, ed. R. H. Hutton. London 1895.
BALL, PATRICIA M. "Browning's Godot", in *Victorian Poetry,* III (1965), pp. 245-53.
BODKIN, MAUD. "A Note on Browning's Childe Roland", in *Literature and Psychology,* X, 2 (1960), p. 37.
BROWN, E. K. "The First Person in 'Caliban upon Setebos' ", in *Modern Language Notes,* LXVI (1951), pp. 392-5.
CHIARENZA, FRANK J. "Browning's 'The Bishop Orders his Tomb at Saint Praxed's Church' ", in *The Explicator,* XIX (1961), §22.
COHEN, J. M. "The Young Robert Browning", in *The Cornhill Magazine,* 975 (1948), pp. 234-48.
COWAN, JAMES. "Literary Criticism and Projection", in *The Kansas Magazine* (1960), pp. 84-7.

CUNDIFF, PAUL A. "The Clarity of Browning's Ring Metaphor", in *PMLA*, LXIII (1948), pp. 1276-82.

DEVANE, W. CLYDE. "The Landscape of Browning's 'Childe Roland' ", in *PMLA*, XL (1925), pp. 426-32.

——. "The Harlot and the Thoughtful Young Man: A Study of the Relation between Rossetti's *Jenny* and Browning's *Fifine at the Fair*", in *Studies in Philology*, XXIX (1932), pp. 463-84.

——. "The Virgin and the Dragon", in *Yale Review*, XXXVII (1947), pp. 33-46.

DREW, PHILIP. "Henry Jones on Browning's Optimism", in *Victorian Poetry*, II (1964), pp. 29-41.

——. "Another View of *Fifine at the Fair*", in *Essays in Criticism*, XVII (1967), pp. 244-55.

DUNCAN, JOSEPH E. "John Donne and Robert Browning", in *The Revival of Metaphysical Poetry*. Minneapolis 1959, pp. 50-68.

ERDMAN, DAVID V. "Browning's Industrial Nightmare", in *Philological Quarterly*, XXXVI, 4 (1957), pp. 417-35.

FRIEDLAND, L. S. "Ferrara and 'My Last Duchess' ", in *Studies in Philology*, XXXIII (1936), pp. 656-84.

GOLDER, HAROLD. "Browning's 'Childe Roland' ", in *PMLA*, XXXIX (1924), pp. 963-78.

GOLDFARB, RUSSELL M. "Sexual Meaning in 'The Last Ride Together' ", in *Victorian Poetry*, III (1965), pp. 255-61.

GRATZ, R. J. "The Journey of Childe Roland", in *Poet Lore*, II (1890), pp. 578-85.

HIGGINSON, THOMAS WENTWORTH. " 'Childe Roland to the Dark Tower Came' ", in *Poet Lore*, XIII (1901), pp. 262-8.

HITNER, JOHN M. "Browning's Grotesque Period", in *Victorian Poetry*, IV (1966), pp. 1-13.

HOLMES STEWART W. "Browning: Semantic Stutterer", in *PMLA*, LX (1945), pp. 231-55.

HOWARD, JOHN. "Caliban's Mind", in *Victorian Poetry*, I (1963), pp. 249-57.

HUEBENTHAL, JOHN. "The Dating of Browning's 'Love among the Ruins', 'Women and Roses', and 'Childe Roland' ", in *Victorian Poetry*, IV (1966), pp. 51-4.

HUGHES, R. E. "Browning's 'Childe Roland' and the Broken Taboo", in *Literature and Psychology*, IX, 2 (1959), pp. 18-19.

KIRKMAN, J. *Browning Society Papers*, I (1881-4), meeting of March 24, 1882, p. 21.

LAW, ROBERT ADGER. "The Background of Browning's 'Love among the Ruins' ", in *Modern Language Notes*, XXXVII (1922), p. 312-3.

LINDBERG, JOHN. "Grail Themes in Browning's 'Childe Roland' ", in *Victorian Newsletter*, XVI (Fall 1959), pp. 27-30.

LOWE, ROBERT LIDDELL. "Browning and Donne", in *Notes and Queries*, CXCVIII (1953), pp. 491-2.

MELCHIORI, GIORGIO. "Cups of Gold for the Sacred Fount", in *The Critical Quarterly*, VII (1965), pp. 301-16.

——. "Browning e Henry James", in *Friendship's Garland, Essays presented to Mario Praz*, ed. Vittorio Gabrieli, Rome 1966, II, pp. 143-80.

PARR, JOHNSTONE. "The Date of Composition of Browning's 'Love among the Ruins' ", in *Philological Quarterly*, XXXII (1953), pp. 443-6.

REA, JOHN D. " 'My Last Duchess' ", in *Studies in Philology*, XXIX (1932), pp. 120-2.

SHANKS, EDWARD. "Robert Browning", in *The London Mercury*, XII (1925), pp. 180-9.

SMITH, FRED MANNING. "Elizabeth Barrett and Browning's 'The Flight of the Duchess' ", in *Studies in Philology*, XXXIX (1942), pp. 102-17.

——. "More Light on Elizabeth Barrett and Browning's 'The Flight of the Duchess' ", in *Studies in Philology*, XXXIX (1942), pp. 693-5.

SNYDER, EDWARD, AND FREDERIC PALMER. "New Light on the Brownings", in *The Quarterly Review*, 269 (1937), pp. 48-63.

STEVENSON, L. "The Pertinacious Victorian Poets", in *The University of Toronto Quarterly*, XXI (1952), pp. 232-45.

TILLOTSON, GEOFFREY. "A Word for Browning", in GEOFFREY AND KATHLEEN TILLOTSON. *Mid-VictorianStudies*. London 1965, pp. 110-117.

TRACY, C. R. "Browning's Heresies", in *Studies in Philology*, XXXIII (1936), pp. 610-25.

——. " 'Caliban upon Setebos' ", in *Studies in Philology*, XXXV (1938), pp. 489-99.

WILLOUGHBY, JOHN W. "Browning's 'Childe Roland to the Dark Tower Came' ", in *Victorian Poetry*, I (1963), pp. 291-9.

WOODWARD, CHARLES R. "The Road to the Dark Tower: Browning's 'Childe Roland' ", *Tennessee Studies in Literature* Special Number—Studies in Honor of John C. Hodges and Alwin Thaler. Knoxville 1961, pp. 93-9.

III. OTHER BOOKS CITED IN THE TEXT

AFFÒ, P. IRENEO. *Vita di Vespasiano Gonzaga*. Parma 1780.

ALIGHIERI, DANTE. *Divina Commedia*.

ARIOSTO, LODOVICO. *Orlando Furioso*.

BALDINUCCI, FILIPPO. *Notizie de' Professori del Disegno*. Florence 1767-74.

BARRETT BROWNING, ELIZABETH. *Poetical Works*. London 1850.

BARTOLI, DANIELLO. *Dei Simboli Trasportati al Morale*. Rome 1677.

BAUDELAIRE, CHARLES. *Les Fleurs du mal*.

BUNYAN, JOHN. *The Pilgrim's Progress*, ed. J. B. Wharey. Oxford 1928.

BUTLER, SAMUEL. *The Way of All Flesh*. Oxford 1944.

COLERIDGE, SAMUEL TAYLOR. *Collected Poems*. London 1924.

COMINES, PHILIPPE DE. *Mémoires*. Paris 1524-8.

DARWIN, CHARLES. *The Origin of Species*. London 1859.

DICKENS, CHARLES. *A Christmas Carol*.

DONNE, JOHN. *Poems*, ed. H. J. C. Grierson. London 1912.

DRYDEN, JOHN. *The Poems and Fables*, ed. James Kinsley. London 1962.
ELIOT, THOMAS STEARNS. *Collected Poems, 1909-35*. London 1936.
EMPSON, WILLIAM. *Seven Types of Ambiguity*. London 1930.
EVELYN, JOHN. *The Dairy of John Evelyn*, ed. E. S. de Beer. 6 vols. Oxford 1955.
FREUD, SIGMUND. *Works*. "Standard Edition." 24 vols. London 1953-66.
FRIEDLAENDER, MICHAEL. *The Commentary of Ibn Ezra on Isaiah*. London 1873.
GOLDING, WILLIAM. *The Spire*. London 1964.
HALLIDAY, JAMES L. *Mr Carlyle, My Patient: A Psychosomatic Biography*. London 1949.
HILLARD, GEORGE STILLMAN. *Six Months in Italy*. New York 1853.
HODELL, CHARLES W. See *The Old Yellow Book*.
JAMES, HENRY. *The Complete Tales*, ed. Leon Edel. 12 vols. London 1962-4.
JAMES, HENRY. *William Wetmore Story and his Friends*. Edinburgh 1903.
JAMIESON, ROBERT. Translator, *Illustrations of Northern Antiquities from the Earlier Teutonic and Scandinavian Romances*. Edinburgh 1814.
JOYCE, JAMES. *Finnegans Wake*. London 1939.
KAYSER, W. *The Grotesque in Art and Literature*. Bloomington 1963.
LAIRESSE, GERARD DE. *The Art of Painting in All its Branches*. Translated by J. F. Fritsch. London 1778.
LANDOR, WALTER SAVAGE. *Imaginary Conversations and Poems, a Selection*, ed. Havelock Ellis. London 1933.
MELCHIORI, GIORGIO. *The Tightrope Walkers: Studies of Mannerism in Modern English Literature*. London 1956.
MUSSET (DE), ALFRED. *André del Sarto*, in *Oeuvres*, III. Paris 1876.
PARKER, THEODORE. *A Discourse of Matters pertaining to Religion*. Boston 1907.
PIRANDELLO, LUIGI. *Maschere Nude*, Vol. I. Milan 1919.
POE, EDGAR ALLAN. *The Complete Tales and Poems*, intr. Hervey Allen. New York 1938.
POUND, EZRA. *Personae*. London 1952.
PRAZ, MARIO. *The Hero in Eclipse in Victorian Fiction*, tr. Angus Davidson. London 1956.
Reime und Gedichte des Abraham Ibn Ezra, ed. David Rosen. Breslau 1885-8.
ROSEN, DAVID. See *Reime und Gedichte*. . . .
ROSSETTI, DANTE GABRIEL. *Poems and Translations*. London 1912.
SHAKESPEARE, WILLIAM. *The Tempest*, ed. Kermode. London, 1954.
TENNYSON, ALFRED. *The Poetical Works*. London 1907.
The Old Yellow Book, ed. Charles W. Hodell. Washington 1908.
VASARI, GIORGIO. *Le Vite dei più Eccellenti Pittori, Scultori, e Architetti*. Florence 1550, 1568.
WALTON, MRS O. F. *A Peep Behind the Scenes*. London 1877.
WHITING, LILIAN. *The Brownings*. Boston 1917.
WILDE, OSCAR. *Selected Works*, ed. R. Aldington. London 1947.
WILSON, EDMUND. *The Triple Thinkers*. Harmondsworth 1962.

Index

I. General Index

Abel: 144.
Aberdeen Journal: 92, 112.
Abraham: 41, 52, 94.
Affò, Ireneo: *Vita di Vespasiano Gonzaga*, 21, 22, 223.
Aldington, R.: 140n, 224.
Alfonso II, Duke of Ferrara: 22.
Alighieri, Dante: *Divina Commedia*, 2n, 223.
Amsterdam Stedelijk Museum: 19n.
Andromeda: 120, 130, 131n, 132.
Apollyon: 128, 129, 211.
Ariosto, Ludovico: *Orlando Furioso*, 23, 223.
Ashburton, Louisa Lady: 18, 161, 165.

Bacchus: 30, 33, 34, 35.
Bagehot, Walter: "The Grotesque in Art and Literature", 16n, 83, 180n, 221.
Baldinucci, Filippo: *Notizie de' Professori del Disegno*, 2, 68, 199, 200, 206, 223.
Ball, Patricia M.: 131n, 221.
Balzac, Honoré: 17n.
Bartoli, Daniello: *Dei Simboli trasportati al Morale*, 2, **27-9,** 223.
Baudelaire, Charles: 121n, 223.
Ben Ezra: *see* IBN EZRA.
Benziger, James: *Images of Eternity*, 102n, 220.
Berlifitzing, Wilhelm Von: 208, 209, 210, 212.
Berlin-Lieberman, Judith: *Robert Browning and Hebraism*, 104n, 220.
Bible, The: 2, 40, 41, 42, 53, 55, 73, 88, 92, 93, 104, 105, 139, 147, 148. Quoted: Genesis (XIII. 2) 41, (XXII. 17) 52; Numbers (XI. 29-35) 155; Deuteronomy (XXVI. 5-9, 18-19) 96; Psalms (L) 143, 145, 146; (LI) 144; Proverbs (XXXI. 6) 97; Ecclesiastes (XII. 7-8) 39; Song of Solomon (II. 1) 79;

Isaiah. (VII. 18-20) 100n, (XVI. 1-2) 106; Jeremiah (III. 17-19) 111. (XIX. 8, 11) 118, (XXXI. 12-13, 17) 106, 139; Lamentations (IV. 1) 41, 102; Malachi (IV. 4-5) 107, 108; Matthew (VII. 6) 101, (XI. 14) 108, (XV. 24-7) 95, (XXIII. 17) 41, (XXVI. 34, 40-3) 109; Mark (XIII. 31-7) 107, (XV. 35-7) 108; Luke (I. 72-5, 76-8) 94; John (I. 21) 108; I Corinthians (IX. 16-20) 98; (X. 27, 30) 97; (X. 20, 21) 110; Galatians (V. 16) 155; I Timothy (VI. 10) 79n; Revelation (XXI. 18, 21) 41, 42, 73, 76, 130.
Biographie Universelle: 173n.
Birrell, Augustine: 12, 220.
Blake, William: 48, 139.
Bodkin, Maud: 123n, 221.
Bosch, Hieronymus: 13.
Brooke, Stopford A.: *The Poetry of Robert Browning*, 162, 180, 220.
Brown, E. K.: 141n, 221.
Browning, Elizabeth Barrett: 4n, 7, 87, 104n, 119, 165, 167, 184-6, 199, 200, 209, 219, 220; *Aurora Leigh*, 99; "The Cry of the Children", 72n, 114; "The Cry of the Human", 72n; "A Vision of Poets", 125; "Wine of Cyprus", 63n.
Browning, Robert: see INDEX TO WORKS AND CHARACTERS.
Buchanan, Robert W.: 161.
Buloz, M.: 199.
Bunyan, John: *The Pilgrim's Progress*, 119, 128, 129, 130, 223.
Burnett, Ivy Compton: 160.
Burrows, Leonard: *Browning, an Introductory Essay*, 17n, 145, 220.
Buti, Ludovico: 104n.
Butler, Samuel: 67, 160, 223.
Byron, George Gordon: 158, 160, 192.

Cain: 144.
Carew, Thomas: 169.

II. INDEX TO BROWNING'S WORKS AND CHARACTERS